Monetary Policy in the Euro A

How the European Central Bank (ECB)
forms, is one of the most important issues
the subject of vast media and academic interest. Almost daily the ECB
is a topic of discussion in the press and among 'Euro Watchers'. Much
of this discussion has been of a confused and political nature and has
served to blur rather than inform.

This book, written by a team at the ECB including Otmar Issing, the
ECB's Chief Economist, provides the first comprehensive, insider, non-
technical analysis of the monetary policy strategy, institutional features
and operational procedures of the Eurosystem.

The goals and the transmission mechanism of monetary policy are
explored, as are the theoretical and empirical results underpinning the
'stability-oriented monetary policy strategy' adopted by the ECB. The
characteristics of this strategy are also discussed in comparison with
suggested alternatives.

OTMAR ISSING is a Member of the Executive Board of the European
Central Bank.

VÍTOR GASPAR is Director General, DG Research at the European
Central Bank.

IGNAZIO ANGELONI is Deputy Director General, DG Research at the
European Central Bank.

ORESTE TRISTANI is a senior economist in DG Research at the
European Central Bank.

Monetary Policy in the Euro Area

Strategy and Decision Making at the European Central Bank

Otmar Issing
Vítor Gaspar
Ignazio Angeloni
Oreste Tristani

All at the European Central Bank

CAMBRIDGE
UNIVERSITY PRESS

PUBLISHED BY THE PRESS SYNDICATE OF THE UNIVERSITY OF CAMBRIDGE
The Pitt Building, Trumpington Street, Cambridge, United Kingdom

CAMBRIDGE UNIVERSITY PRESS
The Edinburgh Building, Cambridge CB2 2RU, UK
40 West 20th Street, New York, NY 10011-4211, USA
10 Stamford Road, Oakleigh, VIC 3166, Australia
Ruiz de Alarcón 13, 28014 Madrid, Spain
Dock House, The Waterfront, Cape Town 8001, South Africa

http://www.cambridge.org

First published 2001

Printed in the United Kingdom at the University Press, Cambridge

Typeface Plantin 10/12 pt.   *System* LATEX 2$_\varepsilon$ [TB]

A catalog record for this book is available from the British Library.

Library of Congress Cataloguing in Publication Data
Monetary policy in the euro area / Otmar Issing . . . [et al.].
    p. cm.
Includes bibliographical references and index.
ISBN 0-521-78324-0 – ISBN 0-521-78888-9 (pb.)
1. Monetary policy – Europe.   2. European Central Bank.   I. Issing, Otmar.
HG925 .M6595   2001
332.4'94 – dc21   2001025440

ISBN 0 521 78324 0 hardback
ISBN 0 521 78888 9 paperback

Contents

Figures

Tables

Acknowledgements

Although the cover of this book bears only four explicit signatures, many of the ideas it presents are the result of a collective endeavour, which embodies intellectual input from many sources.

We feel, first of all, a deep intellectual debt to the ECB colleagues who have contributed, through suggestions, discussions, comments and criticisms, to sharpen our thoughts on the strategy, namely Frank Browne, Hans-Joachim Klöckers, Klaus Masuch, Huw Pill, Frank Smets and Bernhard Winkler. Among the other colleagues who provided specific comments and criticisms on the draft we wish to mention Denis Blenck, Claus Brand, Nuno Cassola, Dieter Gerdesmeier, Philipp Hartmann, Sergio Nicoletti-Altimari, Barbara Roffia, Massimo Rostagno and Juan Luis Vega. Second, we are indebted to the colleagues of the National Central Banks for their contribution of thought and experience. Thirdly, we are grateful to a number of academic economists who provided inspiration for our thinking on the strategy. Among them, we wish to mention Marvin Goodfriend, Charles Goodhart, Daniel Gros, Allan Meltzer, Rick Mishkin, Ulf Söderström, Lars Svensson and Guido Tabellini, who provided comments on an early draft of this book. Finally, we thank Sandrine Corvoisier and Andres Manzanares for excellent research assistance and Patricia Kearns-Endres, whose organisational skills have contributed to a speedier completion of this endeavour.

All remaining errors must be attributed exclusively to the four of us.

Frankfurt am Main, November 2000   IGNAZIO ANGELONI,
                                            VÍTOR GASPAR,
                                            OTMAR ISSING,
                                            ORESTE TRISTANI

Introduction

A short message, flashing on Reuters screens at 15:36 Frankfurt time on 4 January 1999, announced the launch of the first open market operation of the Eurosystem,[1] a two-week repurchase tender at a fixed interest rate of 3 per cent. This simple act symbolised the birth of the monetary policy for the new single European currency, the euro.

The introduction of the euro (technically, the start of 'Stage Three' of Economic and Monetary Union, EMU) marked at the same time the beginning of the new currency and the end of a long preparatory process. The key initial steps in this process date back to the 1950s, when the European Economic Community was created and began to take action in the field of monetary and financial co-operation. After the relatively prosperous decade of the 1960s, the time for a single European money seemed ripe: the Werner Plan (1970) proposed a first blueprint for a monetary union. But the plan failed in the climate of generalised monetary instability that dominated Europe and the world in the following years. Yet, efforts to promote monetary integration and stability in Europe continued, first in the so-called monetary 'snake', then in the European Monetary System. The process regained momentum in the 1980s, with the approval of the Single Act (1986), eventually leading to the completion of the single market and the elimination of capital controls. Free movement of goods, services and capital in the continent would eventually prove incompatible with stable exchange rates and autonomous national monetary policies, a point forcefully made by Padoa-Schioppa (1987). In 1989, the Delors Report provided a new 'plan' that, embodied in the Maastricht Treaty, eventually proved successful.

At the technical level, the preparation for the single currency, its central bank and its monetary policy is much more recent. Most of it was undertaken by the European Monetary Institute (EMI) and the participating

---

[1] The Eurosystem comprises the ECB and the national central banks (NCBs) of the Member States of the European Union (EU) that have adopted the euro. The European System of Central Banks (ESCB) also includes the NCBs of the other EU Member States that still retain national currencies and monetary policies.

national central banks during EMU's Stage Two (1994–1998). In this period, the basic infrastructure for the new currency to function was created essentially from scratch, building on the experience of the participating central banks. A full set of operating instruments, basic analytical and statistical tools, a new pan-European interbank payment mechanism, internal organisational rules for the new central bank, all these and other things necessary for a new central bank to operate were set up. The technical background was very advanced when, in mid-1998, the ECB was established and the final six-month preparatory period started.

This book focuses on a fundamental and far reaching decision adopted by the Governing Council of the ECB in that period: the choice of monetary policy strategy (in short, the *ECB strategy*). Following a common terminology, by strategy we mean the framework and the procedures that the central bank uses to translate relevant information into monetary policy decisions. The strategy is a key factor shaping monetary policy making in the ECB, as it ensures that all elements relevant for monetary policy decisions are brought together in a logically consistent framework. As we will explain, the ECB strategy is also closely related to its communication policy and its operating procedures, other aspects that are discussed extensively in this book.

The broad lines of the ECB's strategy were announced by the Governing Council on 13 October 1998. The Council took the view that the strategy, aimed at ensuring price stability in accordance with the EU Treaty (henceforth 'the Treaty'), would be new and original. This originality reflects the unique characteristics of the euro area that, composed of a multiplicity of sovereign states sharing a single monetary policy, represents an unprecedented experience of monetary integration.

Nevertheless, the strategy bears marks of the influence of a number of factors. First, the process of European integration, whose general guiding principles have also inspired monetary integration. The single monetary policy has an area-wide objective (*price stability*), and is concerned with national developments only to the extent that these are significant for the area as a whole. Moreover, the influence of the principle of open and free competition can be traced in many of the features that complement the strategy, namely in the operational framework and in the architecture of payment systems. While reflecting a more general process of European integration, Monetary Union can in itself represent a catalyst for deeper integration, in goods and financial markets alike.

Second, as already emphasised, the single monetary policy culminates a long preparatory process, reflecting experiences that belong to the whole central banking profession in Europe. Among these experiences, a crucial one is, we believe, the 'Great Inflation' of the 1970s and the ensuing period of monetary instability. Originated from global factors – an unsustainable expansion of international liquidity; excessive government spending in the USA, partly associated with the military effort; and the first oil shock – the monetory instability was compounded in Europe by domestic factors, namely the structural characteristics of labour and product markets and the response from monetary and fiscal policies. The results were stagflation, currency instability, persistent budget deficits and high and volatile interest rates. A consensus gradually emerged from this experience, and was eventually incorporated in the Treaty and the ECB Statute, that EMU should be built around the concept of a stable money.

Finally, the ECB's monetary policy strategy has been influenced by academic work on macroeconomics and monetary policy. In fact, a key aim of this book is to describe how the ECB's strategy fits in the recent monetary economics thinking. From this viewpoint, the book can be split into three parts. The first, composed of chapters 1 and 2, provides a description of the analytical background for the ECB strategy. Although we refrain from using mathematical notation, these chapters will probably be of interest mainly to professional economists. The second part, including chapters 3 to 7 could, in our view, reach a broader audience. After an introduction to the basic features of the euro area economy, this part provides a detailed description of the main elements composing the monetary policy strategy, thus representing the core of the book. The remaining chapters are dedicated to complementary aspects. Chapter 8 describes how the strategy is implemented, chapter 9 focuses on political economy aspects and chapter 10 concludes with an overview of monetary policy decisions in the first year of the single monetary policy.

More precisely, the book is organised as follows.

In chapter 1, we address the long-standing issue of 'what monetary policy can and cannot do'. We emphasise that a large consensus, supported by theoretical and empirical studies, appears to exist on a few results concerning the long run effects of monetary policy, in particular the relationship between money and prices. However, substantial elements of uncertainty still characterise economists' knowledge of the transmission channels and effects of monetary policy in the shorter run, in spite of great advances made in the literature. According to these results, central banks are able to contribute to improve welfare if they minimise the distortions caused by inflation. They should, however, refrain from policies that crucially hinge on specific assumptions on the functioning of the economy, which could be proven incorrect.

Chapter 2 describes the approaches suggested by the economic literature to cope with the aforementioned elements of uncertainty. In this light, we argue that a central bank's 'strategy' can be seen as a complex set of policy prescriptions. As such, it is optimal, to the best of the central bank's knowledge, but implicit, in the sense that it cannot be expressed in a simple mathematical function. By announcing its strategy, the central bank aims to convey the systematic character of policy and to characterise to the best possible extent how it will respond to the available information set. The announcement of a strategy reflects an effort towards transparency and commitment, and it signals central banks' awareness of the importance of credibility and of being able to influence markets' expectations.

Chapter 3 describes some key features of the euro area. It opens with a comparison of the new monetary area, in terms of a number of available statistics, to the Member States, the United States and Japan. Like the latter two regions, the euro area is a 'large' economy. The chapter then introduces the reader to some new statistics: the Harmonised Index of Consumer Prices (HICP) and the monetary aggregates. In a final section, some tentative evidence is presented on the functioning of the euro area economy and on its monetary policy transmission mechanism.

In chapter 4, we begin discussing the specifics of the monetary policy strategy adopted by the ECB, starting with a critical description of its first element: the announcement of a precise quantitative definition of the price stability objective. On 13 October 1998, price stability was defined as 'a year-on-year increase in the Harmonised Index of Consumer Prices (HICP) for the euro area of below 2 per cent'. This definition is analysed, first, in relation to the ECB Statute, which is part of the Treaty. We then discuss various issues related to the announced definition of price stability, such as the motivation and implications for the choice of the 2 per cent upper bound, and the geographical and temporal reference frame for price stability.

The prominent role attributed to money in the ECB strategy is discussed next, in chapter 5. We argue there that such a role is consistent with economic theory and empirical evidence. However, we also stress that a number of caveats must be borne in mind when using monetary data in day-to-day policy making. After a detailed description of the role that money plays in the ECB strategy, we present the available evidence on money demand and on the leading indicator properties of monetary aggregates for prices in the euro area.

Chapter 6 describes the second main element of the ECB strategy, the broadly based assessment of a wide range of economic and financial indicators. We start justifying why, in spite of the prominence of money, it is necessary for the central bank to analyse other economic indicators, and then provide an account of the main variables that compose the ECB's information set. The broadly based assessment is reached through a combination of informal judgment and the input from a number of formal econometric models.

An overview of the ECB strategy as a whole is provided in chapter 7. We discuss here the special historical circumstances, with associated difficulties, that contributed to shape the strategy. The differences from the frameworks adopted by other central banks are explained in the light of the key findings of the monetary economics literature and of the specific features of the euro area. The ECB strategy is presented as an information-processing framework, used both in internal analyses and decision making and in external communication. We conclude the chapter with a brief discussion of some of the objections that have so far been raised to the ECB strategy.

In the following two chapters, we discuss two complementary aspects of the ECB strategy. Chapter 8 concentrates on the operational framework, i.e. the set of instruments, procedures and practices that are used by the Eurosystem to intervene in the financial market, in order to achieve its objectives. The operational framework is clearly linked to, and must be consistent with, the monetary policy strategy. Moreover, it is designed to ensure an effective communication between the central bank and the market and to respect the principles of a market economy. The performance of the operational framework in the first year of the single monetary policy is also discussed in some detail, with special emphasis on the challenges faced in the 'changeover period'.

Transparency and accountability are analysed in chapter 9. We discuss first the relationship between accountability and independence, and the way in which accountability of central banks should be measured. The relationship between transparency and the publication of the internal inflation forecast, an issue that has recently attracted considerable attention in the academic literature, is considered next. We conclude with a description of the statutory requirements for the accountability of the ECB and of the ways in which it tries to achieve a high degree of transparency.

Chapter 10 concludes with a description of the practical application of the ECB strategy in the first year of EMU. We emphasise the smooth transition from the last phase of Stage Two of EMU, when national central banks retained full monetary independence in each Member State, to the beginning of Stage Three, when the responsibility for monetary policy in the euro area was handed over to the ECB. The monetary policy decisions of the period going from the final months of 1998 to the end of 1999 are discussed in some detail. We conclude that the stability oriented strategy proved to be a well-functioning and efficient framework for policy decisions in the newly created monetary area.

1 Money, output and prices: the scope of monetary policy

In this chapter, we draw some basic lessons from the economic literature on what monetary policy can and cannot do. This is not an attempt to find prior justifications for an over restrictive interpretation of the central banker's mandate. Understanding the limits to monetary management is essential for the central banker to avoid mistakes. To be effective and credible, monetary policy makers need to be modest, or, to put it better, realistic, in the way they see the potential scope for their action.

The literature offers a wealth of analyses, evidence and suggestions on 'what monetary policy can and cannot do', an issue which has constantly been at the core of monetary economics (see Friedman, 1968).

Unfortunately, however, the discipline is still characterised by a substantial lack of agreement on the 'appropriate model' suitable for a unified analysis of monetary policy issues. 'Whatever the particular model component that is singled out for special criticism, it seems extremely hard to avoid the conclusion that agreement ... is predominantly absent' (McCallum, 1999). Specifically, the key issue of how exactly monetary policy impacts on real variables over time is still only imperfectly understood and 'different models carry highly different alleged implications for monetary policy' (again, McCallum, 1999).

Moreover, empirical studies often cannot discriminate across competing models. Each model appears capable of replicating some stylised facts of modern economies, but it fails to portray the complex and multifaceted characteristics of the real world.

As a result, the monetary policy maker must take decisions without the help of a comprehensive and reliable body of knowledge of the interaction of monetary policy with the rest of the economy, both in the long run and at the business cycle frequency. There are, however, a few basic principles on which broad consensus can be registered both at the theoretical and empirical levels. A risk-averse central banker should place on them as much emphasis as possible.

Accordingly, we review the literature with the aim of identifying the results of monetary theory and of the empirical analyses that, in our view, represent key and reliable benchmarks. Section 1.1 concentrates on the important lessons we have learned concerning the long run effects of monetary policy. The limits to economists' knowledge of the short run effects of policy are discussed in section 1.2. For the sake of orderly thinking, we have decided not to tackle here the normative question of what monetary policy *should* do, an issue that is touched upon in the next chapter. Rather we address the positive question of whether monetary policy *can* affect two key macroeconomic variables of interest (inflation and output) on the basis of both theoretical and empirical considerations. We conclude each section with a discussion of the policy or institutional implications of the main results of the literature surveyed.

An inherent limitation of our exposition is, clearly, that a satisfactory and agreed distinction between the long and the short run is not available, either to us or to the economic profession as a whole. We therefore follow the common practice of assigning to the 'long run' all effects of economic shocks that, other things been equal, materialise after all adjustments to the initial shock have worked through. Though the transition to equilibrium can take a long time, when the distinction is not essential, we will use the term in a looser sense, to indicate all frequencies beyond the standard business cycle. Short run effects are obviously defined as a complement.

1.1   The long run

A large consensus appears to exist in the academic literature on the direction and the dimension of the effects of monetary policy on prices and real output in the long run. It appears consensual that, in equilibrium, monetary policy is 'neutral':[1] eventually, a monetary policy shock is reflected, *ceteris paribus*, into a permanent change of the price level and no permanent changes in real variables. This proposition is often illustrated through the example of a permanent policy shock, such as a doubling of the quantity of money: when this becomes common knowledge in the economy, it will be recognised as a simple change of *numéraire*, thus leading to a one-to-one effect on the price level, but no permanent consequences on the allocation of real resources.

In the long run, there is therefore a clear dichotomy between the real and nominal variables in the economy. In this section we review the nature of the long run results focusing, in turn, on the effects of policy on prices and on output.

[1] This terminology is based on Patinkin (1965).

1.1.1   Money and prices

The one-to-one relationship between money and prices in the long run is one of the few results that have remained undisputed over time and across economists. The robustness of this relationship derives from the fact that, as stressed by Lucas (1980), it appears to be a consistent characteristic of the long run equilibrium of virtually all models of monetary economies. Lucas goes so far as to say: 'I should think we would view any monetary model that did *not* have this neutrality property with the deepest suspicions, the way we would view a physical model that predicted different times for the earth to complete its orbit depending on whether the distance is measured in miles or kilometres' (Lucas, 1987).

This relationship is traditionally derived within the quantity equation, where it is obtained if money velocity and output are assumed to be approximately constant in the long run. It does not amount, however, to adopting the viewpoint of the monetarist doctrine. As emphasised by Lucas, 'the interpretation of the quantity theory of money as a set of predictions about the long-run average behaviour of a general equilibrium system is different, though not inconsistent with, Milton Friedman (1956). There Friedman stresses the stability of the market demand function for money, a property which is neither necessary nor sufficient for the quantity theory to obtain' in the long run (Lucas, 1980, p. 1005, fn. 1).

As a long run relationship, the quantity theory of money can be traced back to David Hume (1752a, b), who also provides its clearest statement: 'Were all the gold in England annihilated at once, and one and twenty shillings substituted in the place of every guinea, would money be more plentiful or interest lower? No surely: we would only use silver instead of gold. [...] No other difference would ever be observed, no alteration on commerce, manufacturers, navigation, or interest, unless we imagine that the colour of the metal is of any consequence' (Hume, 1752b). The main macroeconomic paradigms proposed during the last century, of both neo-Keynesian or neo-classical variety, from Hicks (1937) to Modigliani (1944), from Friedman (1956) to Patinkin (1965) and Sidrausky (1967), embody, explicitly or implicitly, the same properties, although different specifications of different models play a role in the determination of price and quantity effects.

Models incorporating features of staggered price adjustment differ only in the sense that a certain period of time must elapse before the money–price relationship emerges. A sign of the broad agreement on the long run quantity equation is the fact that neo-Keynesian economists are apparently ready to subscribe to it, declaring that 'when it comes to understanding inflation over the longer term, economists typically emphasise just one factor: growth of money supply. The reason for this emphasis is that no other factor is likely to lead to persistent increases in the price level' (Romer, 1996). The same features are present in the 'new neoclassical synthesis' model of Goodfriend and King (1997), in which short run Keynesian adjustment coexists with real business cycle properties in the long run. McCallum (1990) registers the consensus, stating that: 'there is in fact little professional disagreement with Friedman's position [that 'Inflation is always and everywhere a monetary phenomenon'] when the latter is properly interpreted. In that regard ... Friedman states that "inflation" will be taken to mean "a steady and sustained rise in prices" (1963, p. 1)'.

Theory does not predict that money is the sole economic variable that can affect prices. Other factors – from technological to aggregate demand shocks, of a transitory or permanent nature – will of course influence the rate of change of prices. Over time, however, the effects of all these 'other factors' on the price level can be offset with some degree of adjustment of the money stock. The nature of the 'other factors' is therefore irrelevant for the long run course of prices or inflation, which can be seen as entirely in the hands of the central bank. It is in this sense that inflation is ultimately a monetary phenomenon.

This theoretical consensus is corroborated by a substantial support from empirical studies. The money–price relationship appears indeed robust throughout analyses conducted across a number of dimensions: specifically, over time (Friedman and Schwartz, 1963; Lucas, 1980), across countries (e.g., Barro, 1993; Dwyer and Hafer, 1988; McCandless and Weber, 1995; Schwartz, 1973), with pooled data (Vogel, 1974), across regimes (Lothian, 1985; Rolnick and Weber, 1997) and using various definitions of money (an explicit comparison between three increasingly broad definitions can be found in McCandless and Weber, 1995). All these tests provide support to the theory.

The most straightforward results are obtained from cross-country studies. A typical cross-country diagram of the sort considered in the literature is presented in McCandless and Weber (1995, figure 1). The figure, constructed on the basis of thirty-year averages in 110 countries, shows a remarkably high and positive correlation between inflation and money growth.

Figure 1.1 presents a similar cross-country plot of long term averages (over the 1960 to 1994 period) of inflation and money growth. In order to filter out the influence of high inflation countries, graph (a) focuses on all IMF member countries with an average annual inflation rate of less than 20 per cent, while graph (b) further restricts the sample to twenty-three

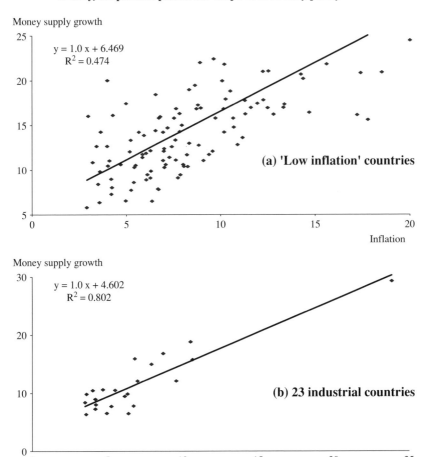

Figure 1.1 Cross-country inflation rates and money supply growth in selected countries
Source: IMF.
Notes: F-tests of the restriction that the slope coefficient is 1: (a) $F(1,115) = 0.681$; (b) $F(1,21) = 0.844$; 'low inflation' countries: all IMF member countries with an annual inflation rate of less than 20 per cent; 23 industrial countries: OECD countries excluding Turkey, Mexico, Korea and the economies in transition.

industrial countries.[2] The figure shows that the money–price relationship holds also at moderate inflation levels. In both cases, the relationship is strong and positive, and the slope coefficient in the regression is insignificantly different from unity.

This result is not sensitive to alternative definitions of money. A variety of monetary aggregates, from base to broad money, has been used in the empirical analyses and the results on the money–price relationship appear to be robust also to changes in the definition of money. This is most clearly evident in the study by McCandless and Weber (1995), where three definitions – base money, M1 and M2, as reported in the IMF International Financial Statistics – are adopted with no significant change in the results.

The main drawback of the simple techniques used in these analyses is of course that they do not allow attaching a causal interpretation to the results. Indeed, both money and prices can be regarded as endogenous variables and there is no reason, in general, to assume a specific chain of causation between them. It remains true, however, that money and prices are tied together in the long run. Large and persistent deviations of these two variables from each other, therefore, are highly unlikely, so that unusually robust money growth for a prolonged period is almost surely a signal of ensuing inflation risks. Conversely, inflationary pressures are unlikely to persist without monetary accommodation.

1.1.2   Money and output

In spite of the aforementioned empirical results on the relationship between money and prices, long run effects of monetary policy on output should not be excluded altogether. In addition to 'neutrality', there is the issue of 'superneutrality': money is said to be superneutral if an increase in its rate of growth (rather than its level) is eventually reflected, *ceteris paribus*, in an equal increase of the inflation rate and it has no influence on real output. Unlike neutrality, superneutrality is not a widespread theoretical result: a number of models show that a change in the rate of growth of money can have either positive or negative effects on real variables.[3]

Many studies have investigated directly the relationship between money and output, including the superneutrality issue. The prevalent view in the discipline appears to be that, at least to a first order approximation, superneutrality holds for small changes in the rate of growth of money.

[2] All OECD countries minus Turkey, Mexico, Korea and the economies in transition.
[3] Results depend, in particular, on the way in which the demand for money is introduced in the models and on the length of individuals' horizons when taking consumption and investment decisions (see, e.g., Orphanides and Solow, 1990).

Short-term interest rates

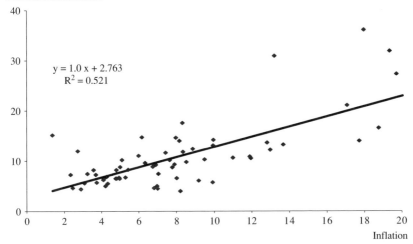

$y = 1.0 x + 2.763$
$R^2 = 0.521$

Inflation

Figure 1.2 Cross-country short term interest and inflation rates in 'low inflation' countries
Source: IMF.
Notes: F-tests of the restriction that the slope is 1: $F(1,63) = 0.004$; 'low inflation' countries: all IMF member countries with an annual inflation rate of less than 20 per cent.

Larger changes, however, such as those involving a shift from price stability to relatively high inflation and especially hyperinflation, have disruptive effects on the real economy (the 'costs of inflation') that invalidate the superneutrality result.

The existing empirical studies on these issues can be divided into two main strands. The first, comprising Geweke (1986) and Kormendi and Meguire (1985) as examples of the time-series and cross-country approaches, respectively, attempts to test directly the money–output relationship (often using the same approach as in the money–price empirical literature). Other examples of this strand of research can be found in the work of Dwyer and Hafer (1988), Lothian (1985) and McCandless and Weber (1995). More recent studies address more precisely the issues of neutrality and superneutrality of money, on the basis of methodologies that take into account explicitly the low frequency characteristics of the data. Fisher and Seater (1993) and King and Watson (1997) develop novel econometric approaches and apply them to US post-war data, while Serletis and Krause (1996), Serletis and Koustas (1998) and Weber (1994) apply the new methodologies to a range of other countries.

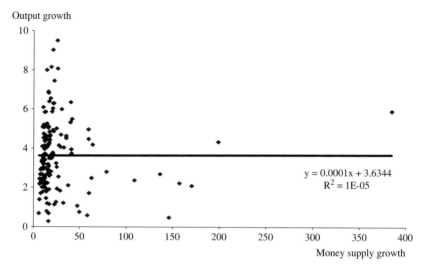

Figure 1.3 Cross-country output and money supply growth in IMF member countries
Source: IMF.

This literature highlights a lack of correlation between the rates of growth of output and money. In general, simple regression coefficients are insignificantly different from zero (see figure 1.3 for an example of such cross-country evidence). Significant and negative results can, however, be obtained for countries experiencing very fast money growth in selected sample periods.

Fisher and Seater (1993) and King and Watson (1997) complement these results through analyses of time-series evidence for the main industrial countries. Both papers explicitly tackle the issues of neutrality and superneutrality. They show, first, that meaningful neutrality tests can only be conducted if the data satisfy certain nonstationarity conditions, which therefore need to be carefully checked at the outset of the analysis. If these conditions are satisfied, neutrality (superneutrality) can be studied on the basis of reduced form models through a test of the restriction that the sum of all coefficients attached to money (or money growth) in a regression of real economic activity be zero.

By and large, the tests cannot reject the neutrality hypothesis for the USA and for a number of other countries. This result is consistent across methodologies: the Fisher and Seater test assumes that money is exogenous in the long run, while the King and Watson methodology accommodates a broad range of identifying hypotheses. The results of superneutrality tests, on the other hand, are not conclusive and they prove sensitive to changes in the identifying assumptions.

The second strand of empirical literature that is relevant for the analysis of the superneutrality issue does not focus directly on money. However, evidence can also be obtained *indirectly* from studies of the relationship between output growth and inflation, relying on the long run link between inflation and money growth. The traditional way to approach this issue is in terms of the slope of the long-run Phillips curve. King and Watson (1994, 1997) tackle it again in these terms making use of recent advances in econometric analysis. From a different angle, Barro (1996, 1997), Barro and Sala-i-Martin (1995) and Fischer (1993) approach the issue as part of a general investigation of the long run determinants of economic growth.[4] Bruno (1995) and the literature cited therein also provide evidence on the relationship between inflation and growth (see also Bruno and Easterly, 1998). Given the issues being investigated, this literature is concerned with the effects of ongoing, largely anticipated, inflation. Unanticipated inflation, more likely to be of an irregular or cyclical nature, is not taken into account.

Testing the slope of the long-run Phillips curve, King and Watson (1994, 1997) show that the evidence is very difficult to interpret. In particular, they highlight that there is a relationship between identifying assumptions and long run results. If inflation is maintained to have no impact effect on unemployment, then the estimated long run effect is very small; this result, however, is not robust to changes in the maintained assumption. The authors conclude that the shape of the long run Phillips curve is likely to be very steep, if not vertical.

The empirical literature on economic growth adds an important qualification to this result. When inflation is included in a regression with all other potential determinants of economic growth – from the level of schooling, to life expectancy and indices of the degree of democracy enjoyed by the country – then the evidence strongly points to a predominantly negative relationship between growth and inflation. This result has been argued to depend on the *level* of inflation – whereby it would hold at medium to high inflation levels, but not necessarily at low levels – leading some scholars to formulate the hypothesis of a possible nonlinearity in the relationship. Bruno (1995), for example, shows that the relationship is stronger at very high inflation levels, but tends to fade at low levels. Fischer (1993), however, argues that if separate coefficients are calculated for low, medium and high inflation levels, it is the first two that

---

[4] Durlauf and Quah (1999) provide a survey of this literature.

tend to account for the negative effect typically found in the literature. In contrast, Barro (1997) holds the view that the hypothesis of linearity cannot be rejected, so that inflation is detrimental also at low levels.

Some doubts remain about the correct way to interpret these regressions.[5] Widespread consensus seems to exist about the negative effect on growth of double-digit inflation. Though the evidence may be weaker at lower inflation rates, the recent experience showed us that the public tends to lose confidence in the central bank's ability or willingness to ensure price stability once the rate of change of prices becomes non-negligible. Only low inflation appears to secure the central bank with the level of credibility that is necessary for any inflation rate to be sustainable.

1.1.3   The costs of inflation

These results are among the most important in shaping the view that price stability is a desirable goal for society, because inflation entails a number of welfare costs for the economic system. The exact nature of the costs of inflation has been thoroughly investigated in the literature and found to be both economic and social. Economic costs are mainly related to the distortions that inflation introduces in the economy through the general disruption of the stable economic and social environment that is conducive to economic growth. The distortion can affect the intertemporal allocation of resources and also determine arbitrary redistributions of wealth.

Fischer (1995) presents a detailed description of the economic costs of inflation,[6] which can be briefly summarised in the following categories. First, the so-called 'shoe-leather costs', that is the costs of economising on the use of money, a non-interest-bearing asset. Second, the tendency to invest less in the 'productive' sectors of the economy and over-invest in the financial sector and in a number of indexing technologies aimed at neutralising the real effects of inflation. Another category of costs pertains to the observed increase in the volatility of inflation when its level rises, which fosters a rise in the overall level of uncertainty in the economy.

---

[5] Levine and Renelt (1992) have pointed out that the inclusion in growth-regression equations of a number of controls aimed at capturing the most disparate effects has important consequences on the robustness of the results. The statistical significance of a given regressor may be *fragile*, i.e. entirely due to the presence of other controls whose presence or absence is not strongly motivated by the theory. Using a statistical methodology, Levine and Renelt argue that most regressors, and notably inflation, are indeed fragile. Durlauf and Quah (1999), however, question the appropriateness of a purely statistical approach to deal with this problem and maintain that the dimensions along which robustness can be investigated are determined by the goals of the researcher.

[6] See also Fischer and Modigliani (1978) and Fischer (1981).

Finally, distortions arise in conjunction with the tax system. Since this is only imperfectly indexed to inflation, any positive inflation rate raises the effective tax rate on households and firms. Feldstein (1997) argues that these distortions are such that, for the US economy, the annual welfare gains of going from a 2 per cent rate of inflation to price stability would be equivalent to a 1 per cent rise in real GDP. The general hypothesis that reducing inflation leads to an increase of the level of real GDP, though possibly not of its rate of growth, is analysed thoroughly in Feldstein (1999). From the analysis of a number of OECD countries during a period of relatively low inflation, Andrés and Hernando (1999) argue that even low inflation has a permanent and sizeable negative effect on the level of real income.

Social costs are more difficult to classify, but the existing evidence normally confirms that people dislike inflation. Fischer (1996) reports the results of systematic opinion polls, conducted in the US by the Gallup Organisation since the Second World War, asking the public about the most important problem facing the nation. Inflation is regarded as such by up to 80 per cent of respondents over the seventies and early eighties, while the concern disappears when the actual inflation rate drops to recent levels. Even stronger evidence in this sense usually emerges in countries that have suffered from prolonged and pronounced inflationary processes in their recent history.

While this evidence points to the desirability of the lowest possible inflation rate, it is not conclusive on whether exactly zero is the rate that maximises social welfare. The issue of the optimality of inflation rates 'around' zero can be seen as slightly distinct from the more general one of the costs and benefits of low vs. high inflation. It is noticeable that the *Friedman rule*, prescribing deflation and a zero nominal interest rate in order to minimise the private opportunity cost of holding money, has proven to be a remarkably robust result in general equilibrium models.[7] Recently, however, price stability is starting to appear as an optimum in general equilibrium, within arguably more realistic models including nominal rigidities (for example, Khan, King and Wolman, 2000).

However, a few arguments have been put forward in favour of small positive inflation rates. Akerlof, Dickens and Perry (1996), for example, formalise the argument according to which the optimality of small, but positive, inflation rates is related to the existence of downward nominal and real rigidities in relative prices and wages. Another reason to pursue a small positive inflation rate has to do with the lower bound (at zero) to

---

[7] See Corretja and Teles (1996) and De Fiore and Teles (1999) for recent restatements of the Friedman rule. Wolman (1997) makes the point that the welfare gains in moving from zero inflation to deflation may be relatively small.

nominal interest rates (originally pointed out by Vickrey, 1954, and elaborated in Okun, 1981). It has been argued that this would prevent monetary policy from engineering negative *ex ante* real interest rates whenever such a stance was deemed appropriate, with potential consequences in terms of excessive volatility of output.

The empirical evidence appears to support the conclusion that a very low, but nonzero, inflation rate could be a more desirable, practical goal for society. Recent estimates concerning the US economy (e.g., Fuhrer and Madigan, 1997; Orphanides and Wieland, 1998) appear to indicate that the zero bound on nominal interest rates is unlikely to constitute a binding constraint for monetary policy when the inflation rate is already just slightly higher than zero. Orphanides and Wieland (1998) conclude: 'the consequences of the zero bound are negligible for target inflation rates as low as 2 per cent. However, the effectiveness of the constraint becomes increasingly important to determine the effectiveness of policy with inflation targets between 0 and 1 per cent'.[8]

Our sense of the message emerging from this literature, in terms of the question 'what can monetary policy do?', is that the best maintained hypothesis is that monetary policy can contribute to improve the overall performance of the economic system and collective welfare, in the medium to long run, if it minimises the distortions caused by inflation or deflation.[9]

Concerning the issue of what exactly should be interpreted as price stability, it appears that this could be an inflation rate slightly higher than zero. However, the issue of which inflation goal is optimal is far from settled, considering also the shortcomings that existing consumer price indices have in accurately measuring the inflation rate. On the whole, more research seems needed to settle this issue.

1.2   The short run

The relatively large consensus existing on the effects of money on real output and prices vanishes when one moves on from the long to the short

---

[8] It goes without saying that a small positive inflation objective does not ensure against the risk of large deflationary shocks that, in principle, can make the zero interest rate constraint binding in the economy. We touch upon this issue when we discuss so-called 'price level targeting' in chapter 4.

[9] It should be pointed out that, though consensual amongst economists, this conclusion is not unanimous. In particular, labour market theories emphasising the possibility of hysteresis in unemployment (Blanchard and Summers, 1986) would imply that the NAIRU is affected by changes in aggregate demand (and not only by structural policies). Monetary policy would therefore have permanent effects on real economic growth. A forceful defence of this heterodox viewpoint (which is not supported by the empirical analyses mentioned in the text) can be found in Ball (1999).

run. The issue concerning the mechanism through which monetary policy has short run effects on output is still far from being settled.

The advent of more complex and detailed models has greatly refined our understanding of the advantages and drawbacks of existing theories, but it has arguably not helped much to settle the issue. One of the few common features of existing dynamic models of monetary economies is that money often plays no role in monetary policy. The transmission mechanism operates entirely through the effects on aggregate demand of changes in the monetary policy instrument, a short term nominal interest rate. The stock of money adjusts endogenously, in this theoretical scheme, and money is not even included – given its purely passive role – in most model specifications.

While currently successful in the economic discipline, hence in quantitative analyses within all central banks, these models do not capture important features of the monetary transmission mechanism in the view of distinguished scholars (Meltzer, 1999). The apparent empirical success of schemes, such as the so-called *P-star* model, that fail to be easily incorporated in the standard framework, can also be seen as a signal that all the secrets of the transmission mechanism have not yet been uncovered. Some role for money, in particular, appears readily to crop up again in the standard models when relatively minor modifications are undertaken (see Nelson, 2000).

In the rest of this chapter, we document some important advances in economists' understanding of the transmission mechanism thanks to existing dynamic general equilibrium models. We also maintain, however, that, by and large, monetary policy is still implemented in conditions of very imperfect knowledge of the functioning of monetary economies.

1.2.1   Money, prices and output

Against the background of long run neutrality, theoretical arguments and empirical evidence suggest that monetary policy produces real effects, and has therefore scope for responding to shocks, in the short run. After a monetary policy shock, one typically observes a reaction of both prices and quantities, so that the long-run dichotomy between real and nominal variables breaks down and the reaction of output and prices to the monetary shock must be analysed jointly.

The short run non-neutrality of money can be understood in the context of departures from the pure competition (Walras–Arrow–Debreu) paradigm, due to imperfect information, imperfect competition or both. Lucas (1972, 1973) is the classic reference on the role of imperfect information. Under complete information, a shock to the supply of money would translate into an immediate equiproportional change in the general price level and firms would make no adjustment to the quantity of goods that they supply. They would, however, adjust their output following a relative price shock. Lucas' model shows that, if firms confuse absolute and relative price shocks, they can end up adjusting their output to changes in the general level of prices, thus leading to real effects of money supply changes.

The main alternative mechanism is that suggested by sticky-price and sticky-wage theories, whereby the seminal contributions based on rational expectations are Fischer (1977) and Taylor (1979) (see Taylor, 1999, for a comprehensive survey of the evolution of sticky-price models). More recent fundamental contributions are those by Mankiw (1985) and Akerlof and Yellen (1985), showing that large nominal rigidities can arise from the existence of small costs of adjusting prices ('menu costs'). Blanchard and Kyotaki (1987) adopt the model of monopolistic competition (originally proposed by Dixit and Stiglitz, 1977) that still plays an essential role in most recent models (from Goodfriend and King, 1997, to Obstfeld and Rogoff, 1995). These theories can explain short run monetary effectiveness because, if some prices or wages are set in advance, they cannot immediately adjust when a monetary shock is observed and real effects of the shock ensue. The effects of nominal rigidities have been shown to be magnified by the interaction with real rigidities, e.g. in the labour market (Ball and Romer, 1990).

An additional channel of short-run effectiveness of monetary policy, which has recently attracted attention, is based on financial market frictions, namely the assumption that a group of agents cannot readily access the money market after a monetary injection (thus the name 'limited participation models'; see Lucas, 1990, for an early general equilibrium contribution).

All these explanations are obviously not mutually exclusive and the most fruitful results, in terms of capacity of the models to provide a reasonable description of the data, have been obtained within eclectic frameworks, taking into account different imperfections at the same time. For example, Erceg, Henderson and Levin (2000) allow for both wage and price staggering, while Roberts (1997) argues that a small amount of imperfect information about the determinants of inflation combined with staggered prices could – unlike staggered prices on their own – explain the observed serial correlation of inflation.

Regardless of one's preferences towards one approach or the other, these theories provide rigorous economic arguments showing that money supply does, through various channels, have real short run effects. Importantly, this can be the case also for monetary policy actions implemented in accordance with a systematic, rule-type, behaviour – that is, a rule of reactions to given macroeconomic outcomes – thus contradicting the 'policy ineffectiveness proposition' most notably stated in Sargent and Wallace (1975).

Formal empirical investigations of the precise channels through which monetary policy has short-run effects, however, have always had to face a fundamental difficulty. It is not possible to identify the chain of causation between economic variables *before* having assumed a given structural model to explain those causations.

The research strategy has therefore been to postulate a given economic structure and then test whether it appears consistent with the observed behaviour of empirical variables. Depending on the methodologies, the test is conducted by estimating or calibrating the model. From this perspective, different methodologies can be distinguished by the amount of *a priori* assumptions they are willing to postulate before going to the empirical test. Three general approaches can be identified: 'traditional' large macroeconomic models; 'smaller' models, which can be either estimated or calibrated using methodologies originally devised in the 'real business cycle' (henceforth, RBC) literature; and identified, or structural, vector auto-regressions (henceforth, VARs).

All the three approaches have advantages and shortcomings. The unsatisfactory features of large macro-models are well known: they typically impose strong restrictions – not always firmly grounded in theory – on functional forms and the shape of transmission mechanisms and they are often estimated equation by equation. However, they have the advantage of being extremely detailed, thus allowing the researcher to trace the impact of a given shock or simulation exercise on different sectors of the economy. Examples of the 'new' generation of more theory-based rational expectations macro-models are Bryant (1991), Bryant, Hooper and Mann (1993), Taylor (1993a) and forward-looking versions of the ECB area-wide model (Fagan, Henry and Mestre, 2001).

Smaller 'estimated' models are obviously more manageable, their dynamic properties are more easily understood, they can be estimated by full-information techniques. However, they have to resort to short cuts in modelling only broad features of the economies and they are not always built from first principles (although they are often consistent with some underlying fully fledged theoretical model). Examples of these are Coenen and Wieland (2000), Fuhrer (1997), Fuhrer and Moore (1995), Rudebusch and Svensson (1998), Smets (2000). Small 'calibrated' models, also referred to as dynamic general equilibrium models, are measured against the data using methodologies introduced in the RBC literature. They have the advantage of being specified starting from individuals' maximising behaviour, so that they are fully internally consistent. However, at the current level of abstraction, they are not (yet) able to provide a satisfactory description of the stochastic behaviour of actual data. A couple of papers that address specifically the issue of the overall empirical fit of the models – rather than its improvement in describing a specific dimension of reality – are King and Watson (1996) and Christiano, Eichenbaum and Evans (1997).

In terms of the trade-off between model consistency and data fit, the structural VAR approach is probably the most heterodox of all. The studies along this avenue of research attempt to impose a minimal degree of *a priori* 'structure' on the data and can generally reproduce fairly well the characteristics of the data in terms of statistical fit. They remain silent, however, on the effects of 'systematic' monetary policy behaviour, concentrating on the transmission mechanism of monetary policy 'shocks' (e.g., Leeper, Sims and Zha, 1996; Christiano, Eichenbaum and Evans, 1999).

In the rest of this section we briefly discuss a number of empirical results obtained through these approaches. Rather than aiming to provide an exhaustive survey, we simply outline the main empirical regularities against which different theories must be measured. In so doing, we stress the results related to the euro area whenever they are available. Proceeding in increasing order of theoretical structure imposed on the data, we start with a discussion of stylised facts on business cycles. We also report the difficulties encountered by the existing dynamic general equilibrium models when trying to replicate these stylised facts. Structural VAR models are discussed next, with special emphasis on both the limitations and the strengths of this empirical approach. Finally, we mention a few general results obtained through large macroeconometric models and, in the same section, smaller estimated models.

1.2.1.1 Stylised facts on business cycles. One of the standard tools of evaluation of the models in the traditional real business cycle literature and, more recently, in all dynamic general equilibrium models is to compare the models' prediction for the business cycle behaviour of macroeconomic variables to those observed in the data. A key initial step in this process is the measurement of movements and co-movements of the variables of interest along the business cycles in actual economies. Although the RBC literature has initially concentrated on real variables such as output and employment and wages, the models have also been expanded to take into account monetary economies (see Cooley and Hansen, 1995). More recently, approaches based on less neoclassical assumptions have adopted the RBC-type methodology to test the goodness of fit of the models. There is not, as yet, an agreed upon macro-model, but a range of models and empirical evidence is available.

A very interesting contribution in this respect is King and Watson (1996). The authors document, first, the behaviour of money, prices, interest rates and output in the business cycle (for the United States). They then move on to evaluate the performance of three of the currently most popular sorts of models – an RBC model with endogenous money, a sticky-price model and a limited-participation model – through a comparison of their relative abilities to account for the observed behaviour of the aforementioned variables.

It is important to clarify that the significance of 'observed' correlations should not be overstated. Apart from technical measurement issues, such as how best to filter out seasonality and trend components from the raw data, the correlations are also conditional on the historical behaviour of monetary policy. Different policy reactions to economic shocks, for example pre-emptive vs. lagged responses, would obviously induce different dynamics in economic variables and in their correlation to policy variables. In this respect, the evidence summarised in the rest of this section cannot be considered as a structural feature of the economy.

King and Watson identify a few notable features emerging from the US data. There is a strong and positive correlation between nominal (and real) money M1 and output at lag zero. Moreover, money – especially in real terms – tends to lead output over the cycle, with a very high correlation at two-quarter leads. The leading behaviour of money with respect to output had already been stressed in Friedman and Schwartz (1963); King and Plosser (1984) had also stressed that the correlation is larger for the broader concept of M2. Prices tend to lead output in a counter-cyclical fashion, but they are positively correlated with output at long lags (ten quarters).

Since, to our knowledge, little business cycle evidence exists yet for the euro area,[10] we briefly document here some features on the basis of synthetic data.[11] As in King and Watson, we identify business cycle frequencies with periodicities between six and thirty-two quarters and apply the Baxter and King (1999) filter to identify such frequencies.[12] Results obtained on the basis of the Hodrick–Prescott filter are also shown for comparison. It is important to take into account that these results must be considered with great care because they are based on fictitious series

---

[10] The notable exception is Galí, Gertler and López-Salido (2000).

[11] A detailed description of the methodology adopted to construct area-wide data is provided in Fagan, Henry and Mestre (2001).

[12] King and Watson (1996) use both this bandpass filter and an estimate that takes into account the long-run cointegration properties of the variables.

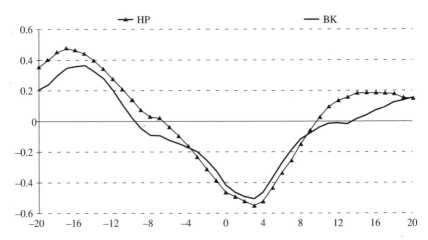

Figure 1.4 Correlation between prices and output over the business cycle
Source: Area-wide model database (see Fagan, Henry and Mestre, 2001).
Notes: HP: Hodrick–Prescott filter; BK: Baxter–King filter.

constructed *ex post* for the euro area. Moreover, they are based on a much shorter sample (typically, 1970:1 to 1998:4), especially concerning monetary aggregates (that are only available for the sample 1980:1 to 1998:4).

None the less, we generally observe patterns similar to those of the US data. Prices and output are negatively correlated at zero lags and only become pro-cyclical when long lags for output are considered. If this positive correlation between prices and lagged values of output is taken to be suggestive of price stickiness, a characteristic of euro area data is probably a higher level of stickiness: while the peak in the correlation for the USA is apparently observed after 2.5 years, in the euro area it is reached only after almost four years. The correlation pattern of nominal interest rates and output is also very similar between Europe and the USA: in particular, the correlation between output and interest rates in Europe peaks after only two quarters (see figure 1.4 and table 1.1).

The most notable difference between euro area and US data concerns the correlation between money and output. Unlike in the USA, narrow money (M1) is only weakly correlated to output at lag zero; although it does, like in the USA, appear to lead output, the maximum correlation between the two is lower and peaks at a longer lag than in the USA. As to broad money (M3), this appears to be a lagging – rather than leading – indicator for output (see figures 1.5–1.6).

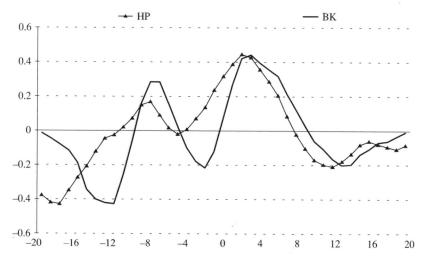

Figure 1.5 Correlation between money M1 and output over the business cycle
Source: Area-wide model database (see Fagan, Henry and Mestre, 2001).
Notes: HP: Hodrick–Prescott filter; BK: Baxter–King filter.

As already mentioned, the results for monetary aggregates should be considered with special care, because of the very short sample period available.[13] Nevertheless, on the basis of King and Watson's theoretical results, the behaviour of money in Europe could also be taken as suggestive of higher price stickiness: the only model – amongst those considered by the authors – that can produce negative correlation between money and output at some lagged values of money is the sticky-price one.

Evidence suggestive of a relatively high degree of nominal stickiness also emerges from the analysis of the correlation of output and the real wage in table 1.1. As also noted by Galí, Gertler and López-Salido (2000), the real wage reacts very little to output fluctuations: the latter appear to be accommodated mainly through adjustments of productivity.

Finally, it is interesting to note that nominal broad money is strongly positively correlated with prices and it would appear to be a leading indicator less than one year ahead. A strong counter-cyclical relationship, however, is also observed between money and prices lagged 3.5 years (see figure 1.7).

As stressed earlier, these correlations say nothing about causation. Most of the movement of nominal money could actually represent

[13] Not only is the sample period short, but it includes 'extraordinary' events such as the ERM crisis and the German reunification.

Table 1.1. *Business cycle statistics for Baxter–King filtered data (1973:01–1995:04)*

					Cross-correlation of Y_{t+j}			
	SD(x)/SD(Y)	$j = -3$	$j = -2$	$j = -1$	$j = 0$	$j = 1$	$j = 2$	$j = 3$
Y	0.08	0.33	0.57	0.78	1.00	0.78	0.57	0.33
P	7.33	−0.53	−0.50	−0.47	−0.42	−0.33	−0.26	−0.21
I	0.61	0.29	0.49	0.66	0.84	0.75	0.63	0.48
N	0.05	0.12	0.29	0.50	0.69	0.78	0.77	0.70
C	0.44	0.37	0.46	0.59	0.71	0.47	0.37	0.30
R	16.15	−0.37	−0.12	0.18	0.44	0.59	0.60	0.52
W	0.59	0.02	0.02	0.11	0.22	0.16	0.19	0.22
Pr	0.96	0.35	0.53	0.71	0.83	0.51	0.24	−0.03
M_1	1.05	0.24	0.33	0.53	0.69	0.18	−0.09	−0.32
M_2	1.28	0.46	0.36	0.13	−0.06	−0.27	−0.37	−0.32
M_3	2.49	0.14	0.05	−0.12	−0.31	−0.45	−0.49	−0.43

					Cross-correlation of P_{t+j}			
	SD(x)/SD(P)	$j = -3$	$j = -2$	$j = -1$	$j = 0$	$j = 1$	$j = 2$	$j = 3$
Y	0.58	0.77	0.85	0.94	1.00	0.94	0.85	0.77
P	0.14	−0.21	−0.26	−0.33	−0.42	−0.47	−0.50	−0.53
I	0.08	−0.18	−0.26	−0.35	−0.46	−0.52	−0.57	−0.61
N	0.01	−0.23	−0.30	−0.38	−0.46	−0.54	−0.60	−0.62
C	0.06	−0.39	−0.45	−0.51	−0.58	−0.55	−0.52	−0.53
R	2.20	0.32	0.30	0.22	0.10	−0.05	−0.20	−0.31
W	0.08	−0.24	−0.25	−0.34	−0.42	−0.33	−0.30	−0.34
Pr	0.15	−0.22	−0.26	−0.26	−0.30	−0.31	−0.25	−0.18
M_1	0.28	0.25	0.26	0.27	0.26	0.24	0.25	0.25
M_2	0.39	0.46	0.47	0.47	0.44	0.40	0.37	0.33
M_3	0.13	−0.12	−0.14	−0.19	−0.26	−0.24	−0.26	−0.29

Source: Area-wide model database (see Fagan, Henry and Mestre, 2001).
Notes: Y, Gross Domestic Product; P, Harmonised Index of Consumer Prices for the euro area (or national CPIs); I, investment; N; employment; C, consumption; R, 3-month nominal interest rate; W, real wage; Pr, productivity. For M_1, M_2 and M_3, the sample period is restricted to 1983:01–1995:04. GDP, investment, consumption, employment and money are per capita (in the labour force); the real wage is defined as nominal wage/MUICP; labour productivity is defined as GDP per employed.

reactions to real economic developments according to the so-called reverse causality effect (see Tobin, 1970, and King and Plosser, 1984). King and Watson try to tackle this issue, testing which of the three classes of models mentioned before does best in fitting the data, but, unfortunately, none of the three models appears to be satisfactory. For suitable specifications of the driving processes for money and technology shocks, the RBC

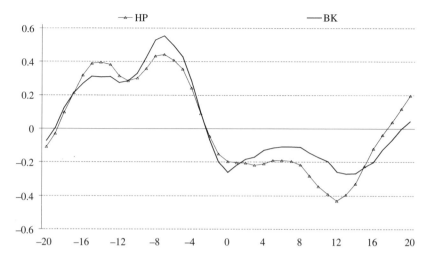

Figure 1.6 Correlation between money M3 and output over the business cycle
Source: Area-wide model database (see Fagan, Henry and Mestre, 2001).
Notes: HP: Hodrick–Prescott filter; BK: Baxter–King filter.

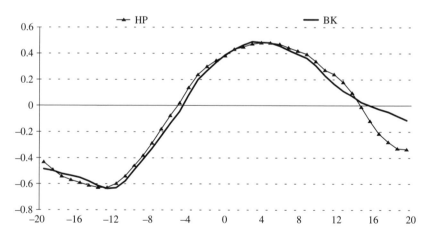

Figure 1.7 Correlation between money M3 and prices over the business cycle
Source: Area-wide model database (see Fagan, Henry and Mestre, 2000).
Notes: HP: Hodrick–Prescott filter; BK: Baxter–King filter.

model is capable of fully replicating the cyclical behaviour of money in US data. The model, however, produces too little volatility for nominal and, especially, real interest rates. A notable feature of the sticky-price model is a negative correlation between money and future output, which is consistent with the evidence on broad money in Europe (but not in the USA). Interestingly, King and Watson argue that this depends on the assumed mean reversion of the money supply process and on the interest elasticity of money demand. Together, these two assumptions imply that when M is high, it is expected to decline; hence, expected future declines in the (sticky) prices, the interest rate and output. However, the cyclical behaviour of nominal interest rates in the sticky-price model is the opposite of that found in the data. The limited participation model also replicates the measured variability and covariation of the data only imperfectly. King and Watson conclude that 'all prominent macroeconomic models – those which stress a single set of economic mechanisms – have substantial difficulties matching the core features of nominal and real interactions'.

1.2.1.2 Structural VARs. The structural VAR literature can also provide information on the lead-lag characteristics of money and prices. Moreover, structural VARs (or SVARs) can be useful in tracing the general features of the monetary policy transmission mechanism – its lags, in particular – and in assessing the role of monetary policy shocks in the determination of business cycle fluctuations. The SVAR literature is of particular interest because it provides relatively more empirical evidence on Europe.

A recent survey of the general results obtained – for the USA – within the SVAR literature is provided by Christiano, Eichenbaum and Evans (1999). A particularly comprehensive analysis can be found in Leeper, Sims and Zha (1996).

Before going on to discuss the results of this literature, its main objective has to be specified carefully. Although this should be an implicit outcome in a well-specified system, VARs do not focus on the identification of the monetary policy reaction function to exogenous shocks (e.g., to technology or tastes). As Christiano, Eichenbaum and Evans (1999, fn. 4) point out, the literature they review 'is silent on this point' (which is sometimes also referred to as the 'systematic' component of monetary policy).

The SVAR literature focuses instead on the effects of unexpected, or unsystematic, monetary policy, typically referred to as monetary policy shocks. The interest in studying this kind of policy behaviour rests on the fact that, in order to analyse the transmission mechanism of a monetary policy move, it is essential to first isolate the policy move. It is necessary, in other words, to be able to separate the endogenous responses of macro-variables to policy from the movements they can display in response to other sorts of exogenous shocks.

Unfortunately, within the common SVAR approach, differences exist in relation to the identifying assumption imposed to isolate monetary policy shocks. As a result, for example, inference about the stance of monetary policy at each moment in time is not invariant to changes in the identifying assumption. More uniform results, however, are obtained concerning the qualitative features of the response of the economy to a monetary policy shock.

In particular, a contractionary policy shock coincides with an increase of policy rates and a decline in monetary aggregates; it is followed by a temporary fall in output and a very slow response of prices. Exactly because of the slow response of prices, money typically tends to lead prices in the transmission mechanism.

The structural VAR literature also provides indications concerning the timing of the responses of the economy to monetary policy shocks. There is obviously a considerable amount of uncertainty regarding these effects – increasingly so, the further away in the future the effects are with respect to the initial policy impulse. Although a certain degree of heterogeneity across models exists, a few unifying features can again be identified.

Within the numerous alternative models considered by Christiano, Eichenbaum and Evans, the response of output to a monetary shock goes from being statistically insignificant to becoming negligible after approximately three years, with the peak effect typically occurring in the second year after the shock.[14] On the contrary, the impact on prices appears more delayed. The effects on prices of a monetary shock often become significant only after three years and in many occasions they only appear to be approaching the new steady state after four years.[15] Similarly, within an 18-variable VAR in which movements in both the discount and the federal funds rates are considered, Leeper, Sims and Zha (1996) report that a change in the two policy rates barely starts having significant

---

[14] It is worth emphasising that Christiano, Eichenbaum and Evans (1999) claim that their results are quite consistent with those obtained through yet another methodology used by Romer and Romer (1989) to identify the effects of monetary policy: the so-called 'narrative' approach. Rather than through a statistical analysis, Romer and Romer single out a number of episodes of monetary contractions on the basis of a careful reading of the records of FOMC meetings along the tradition of Friedman and Schwartz (1963). Romer and Romer argue that their results are not subject to the risk of being based on an incorrect identifying assumption, as is the case for VAR-type studies.

[15] This is the maximum number of steps in the impulse responses shown in the paper.

effects on the price level after four years. Within a different set of identifying assumptions, however, Galí (1992) only finds significant effects on prices up to two years.

Although the aforementioned results only pertain to the US economy, they have largely been confirmed for European countries in a number of studies. Amongst the comparative ones, which analyse many European countries at the same time, see Gerlach and Smets (1995) and Kim (1999). Monticelli and Tristani (1999) and Peersman and Smets (2000) attempt to characterise the effects of the single monetary policy using pre-EMU data.

1.2.1.3 Large macroeconometric models and smaller 'estimated' models. Simulation exercises using large macroeconometric models can in principle give a lot of information about the propagation through the economy of monetary policy moves, such as an increase in the interest rates with respect to the baseline. Their results are obviously conditional on a postulated transmission mechanism and they can only be believed to the extent that one is willing to trust the overall goodness of fit of the model as a signal of the appropriateness of the assumptions on which it is based.

The results of a systematic comparative exercise conducted using large macro-models of a number of central banks are reported in BIS (1995) and summarised in Smets (1995). The exercise typically consists in assuming a change of short-term interest rates over a number of periods and then tracing the effects of the shock on many economic variables. A particularly interesting feature of the exercise is that it is conducted independently in different countries, on the basis of models that can be quite different in terms of underlying assumptions and estimation techniques. Results consistent across countries/models could therefore be considered as relatively more reliable, although typical cautions obviously apply.

The exercise shows that a 1 percentage point increase of policy-determined interest rates sustained for two years has a short-lasting negative impact on the level of output (the effect is typically reabsorbed two years after the policy rate goes back to the baseline). Continental European models tend to produce smaller output effects than models of Anglo-Saxon countries: peak effects are always below 50 basis points of deviation of output from the baseline, and can be regarded as negligible in a few countries.

Concerning the effect of the change of policy interest rates on prices, the most notable feature that emerges is the presence of Milton Friedman's 'long and variable lags' in the transmission mechanism. Different models give quite different answers as to the size and especially the timing of the impact: in a few cases, the effect on prices has not even reached its peak five years after the start of the monetary policy impulse. Although noticeable, this result has to be treated with special care because of the well-known difficulties in ensuring dynamic stability properties in large macro-models.

As already emphasised, one of the points of strength of large macro-econometric models is their capacity to provide a very detailed account of the propagation through the economy of a monetary policy move. It is remarkable, however, that this degree of detail is not always helpful to achieve a better understanding of overall macroeconomic developments. Results broadly comparable to those outlined above can be obtained also within much smaller models, where the economy is stripped down to two equations corresponding to the traditional IS–AS schedules.

Two examples of small macro-models estimated on euro area data are Smets (2000) and Coenen and Wieland (2000). Using a specification consistent with a sticky-price model, but extended to allow for some stickiness also in the rate of inflation, these models are able to replicate reasonably well the behaviour of output and inflation in the euro area in the past twenty years. The results, when compared to those obtained in similar models estimated on US data, are again suggestive of a higher degree of price stickiness in Europe.

2   Monetary policy making: strategies and rules

Having discussed the issue of *what* monetary policy can accomplish, we go on to review the current academic thinking on 'monetary policy making', that is on *how* monetary policy makers can best achieve their objectives. The advances in this field of monetary economics have been remarkable in recent years. Nowadays, we have more precise ways to investigate the comparative effects of different policy actions within rigorous, quantitative frameworks. Nevertheless, though relying partly on theoretical results, actual policy making must also recognise the role of judgmental inputs. While welcoming the advances of the economic discipline, practical monetary policy must not be dazzled by the formal elegance and refinement of theoretical models. In spite of great improvements, formal models continue to be so highly simplified, with respect to the complexities of the real world, that their practical implications must be regarded with considerable caution.

Our starting point is the issue of 'rules vs. discretion'. While in recent practical central banking experience simple rules are the exception – and, *de facto*, always linked to the adoption of a fixed exchange rate arrangement – the issue of rules vs. discretion is far from settled in the academic debate. After a brief account of the 'old' debate, in section 2.1 we review how this has been completely reshaped by the advent of the 'time inconsistency' literature. This literature has helped to clarify the distinction between discretion and activism and, more importantly, has highlighted the fundamental importance of *credibility* in monetary policy.

In section 2.2 we discuss the theory of optimal monetary policy making in the context of a given model. Here, the fundamental results obtained in the seventies within simpler models – results favouring an approach based on all the available information – have recently been restated in terms of more complex frameworks. In most cases, however, these results are strictly model dependent and assume away the problem of achieving and maintaining credibility. Few robust results have been found in the literature, once model uncertainty is taken into account.

In search of robustness, the literature has therefore gone back to explore simple (more or less activist) rules, which express the policy instrument as a function of a limited number of variables. Simple and robust instrument rules have recently attracted attention because of their capacity to approximate reasonably well complex and optimal rules. Moreover, simple rules have, in principle, the advantage of making a formal announcement feasible, thus ensuring commitment. We briefly discuss simple rules in section 2.3, and suggest that, in practice, they can be useful as policy benchmarks *within* a full information approach.

Finally, in section 2.4, we characterise monetary policy strategies in light of the aforementioned results. We emphasise that they represent an attempt to clarify the systematic character of the optimal and complex policy response implemented by the central bank over time. The public announcement of the strategy represents a form of commitment and can therefore contribute to establishing credibility for the central bank.

2.1 Rules vs. discretion: the importance of credibility

The debate on rules vs. discretion has a long history in macroeconomics (for a survey, see Fischer, 1990), arising from the proposals, put forward by a number of academics, in favour of constraining the behaviour of monetary authorities (most famously, Milton Friedman, 1959, but, earlier on, Bagehot, 1873; Fisher, 1920, 1926; Simons, 1936; and Wicksell, 1907 – see McCallum, 1999, for a brief account).

Advocates of fixed rules would typically prescribe setting the policy instrument at a given level once and for all (a typical example is Friedman's so-called k per cent money growth rule). The key element in the argument for rules would typically be to underline the extent of economists' and central banks' ignorance on the functioning of the economy, thus warning against activist stabilisation policies. A famous example is Milton Friedman's statement on the 'long and variable lags' of the monetary policy transmission mechanism, leading to the conclusion that activist and myopic policies could exacerbate, rather than dampen, economic fluctuations.

Fixed rules are characterised by two key features. The first is the elimination of judgmental elements from monetary policy. The second is the aversion to activism, i.e. changes in policy in response to current economic developments.

Before 1977 the case for rules, 'however suggestive it may have been, was vulnerable to the simple criticism that any good rule can always be operated by discretion – and that discretion therefore always dominates rules'(Blanchard and Fischer, 1989). It was hard to see any clear advantage for a central bank to commit to a rule-like behaviour.

This state of affairs changed radically with the advent of the 'time inconsistency' literature. The central idea is simple and convincing: macroeconomic policies cannot be systematically implemented on the basis of the assumption that agents' expectations are given. Since economic outcomes will depend on future policy intentions, as well as on current policy decisions, agents will systematically try to anticipate policy moves when forming their expectations. This kind of interaction between policy makers and the other economic players can be usefully characterised as a policy game in which the credibility of future policy intentions assumes crucial importance.

In the simple examples of Kydland and Prescott (1977) and Barro and Gordon (1983), the existence of distortions in the economy justifies that the monetary authority, and society at large, wish to attain an unemployment level below the natural rate. In such circumstances, the authority will have an incentive to create surprise inflation, that is to announce an inflation goal and renege on it *ex post*. Once the private sector understands the authorities' incentives, however, it will anticipate future inflation. The outcome is dismal: an 'inflationary bias', which translates to a higher than planned level of inflation and which prevents policy from attaining the first best solution even when it does not renege on its announcement *ex post*. A superior outcome is achieved if the authority takes into account the impact of its behaviour on agents' expectations and, consequently, commits not to inflate. The advantage of commitment relative to discretion hinges on the *credibility* that the central bank achieves under this regime.

The distinction between rules and discretion has since been differentiated from that between active and passive policies. Rules do not necessarily imply fixing once and for all the policy instrument; they typically involve changing the instrument in response to the evolution of the economy, as long as the change occurs in a predetermined fashion. 'Roughly speaking, discretion implies period-by-period reoptimization on the part of the monetary authority whereas a rule calls for period-by-period implementation of a contingency formula that has been selected to be generally applicable for an indefinitely large number of decision periods'(McCallum,1999).

In the rest of this section, we focus on the evolution of the commitment vs. discretion debate. We will return to the debate on active vs. passive policies in section 2.3.

2.1.1   Commitment vs. discretion

A main strand of literature originating from the Kydland and Prescott contribution has since tried to devise incentive-compatible institutional arrangements capable of enforcing a rule-like behaviour on the monetary policy authority. A general feature of the proposed arrangements is to appoint an independent central bank in charge of monetary policy. This feature is at the basis of the statutes of many modern central banks, including the ECB (see chapter 9).

Within the common prescription of an independent central bank, however, different forms of 'commitment technology' have been invoked to force it to adopt the commitment-type behaviour. Within the 'standard' Barro–Gordon model, it has been shown that three of them perform as well as the optimal rule under commitment.

The first is to design an optimal contract (Walsh, 1995)[1] that penalises the central bank for deviating from the inflation target. The optimal contract turns out to be linear in the Barro–Gordon world, and it allows elimination of the inflationary bias without costs in terms of output volatility. The second sort of contract has been proposed by Svensson (1997a), who shows that the optimal linear contract is equivalent to the situation in which the central bank has a lower inflation target than society. A third solution to the inflationary bias problem is simply to accept that policy should treat the natural unemployment rate as socially optimal, without trying to push unemployment above its natural rate even when it has an opportunity to do so.

Recent additions to this literature (e.g., Lockwood, Miller and Zhang, 1998, and Svensson,1997a) have shown that things are more complex when employment persistence is taken into account. In this case, a bias due to the possibility of exploiting employment persistence in order to engineer surprise inflation ('stabilisation bias') arises besides the standard ('average') inflationary bias. While the three aforementioned solutions continue to cure the average bias, they must be amended and made contingent on the state of the economy in order to eliminate the inflationary bias completely. In particular, the Walsh inflation contract would have to be made contingent on lagged employment. The solution represented by a lower inflation target for the central bank would also have to be made contingent on the state of the economy and, in addition, coupled with the appointment of a weight-conservative central banker in the Rogoff (1985) sense. The natural employment level to be accepted by the monetary

---

[1] For further elaboration and some institutional insight see also Persson and Tabellini (1993, 1999).

authority should vary over time, so that monetary policy cannot exploit the output–inflation trade-off.

Two general normative results can be taken from this literature (see Persson and Tabellini, 1999). First, the goal of pursuing price stability deserves special emphasis in the statute or mandate of a central bank. 'Intuitively, the whole purpose of optimal contracts is to remove an inflation bias. This is most easily done by means of a direct penalty on inflation, rather than in a more roundabout way, by targeting other variables that are only loosely related to inflation'(Persson and Tabellini, 1999, p. 1435). An inflation objective is also easy to monitor, which enhances accountability. We will return to this issue in its relationship to independence in chapter 9.

The second result is that, in the design of a monetary constitution, society faces a trade-off between credibility and flexibility: strong incentives for the central bank to achieve price stability may result in unnecessary losses in terms of other economic variables. In this respect, the aforementioned three institutional arrangements are optimal since, in principle, they solve the credibility problem at no cost in terms of flexibility. Their complexity within general, more realistic frameworks, however, has prompted doubts as to their practical feasibility. Svensson (1997a), for instance, argues that 'state contingent targets may be too sophisticated to be feasible, especially if there are more state variables than lagged employment. In practice, only constant targets may be feasible' (p. 110).

From the positive viewpoint, therefore, the academic literature has focused on the hypothesis of absence of a feasible 'commitment technology', with the conclusion that central bank behaviour is best described as monetary policy under discretion.

There is, however, an alternative point of view according to which it is not necessarily the case that the central bank is not capable to freely (i.e. without a commitment technology) choose the first best (McCallum, 1995, 1997; also Blinder, 1997a, 1998). The central bank can, simply as a result of the rational expectations assumption, realise that surprise inflation will generate, on average, an inferior outcome. Failing to realise this implies a myopic behaviour, so that monetary policy becomes a sequence of one-period decisions. Optimisation under commitment could therefore be chosen by the central bank by simply realising that this is in its best interest. In practice, this 'just do it' approach (in the words of King, 1997) eventually boils down to the fact that the central bank will systematically avoid exploiting temporarily given inflation expectations for the sake of short-lived output gains.

2.1.2   The importance of credibility

Even if a central bank chose to commit to a (possibly complex) rule, however, the key advantage of the commitment-type solution – achieving credibility – would fail to materialise if the rule was not publicly announced and internalised by the public.

Central bankers are highly conscious of the benefits of credibility. Blinder's (1999) survey documents that they attach to this concept a higher importance than academics. Thus, they can certainly understand that the full benefits of credibility can, if unattainable through institutional arrangements, be achieved through a freely chosen commitment.

It is important to stress that, if forward looking variables exist in the economy, the benefits of credibility materialise *even in the absence of an inflationary bias*. Since forward looking variables react to expected future policy moves, being able to influence expectations of future policy – because it is credible – the central bank can have an effect on current economic outcomes. This channel of monetary policy transmission is independent of whether the central bank tries to engineer surprise inflation.

Clarida, Galí and Gertler (1999) and Woodford (1999a, b, c) have recently demonstrated this point formally. They assume that price setting decisions are taken by forward-looking firms, so that current inflation will depend on future economic conditions. In such a framework, a central bank facing an inflationary shock has an incentive to persuade private agents that it is committed to disinflation in future periods. The expectation of *future* central bank actions will have an effect on current inflation, moderating the current impact of the shock on prices. As a result, the central bank will be able to implement a milder *initial* policy response than would have been the case under discretion.

It is remarkable how this result is consistent with standard central bank jargon. Using the latter, Clarida, Galí and Gertler's results can be characterised as showing that, if the central bank is able to credibly signal that it will maintain a steady course in the face of a persistent (cost-push) inflationary shock, this will immediately curb inflation. The reason is that inflationary expectations have a direct effect on current inflation. Ultimately, the central bank is able to reduce the immediate impact of an inflationary shock through the promise of a tough future course of actions and, in a sense, irrespective of the current response. This implies that a credible central bank can achieve superior outcomes. Since credibility causes a smaller propagation of inflationary shocks, the departure from price stability will be smaller than in the case in which the bank pursues time consistent policies. Consequently, the return to price stability becomes possible through a smaller contraction of aggregate demand, thus with a smaller output loss. It is exactly through an announcement that it cares 'little' about output fluctuations that the central bank effectively smooths out the excess volatility of output.

Since the effects of credibility unfold through forward-looking variables, it becomes clear why central bankers pay great attention to financial asset prices and in particular to bond markets. The importance of the latter is twofold. First, as forward-looking variables incorporating expectations of future inflationary developments, long-term bond prices should reflect the credibility of the central bank. Second, the yield curve represents a 'filter' through which monetary policy is transmitted to real variables.[2]

Consciousness of the benefits of credibility is the driving force behind the trend currently observed amongst central banks to select a strategy. The adoption of a monetary policy strategy is an attempt to characterise to the best possible extent, given the imperfect knowledge of the economy, the way in which the central bank will respond to the arrival of information. The strategy represents exactly an effort to capture the systematic character of the (optimal) policy, i.e. the fact that certain outcomes of the state of the economy will always be met by the same response.

The public announcement of a strategy effectively works as a form of commitment. Since the strategy aims to be 'optimal', however, it will typically be infeasible to provide a complete taxonomy of policy responses to all possible states of the world. This 'imprecision' makes it more difficult to monitor whether the commitment is being enforced at each point in time, but it appears to be the necessary by-product of the attempt to implement an *optimal* policy. As a result, the announcement of a strategy cannot be expected to 'buy' credibility in itself. The peculiar characteristics of the monetary policy response to specific sources of shocks will necessarily have to be clarified over time, as these shocks occur.

Ultimately, however, credibility will have to be built over time by establishing a reputation. Reputation has already been shown capable of producing positive effects on the inflationary bias in applications of the Kreps and Wilson (1982) model. According to Blinder (1999), reputation ('living up to one's words') is the best way to achieve credibility in the opinion of both academics and central bankers. The lack of a track record represents, in this respect, a crucial drawback in the quest for credibility.

Nevertheless, the announcement of the strategy and an appropriate communication policy are also useful for a reputable central bank. They ensure that credibility takes on an institutional character, without which

---

[2] It is certainly more difficult to provide a precise quantitative assessment of the 'value' of credibility, for example in terms of percentage points of long-term interest rates.

reputation can be attached to the personal charisma of a Chairman, President or Governor. In this respect, the strategy helps to avoid the risks of swings in credibility over time arising as a result of changes in the personal composition of the monetary policy decision making body.

2.2   Optimal policy

Once the crucial importance of credibility is recognised, the issue of 'what exactly is the best the central bank can do?' arises.

The first time the issue of optimal monetary policy arose in the literature was probably during the early debate on monetary targeting in the early seventies. Amongst other authors, Friedman (1975), Kalchbrenner and Tinsley (1976) and Kareken, Muench and Wallace (1973) showed that optimal monetary policy must adopt a full information approach, i.e. respond to all the information in the economy which is relevant to gauge the risks of missing the goal. In the case of imperfect information, some variables could have a purely 'informational' role. If they are correlated with the final goal and they either become known earlier or appear to move chronologically before the goal, then they are useful indicators, even if they are not causal determinants of the goal.

A restatement of these results has recently occurred within some variants of the theoretical inflation targeting literature. In these papers, the need to adopt a full information approach is emphasised in the form of the adoption of a *target rule*, i.e. a rule prescribing a *gradual* reduction of the discrepancy between the inflation forecast (at a horizon compatible with the existence of control lags) and the inflation target. Within any given model, the target rule coincides with the optimal policy, since it is *defined* as the first order condition of the optimal control problem of a central bank trying to minimise deviations of the inflation rate from a given target. In this respect, the inflation forecast obviously summarises, within a given model, all the relevant information for the assessment of the risks of missing the inflation target.

It is important to stress, however, that the optimal policy, or target rule, does not imply, even within simple models, that the policy instrument will be set as a function of the sole deviation of the inflation forecast from target (see, e.g., Clarida, Galí and Gertler, 1999). When the policy maker wishes to reduce unnecessary volatility of output around potential, for example, it is not the case, even within simple models, that the optimal decision making process can be represented as a two-step procedure, in which the forecast is formed first, and the interest rate is set next, depending solely on the gap between the forecast and the target. The way in which the policy instrument must be set in order to implement the model-consistent optimal policy is, in general, more complex. What remains true, as in the 'traditional' literature, is that the central bank is required to react to all the potential determinants of inflation within the model, i.e. to all the relevant information. Again, results consistent with those of the 'old' literature, though within a much richer framework, are obtained by Svensson and Woodford (2000) for the case of imperfect information.

An approach consistent, or aiming to be consistent, with an optimal policy – in the sense of taking into account all the relevant information or, equivalently, of monitoring and reacting to all the determinants of inflation – arguably characterises the behaviour of most modern central banks. They typically process large amounts of information in order to achieve the best possible assessment of the risks to price stability. Within a model, optimal policy, full information approach and target rules are perfectly equivalent definitions of the same concept. We will therefore stick to the traditional label 'full information approach'.

Even if, in theory, the full information approach is acknowledged to represent the best a central bank can do, two fundamental complications arise, in practice. The first is that, as we have emphasised at the beginning of this section, the full information approach does not in itself 'buy' credibility for the central bank. Given the important benefits of credibility, alternative policies could be explored. We address this issue in section 2.3.

A second important complication that arises when the concept of optimal policy is applied to practical central banking is that 'the model' – i.e. an accurate description of the functioning of the economy, the determinants of inflation and the exact channel(s) of transmission of monetary policy – is not available. As we argued in chapter 1, different theoretical specifications match only some of the stylised facts that can be observed from modern monetary economies, so that a straightforward selection of the 'best', if not the 'true', reference model becomes a matter of faith.

In the absence of a precise reference model, what exactly the full information approach implies, in terms of how quickly or by how much the policy interest rate should be moved in a certain direction when a certain development in the economy is observed, is unclear. Even within a single class of models, many features of the optimal policy response vary significantly as the assumptions of the model change.

The most striking example of the sensitivity of the optimal policy response to changes in some model assumptions is related to parameter uncertainty. The traditional result on the effect of parameter uncertainty on monetary policy is that obtained by Brainard (1967), according to which policy should be more cautious when its effects on the economy are imperfectly known. The generality of this result has been questioned in the literature and it now appears that there are forms of uncertainty under which policy should optimally behave more aggressively. For example, Craine (1979) confirms that uncertainty about policy transmission leads to gradualism, but shows that uncertainty about the dynamics of the economy leads to a more aggressive policy. Söderström (2000)confirms this result when uncertainty about the dynamics of the economy concerns the degree of inflation persistence.

More generally, the literature on learning (e.g., Wieland, 2000) shows that, in control problems that also involve some sort of estimation, intertemporal optimal learning can involve some degree of experimentation. More precisely, instead of treating the estimation problem separately from the control problem, the policy maker can try to use its control both to steer the economy and to learn about it. This can involve implementing policies that lead to a worse current outcome, but yield significant information to improve future outcomes.

However, in an application to the case in which the policy maker does not know the true level of the natural unemployment rate, Wieland (1998) shows that the cautionary Brainard-type argument typically prevails over the advantages of experimentation. Consequently, optimal policy is typically (though with exceptions) more gradual than in the corresponding certainty equivalent case.

Parameter uncertainty is therefore very important, in the sense that it is likely to lead to a different monetary policy response than in the case in which all model parameters are known. However, it does not have dramatic consequences, in the sense that the policy maker can deal with it by simply estimating'how much you need to tighten or loosen monetary policy to "get it right". Then do less' (Blinder, 1998). Other sources of uncertainty, in particular model uncertainty, have more far-reaching consequences. The result is that, in practice, a considerable amount of judgment must be employed by central banks when trying to evaluate 'all the relevant information', in order to assess which is the 'best' response to observed economic developments. There is no available model within which the central bank can assess 'scientifically', at each point in time, the size and type of structural shocks occurring in the economy, the evolution of a number of unobserved variables, and the change in the policy instrument needed to best ensure the achievement of the statutory objectives.

2.3 Simple rules as policy benchmarks

The lack of professional agreement on a model suited for the analysis of monetary policy issues has led to a 'rediscovery' of simple rules in the academic literature.

A simple instrument rule is a relationship between the central bank instrument – typically, a short-term interest rate closely controlled by the central bank – and a small set of economic variables (the policy objective and closely related variables). The best known example is the Taylor rule (Taylor, 1993b), expressing the policy interest rate as a linear function of the output gap and of the deviations of inflation from a target level. Other examples, in decreasing order of activism, are the so-called McCallum rule (McCallum, 1988)[3] for the monetary base and the aforementioned Friedman k per cent rule (although the latter is no longer an instrument rule, when referred to broad money, because it does not prescribe directly how to set the policy instrument as a function of a given set of variables).

In principle, simple rules can be seen, first, as the means to ultimately ensure that credibility is earned and maintained, because they can easily be monitored by third parties. Since they are simple, they can also be promptly implemented (an often emphasised characteristic of simple rules is that they should only rely on information available at the time the instrument is set). Moreover, simple rules eliminate any uncertainty about the policy response to future economic developments. Finally, they will be incorporated in forward-looking variables, thus helping to facilitate private-sector planning decisions and the general allocation of resources.

Simple rules, in particular of the Taylor type, appear to provide *ex post* a good description of policies actually followed by central banks in the eighties and early nineties (though with notable exceptions, such as the ERM crisis period in Europe). Moreover, simple rules tend to be 'robust' in policy simulation, that is to yield 'reasonably desirable outcomes in policy simulation experiments in a wide variety of models' (McCallum, 1999). Model simulations (e.g., Levin, Wieland and Williams, 1999) apparently show that the Taylor rule is indeed robust across a variety of models, while rules that are optimal within any one model tend to perform much worse when used in other models.

In spite of these good descriptive properties, simple rules are rarely advocated as *prescriptive* policy tools, even by their proponents. A total commitment to a simple rule could lead to sub-optimal policies since, by assumption, they do not take into account all potential sorts of information that can, from time to time, be relevant for monetary policy (for example, financial crises or asset market bubbles).[4] By construction,

---

[3] This rule reflects ideas expressed earlier by Bronfenbrenner (1961), McCallum (1984) and Meltzer (1984).

[4] An additional drawback of instrument rules sometimes pointed out is that they could be infeasible (Goodhart, 1994) or lead to nominal indeterminacy or solution multiplicity (the traditional reference for the first case is Sargent and Wallace, 1975; for a recent example of the second, see Benhabib, Schmitt-Grohé and Uribe, 1999). See McCallum (1999), for a discussion.

they are dominated, within any given model, by the optimal policy consistent with the model (they can, at most, be equivalent to it).

An additional drawback of simple rules is that, if used as prescriptive tools, they may turn out to be only deceivingly simple, if they are functions of variables that are not timely or accurately observed. Incorrect estimates of the unobserved variables would obviously lead to incorrect policies if the rule were to be applied 'blindly'.

The good performance *ex post* of the Taylor rule, for example, has been shown to depend on the availability of correct estimates of the output gap and of the equilibrium real interest rate. Concerning the output gap, in particular, measurement errors are likely to be significant in view of the unavailability of a precise theoretical definition of this aggregate variable (see Galí and Gertler, 1999, for a discussion). A recent confirmation of the potential imprecision of real time estimates of the output gap is provided by Orphanides (2000) concerning the US experience in the seventies. Orphanides shows that, compared to the final estimates obtained at the end of 1994, real time figures available during the seventies were characterised by very large and very persistent measurement errors. In particular, the output gap was severely overestimated over the whole decade (by up to 10 percentage points), owing to both a serious underestimation of the NAIRU and an overestimation of trend productivity growth.

Orphanides also shows through a number of simulations that, if only the 'correct' estimates of the output gap had been available, application of the Taylor rule would have avoided the 'Great Inflation'. He also shows that the policy followed during the seventies was in fact indistinguishable from a Taylor rule, but based, unfortunately, on incorrect estimates of the output gap. Even if, in principle, the Taylor rule could have led to good outcomes, because of measurement errors it could be viewed as the primary cause of the inflationary outburst in the late sixties and seventies. This is a particular example of the general problems likely to be encountered by any activist rule. Although in principle beneficial, they can fail to deliver their promise because of our imperfect knowledge of the functioning of the economy.

Once these important drawbacks have been taken into account, simple rules are not completely useless to the monetary policy maker. Because of their degree of 'robustness', they can be useful to provide (and are indeed typically presented as) 'guidelines' or 'benchmarks' for the instrument setting. This can be particularly useful in day-to-day monetary policy making. Within a full information approach, actual policy decisions will occasionally be different from those strictly consistent with the benchmark. Such differences, however, would not contradict the benchmark but, rather, represent the policy maker's effort to *optimally* improve on it in order to achieve a better outcome. The possibility of improving on the benchmark naturally hinges on the availability of the necessary information: thus, the benchmark is especially useful when information is scarce, uncertainty is at its highest and there is a significant probability of making large mistakes.

At each point in time, many policy guidelines can be monitored within a full information approach, so that the indications provided by each of them can be evaluated against the others, first, and against a more complete information set, subsequently. Clearly, the contribution of each policy benchmark would be automatically incorporated in the optimal response if the available macroeconomic model could be assumed to provide a correct representation of the functioning of the economy. If the latter assumption cannot be made with certainty, however, the benchmark can provide useful 'additional' information, the more so the more it appears to be robust to particular dimensions of uncertainty.

Simple rules with a large emphasis on nominal variables appear particularly useful as benchmarks. Among the various ones proposed in the literature, two general alternatives to the Taylor rule appear to be available (taking as given the choice of the interest rate as the policy instrument): 'strict' monetary targeting[5] and nominal income targeting.[6] The first prescribes that the interest rate should react only to deviations of the rate of growth of a selected monetary aggregate from a target level. The second (Feldstein and Stock, 1994; Hall and Mankiw 1994; McCallum, 1988) prescribes that the interest rate should react only to deviations of the rate of growth of nominal income from a normative path.

These rules can in principle deliver price stability in the medium run. In counter-factual simulations, Orphanides (2000) shows that the implementation of either a Taylor rule with zero weight on the output gap or the nominal income growth rule would have been successful, unlike the Taylor rule with a positive weight on output stabilisation, to avoid the Great Inflation in the United States. Additionally, these rules have the advantage of being able to prescribe changes in the policy instrument as a function of relatively well-measured variables. For the United States, Orphanides shows that the size of potential measurement errors for trend output *growth*, whose estimate is needed for both strict monetary targeting and nominal income targeting, is of an order of magnitude smaller than for the *level* of the output gap.

[5] We use the adjective 'strict' for monetary targeting to distinguish this simple rule from the monetary targeting strategy, which implies a more complex reaction function than that analysed here (e.g., Friedman, 1990).
[6] Here, we stick to the traditional use of the term target, as a variable in response to which the policy instrument is set. Svensson (1999a) has proposed reserving the word target only for a variable entering the loss function of the central bank.

2.4 Monetary policy strategies

A sharp diversity of views still prevails regarding the functioning of modern economies. Acknowledging this diversity, central banks should be wary of fine-tuning policies whose alleged optimality is based on the maintained assumption of a thorough knowledge of the state, prospects and functioning of the economy, including the monetary policy transmission mechanism.

Nevertheless, a variety of models can be helpful to ensure the overall consistency of judgmental inputs. Rather than adopting an optimal feedback rule, this amounts to adopting a 'strategy', that is a *complex* reaction function that is *optimal*, to the best of the central bank's knowledge, but *implicit*, i.e. incapable of expression in a simple mathematical function. Within the strategy, simple rules can be useful to provide policy guidelines. However, actual instrument setting will often differ from the values consistent with any of the available policy benchmarks, as the strategy will try to make the best possible use of all the available information.

In view of the importance of achieving credibility, central banks make the utmost effort to establish a reputation for being committed to their policy objective. Reputation is, however, unavailable, when the institution lacks a track record. In addition, a route to credibility based only on reputation runs the risk that reputation tends to be attached to people (the governor or the chairman of the decision making body), rather than to the institution, so that a loss of credibility can be experienced each time a term of office ends.

The public announcement of the monetary policy strategy can be seen as a complementary means to achieve credibility. The announcement represents exactly an effort to convey the systematic character of the (optimal) policy, i.e. to characterise to the best possible extent how the central bank will respond to the available information set. From this viewpoint, the announcement represents a form of commitment.

The announcement of the strategy, however, cannot be expected to deliver in itself the full benefits of credibility. Since the policy reaction function implicit in the strategy can only be imperfectly characterised – because of the impossibility of providing a complete taxonomy of policy responses to all possible states of the world – it is not straightforward for economic agents to monitor whether the commitment is being enforced at each point in time.

An additional instrument used by central banks to earn and maintain credibility is an appropriate communication policy, i.e. a specific language used to explain to the public, on the basis of the strategy, the bank's assessment of current and expected developments and the reasoning behind policy decisions. For this reason, the communication policy represents an important complement to the strategy, since it helps to define it more precisely over time for the benefit of the public.

Consistently, with the different strategies adopted over time and across countries, different central banks have sometimes chosen to emphasise different particular pieces of information, or elements of their decision making, in their communication policies. Monetary targeting and inflation targeting represent the most prominent examples in recent periods.[7] To these strategies correspond two alternative communication languages used to improve the mutual understanding between the central bank and the public. The publication of the monetary growth figures and of the inflation forecast, respectively, provide a convenient focal point around which a central bank's explanations are organised. Official publications, i.e. long and detailed verbal explanations of the information processing that underlies policy decisions, are in both cases a key component of the communication process.

---

[7] Since our discussion ultimately aims to shed light on the choices of the ECB, we concentrate on strategies available to central banks of 'large' countries. This leaves out exchange rate targeting, a strategy mainly used in small, open economies.

3 The euro area: an overview

After the general discussion of the functioning of monetary economies and of different theoretical approaches to monetary policy making, this chapter starts to focus on the economic area that adopted the
single currency at the beginning of 1999. The euro area is characterised
from three different viewpoints. Section 3.1 describes its broad economic
features, as compared to those characterising both its constituent countries and other large world economies. The important challenges faced in
the field of data construction are analysed next, in section 3.2, with special emphasis on two entirely new statistical products: the Harmonised
Index of Consumer Prices (HICP) and the new monetary aggregates.
Section 3.3 concludes, providing some tentative quantitative evidence on
the basic features of the monetary policy transmission mechanism.

3.1 Salient features of the euro area economy

The economic area emerging from the launch of Stage Three of the process of European monetary unification, namely the euro area, is, for evident reasons, very similar to the economies of all participating countries.

Some common traits are rather obvious. All national economies are
characterised by broadly similar sectoral patterns of production (see table
3.1). The services sector is by far the largest in all countries, accounting
for an average of 69 per cent of total GDP in the area, with Luxembourg
and Ireland being the countries in which it is largest and smallest, respectively. The industrial and 'primary' sectors only represent an average of
29 and 3 per cent of GDP, respectively, a pattern that is again common
to the economies of most participating countries. The largest deviations
from average are again observed in Ireland, where the primary sector accounts for 5 per cent of GDP, and in Luxembourg, where the industrial
sector is particularly small (21 per cent of GDP). These broad patterns of
production in the euro area are also similar to those of the United States
and Japan (see table 3.2).

Table 3.1. *Key features of euro area member countries* (1999, in % of GDP, unless otherwise stated)

	Area	BE	D	E	F	IRL	I	L	NL	A	P	FI
Population (million)	292.2	10.1	82.1	39.4	59.1	3.7	57.3	0.4	15.8	8.2	10.0	5.2
GDP (share of world GDP, %)	15.8	0.6	4.7	1.8	3.3	0.2	3.1	–	0.9	0.5	0.4	0.3
GDP per capita (€thousand)	21.0	23.0	24.1	14.2	22.8	22.6	19.2	40.7	23.4	24.0	10.4	23.3
Sectors of production[1]												
Agriculture, fishing, forestry	2.6	1.5	1.2	4.2	3.1	5.4	3.0	0.7	3.1	2.3	3.9	3.7
Industry (including constr.)	28.6	28.2	30.9	29.5	25.3	38.6	29.1	20.6	26.7	31.4	33.5	32.3
Services	68.7	70.4	67.9	66.3	71.3	56.0	67.9	78.7	70.3	66.3	62.7	63.9
Exports of goods and services	17.2	76.1	29.4	27.5	26.0	90.4	25.5	117.5	61.4	45.1	30.4	37.7
Imports of goods and services	16.1	72.1	28.5	28.8	23.5	76.2	23.5	100.9	56.4	45.5	41.1	29.5
Domestic credit[2]	131.4	147.3	145.2	108.9	102.0	95.3	92.0	89.3	126.8	131.7	105.3	56.1
Bank assets[3]	253.5	306.3	286.4	186.3	268.2	345.3	149.4	3585.1	262.8	246.9	285.1	98.4
Loans to the corporate sector	45.2	46.8	39.7	43.3	37.2	75.4	50.2	268.5	64.5	66.6	57.9	23.7
Domestic debt securities	98.8	146.5	90.6	60.5	81.5	37.1	125.4	–	62.4	76.0	58.8	64.1
Issued by the corporate sector	7.4	12.0	0.7	4.5	7.6	7.8	1.0	–	4.1	1.9	10.4	6.0
Stock market capitalisation	90.1	78.7	72.0	76.9	111.1	80.7	66.0	204.6	187.2	16.8	65.2	288.4
Unemployment rate[4] (%)	9.0	8.5	8.3	14.2	9.6	4.5	10.5	2.2	2.5	3.2	3.9	9.5
General government												
Receipts	47.8	51.0	47.6	39.1	53.5	36.7	48.1	49.1	48.2	52.3	41.3	54.1
Expenditure	49.1	51.6	49.0	40.2	55.3	34.7	50.0	45.6	47.3	54.3	43.3	52.2

Source: ECB, BIS, OECD, IMF, Eurostat.
Notes: [1] 1998. For Ireland: 1997.
[2] For Austria, Belgium, France, Luxembourg and the Netherlands: 1997; for Finland, Germany, Ireland, Italy, Portugal and Spain: 1998.
[3] MFIs excluding the NCBs for the euro area. Credit institutions and other MFIs for the countries of the euro area.
[4] July 2000.

Table 3.2. *Key features of the euro area vis-à-vis the United States
and Japan*
(1999, in % of GDP, unless otherwise stated)

	Euro area	United States	Japan
Population (million)	292.2	272.9	126.7
GDP (share of world GDP, %)	15.8	21.9	7.6
GDP per capita (€thousand)	21.0	31.9	32.2
Sectors of production[1]			
Agriculture, fishing, forestry	2.6	1.6	1.8
Industry (including constr.)	28.6	27.3	36.4
Services	68.7	71.1	61.9
Exports of goods and services	17.2	10.3	10.7
Imports of goods and services	16.1	13.2	9.1
Domestic credit	131.4	83.3	143.9
Bank assets[2]	253.5	98.8	155.1
Loans to the corporate sector	45.2	12.6	83.5
Domestic debt securities	98.8	178.4	156.2
Issued by the corporate sector	7.4	31.2	18.4
Stock market capitalisation	90.1	192.9	111.5
Unemployment rate[3] (%)	9.0	4.2	4.5
General government			
Receipts	47.8	32.5	31.0
Expenditure	49.1	31.9	39.9

Source: ECB, BIS, OECD, IMF, Eurostat, Federal Reserve and Bank of Japan flow of funds.
Notes: [1] For USA and Japan: 1997.
[2] MFIs excluding the NCBs for the euro area. Commercial banks, savings institutions, credit unions and money market funds for the United States. Domestically licensed banks for Japan.
[3] July 2000.
  Owing to differences in reporting, numbers are not fully comparable between the euro area, the United States and Japan.

Euro area countries are also similar in terms of the contribution of the public sector to GDP. On average, government expenditure is equal to 49 per cent of GDP, a proportion that is significantly smaller only in Ireland, Portugal and Spain. By contrast, lower figures are observed in Japan and especially in the United States, where government expenditure accounts for 40 and 32 per cent of GDP, respectively. This is largely due to the different characteristics of social security systems and, more generally, the provision of collective services by the government.

The financial structure in most euro area countries is also broadly similar. Firm financing takes place predominantly through the interme-diation of the banking sector. At the end of 1999, outstanding loans to the corporate sector by Monetary and Financial Institutions (see section 3.2, for a precise definition) was approximately equal to 45 per cent of GDP in the euro area, as opposed to 13 per cent in the United States. The ratio of total bank assets to GDP exceeded 250 per cent in the euro area, while being equal to 155 per cent in Japan and remaining below 100 per cent in the United States. On the contrary, the outstanding value of corporate debt securities was approximately 7 per cent of GDP in the euro area, as opposed to 18 and 31 per cent in Japan and in the United States, respectively. On a similar note, stock market capitalisation in the euro area is, in percentage of GDP, approximately half of the corresponding figure in the United States and smaller than in Japan.

The geographical distribution of production also shares some common features across countries, especially if one focuses on relatively large ones. Most of these are characterised by some degree of regional imbalance, whereby extremely rich districts coexist with relatively poorer regions (the eastern *Länder* in Germany, Italy's Mezzogiorno, Extremadura in Spain, to mention a few examples). Similar imbalances characterise the euro area as a whole, where per-capita GDP varies from over €24,000 in Germany (and €40,000 in Luxembourg) to €10,452 in Portugal. On the whole, it does not seem that economic imbalances in the euro area are significantly different from those prevailing in the larger member countries. Imbalances in output are also reflected in the unemployment figures, where important structural differences between national labour markets – ranging from employment protection legislation to the duration of unemployment benefits – also play a role. The euro area unemployment rate, equal to 9 per cent in mid-2000, is not only much higher than in both the United States and Japan, but also than in some participating countries, such as Ireland and the Netherlands.

Nevertheless, one main difference exists between the euro area and each of its participating economies. The euro area is 'large' in terms of its weight in world GDP and relatively close to international trade. Together, Member States account for approximately 16 per cent of world GDP, a share comparable to, even if lower than, that of the United States and twice as large as Japan's. In contrast, Germany, the largest euro area economy, can account for only 5 per cent of world GDP. The degree of openness, as measured by the average of exports and imports of goods and services as a percentage of GDP, is approximately 16 per cent in the euro area. While larger than in the United States and Japan, where the corresponding figures are 12 and 10 per cent, respectively, this degree of openness is significantly lower than in any Member State, whose trade mostly takes place with other euro area countries.

These characteristics have implications for the conduct of monetary policy. The most important one is that the single monetary policy must be aware of the impact of its own actions on the rest of the world, an impact that could be considered negligible for each of the 'small' participating countries. Moreover, the impact of exchange rate developments on domestic output and inflation in the euro area is more muted than it was in each participating country.

3.2   Euro area data

By definition, the adoption of the single currency and the establishment of a new institution in charge of monetary policy for the whole euro area-involved a change of focus from national to area-wide economic variables. For virtually all economic variables, the ECB needed, in principle, to have at its disposal new harmonised economic series, constructed with the specific aim of fitting the new Europe-wide policy perspective and possibly reconstructed backwards to allow sufficiently accurate econometric analyses. In most cases, however, there has been no specific revision directly motivated by the changeover to the single currency. Evidence and analyses have therefore been obtained, by necessity, on the basis of synthetic data created *ad hoc* using many simplifying assumptions.

The two variables whose definitions have been substantially revised to ensure maximum consistency across the euro area are the consumer price index and the monetary aggregates.

The design of a new harmonised index of consumer prices was originally prompted by the need to have comparable measures of inflation across Europe for the purpose of monitoring compliance with the inflation criterion laid out in the Maastricht Treaty. Consequently, national HICP series have been available for a few years. Nevertheless, their characteristics have continued to be improved quite significantly over the recent past. The quantitative differences sometimes observed in Member States between 'new' HICPs and 'old' CPIs could appear surprising. For this reason, section 3.2.1 provides a short overview of the main characteristics of HICPs, and also points out the areas where further research is still needed.

The redefinition of area-wide monetary aggregates is more closely related to the beginning of Stage Three of European monetary unification. We provide a brief description of the main innovations in the new definitions in section 3.2.2. The exposition is based on ECB (1999b), where the interested reader can find a more detailed discussion of all the characteristics of monetary aggregates.

3.2.1   *The harmonised index of consumer prices*

The HICP has been designed to meet the Treaty's requirement to measure inflation 'by means of a consumer price index on a comparable basis taking into account differences in national definitions' (see Astin, 1999). In this context, it has been necessary to define the coverage of goods and services, the population of consumers, the geographical coverage and, finally, prices and weights to be used.

Specifically, coverage includes goods and services consumed in both periods being compared. The index measures the change in expenditure necessary to maintain unchanged, with respect to the base period, the consumption pattern of households and the composition of the consumer population. The underlying concept of final monetary consumption expenditure differentiates HICPs from cost of living indices, that aim to measure the change in the minimum expenditure required to achieve the same level of utility ('standard of living') from two potentially different consumption patterns realised in the two periods being compared.

Moreover, the index only measures expenditure resulting in actual monetary or market transactions; thus, it excludes imputations, such as those used for owner-occupied housing, and interest rates or interest costs (see Astin, 1999, or Diewert, 1999). The elementary prices entering the index include indirect taxes and exclude discounts for bulk or off-peak purchases.

Consumption expenditure is included irrespective of the nationality or residence of the household, as long as it takes place in the territory of the Member State. This 'domestic concept' was necessary to avoid gaps or double counting when national indices are aggregated across the euro area.

The weights of the HICP in each Member State are the aggregate expenditures by households on each good or service, expressed as a proportion of the total expenditure on all goods and services covered by the HICP. As a consequence, HICPs of different Member States are not related to a uniform consumption basket.

From the technical viewpoint, the HICP is a Laspeyres-type index, whose weights must be updated at least every seven years.

An issue that has recently attracted considerable attention in the construction of consumer price indices is how to ensure the high degree of precision necessary when central banks explicitly define their primary 'objective' or 'target' as price stability. These definitions obviously require that measurement errors, unavoidable in any price index, be kept within a very small quantitative range. The Boskin Report (Boskin, 1996) emphasised a number of so-called biases in the US CPI, among which the outlet substitution bias, the new goods bias and especially the quality adjustment bias have attracted a lot of attention.

The *outlet substitution bias* indicates the errors made when households change their habits and purchase the same commodities from lower cost outlets. The *new goods bias* arises as price indices fail to keep up with the progressive increase in the number of goods and services available to households. Finally, the *quality adjustment bias* arises when new varieties or models of certain goods are introduced in the market. More precisely, it must be taken into account that statistical agencies are always required to assess whether any new model of a certain commodity truly represents a change in the characteristics (quality) of the good. If this is the case, statistical agencies also have to try to isolate the portion of the observed change in price that reflects the quality change from the remaining portion, which is inflation by all means. The potential errors in the estimate of quality changes are the sources of quality (adjustment) bias in the overall price index. The Boskin report argues that the quality bias due to changes in the quantity or the quality of goods is likely to be upwards in the case of the US CPI, mainly because of the difficulties encountered in adjusting for the quality change in high-tech goods (such as PCs).

For the euro area, Eurostat has pointed out that the quality adjustment issue is likely to play a non-negligible role for a large number of individual goods and services.[1] Since it is unclear whether all the potential errors go in the same direction (quality adjustment for clothing, for example, is likely to be too high and to result in an underestimation of inflation), it is not necessarily the case that these will not cancel out in the aggregate. It therefore remains unclear whether quality adjustment problems affect the headline HICP and, if this is the case, what is their quantitative relevance. Considerable research efforts are being made in order to attain a reasonably accurate estimate of quality adjustments, for example through the use of hedonic regressions that allow the researcher to estimate the portion of change in prices due to changes in quality (see, e.g., Hoffman, 1998).

The HICP for the euro area, or MUICP (Monetary Union Index of Consumer Prices), is itself a weighted average of the indices of the eleven countries comprising the area. These weights are given by the share of each country's household final monetary consumption expenditure as a percentage of total expenditure in the area, and they are allowed to change every year. The MUICP is therefore itself a chain index.

New data on the HICP for each EU Member State, on the MUICP and on approximately a hundred sub-indices are released to the public every month by Eurostat. The country weights used in the construction of the MUICP are also available to the public. Moreover, Eurostat publishes a number of 'special aggregates', ranging from the 'all items excluding energy' to the 'seasonal food' index.

[1] See, e.g., Commission of the European Communities (1998).

Finally, the HICP is being constantly revised and improved over time. As of January 2000, the coverage of goods and services has been significantly extended, with a non-negligible impact on sub-indices related to technical sectors such as 'telephone and telefax services' and others.

Table 3.3 shows the weights of broad categories of goods and services in the HICPs for the euro area (MUICP) and for each Member State. The most important components of the MUICP, with weights exceeding 15 per cent of the index, are the 'Food and non-alcoholic beverages', 'Housing, water, electricity, gas and other fuel' and 'Transport' categories. The 'Recreation and culture' category has a weight of approximately 10 per cent, while 'Education' and 'Communication costs' (including telephone and telefax equipment and services) have the smallest weights.

3.2.2   The new monetary aggregates

The definition and precise measurement of money is not straightforward in practice. Given the close substitutability between many different financial assets and the changing nature of means of payment over time, it is not always immediately clear whether a certain asset should, or should not, be included in the definition of 'money'. Hence, central banks typically use different concepts of money, or monetary aggregates, ranging from those that mainly include currency to those that also include certain types of short term securities. To make these definitions operational and consistent across the area, the ECB also had to ensure that the definitions of the basic components of money used in different Member States were uniform.

Specifically, a definition has been agreed for the money-issuing sector in each national economy, i.e. those entities (excluding central government) that issue liabilities with characteristics ('moneyness') – as medium of exchange, unit of account, store of value – similar to cash. The money-issuing sector is represented by the *Monetary and Financial Institutions* (MFIs) resident in the euro area. These, in turn, comprise three main groups of institutions: central banks, 'credit institutions' (as defined in Community law) and other resident financial institutions with similar characteristics to credit institutions (mainly, money market funds).

Moreover, a definition has been agreed for the money-holding sector, which includes all non-MFI resident entities (excluding central government).

The central issue in the calculation of monetary aggregates is, as mentioned before, the selection of the categories of MFIs' liabilities to be included, distinguished by their degree of 'moneyness'. The redefinition of national aggregates in the euro area eventually involved a general

Table 3.3. *HICP weights in 2000, by item and country (‰)*

	MUICP	BE	D	E	F	IRL	I	L	NL	A	P	FI
01 Food and non-alcoholic beverages	166.8	183.3	140.3	243.7	170.0	189.8	174.0	120.2	157.6	131.1	215.5	173.2
02 Alcoholic beverages, tobacco and narcotics	41.7	33.6	47.8	34.1	41.0	90.4	29.0	101.3	50.2	39.8	32.6	72.8
03 Clothing and footwear	80.3	77.8	74.9	106.5	59.0	52.8	110.9	75.6	67.5	82.7	69.9	54.5
04 Housing, water, electricity, gas and other fuels	157.8	150.0	207.9	104.7	151.0	80.4	101.3	109.5	194.3	139.3	93.3	158.3
05 Household furnishings, equipment and routine maintenance	81.1	81.3	76.9	59.1	72.0	45.4	109.7	107.7	92.2	90.0	78.7	51.3
06 Health	31.9	32.2	34.2	22.9	32.0	20.1	34.0	14.2	21.7	19.1	56.7	45.3
07 Transport	156.5	148.8	154.3	136.8	180.0	118.1	150.3	192.2	134.5	145.2	205.2	162.6
08 Communications	23.3	22.6	21.1	14.1	27.0	16.2	28.2	13.3	20.4	32.1	20.6	23.9
09 Recreation and culture	96.9	111.3	114.6	64.6	93.0	114.3	73.5	110.0	120.6	116.3	39.2	115.1
10 Education	8.8	4.7	7.1	15.8	5.0	19.8	10.8	1.1	15.9	7.4	18.2	2.1
11 Restaurants and hotels	85.3	83.2	51.4	151.6	84.0	196.9	101.9	96.1	71.7	143.3	130.9	93.9
12 Miscellaneous goods and services	69.8	71.3	69.6	46.4	86.0	55.8	76.3	58.8	53.4	53.8	39.4	46.9
Country weights	*1000.0*	*39.9*	*346.5*	*90.8*	*209.1*	*9.8*	*183.1*	*2.0*	*56.5*	*29.1*	*18.1*	*15.1*

Source: Eurostat.

Table 3.4. *Definition of euro area monetary aggregates*

Liabilities	M1	M2	M3
Currency in circulation	√	√	√
Overnight deposits	√	√	√
Deposits with agreed maturity up to two years		√	√
Deposits redeemable at notice up to three months		√	√
Repurchase agreements			√
Money market fund shares/units and money market paper			√
Debt securities up to two years			√

Source: ECB *Monthly Bulletin*, February 1999.
Note: Liabilities of the money-issuing sector and central government liabilities with a monetary character held by the money-holding sector.

review of statistical reporting systems, to allow for a consistent breakdown by financial instrument and maturity.[2] The degree of moneyness of each instrument was defined according to four criteria: transferability, convertibility, period of notice and maturity. Transferability is the ability to mobilise funds placed in a financial instrument by means of payment facilities such as cheques, direct debits etc. Convertibility refers to the ability to convert a financial instrument into cash or transferable deposits. Period of notice refers to the time between the moment in which the holder of an instrument gives notice of its intention to redeem it before its maturity and the moment at which the instrument can effectively be converted into cash without extra costs. Finally, maturity refers to the time between the contract date and the redemption date. The degree of moneyness of a financial instrument is higher the easier the transferability and convertibility and the shorter the maturity and the period of notice.

Based on these characteristics, certain liabilities of MFIs have been identified as characterised by a sufficient degree of moneyness to be included in a monetary aggregate (see table 3.4). These instruments are included when they are held by residents in the euro area with MFIs that are also located in the euro area (i.e., including cross-border deposits in the area itself) and irrespective of the currency of denomination. Three different monetary aggregates have been defined in decreasing order of

---

[2] Initially, the harmonisation process had largely been based on the identification of broadly homogeneous categories amongst existing national instruments, without revising national statistical definitions and classifications.

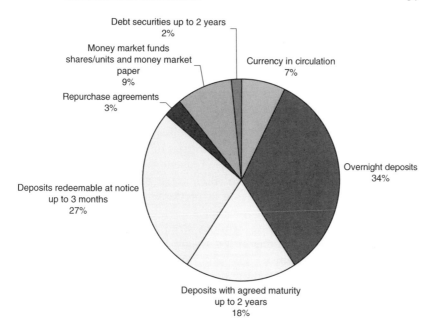

Figure 3.1 Percentage share of the components of M3
Source: ECB.

moneyness of the instruments they include: a 'narrow' (M1), an 'inter-mediate' (M2) and a 'broad' (M3) aggregate.

The narrow aggregate M1 only includes instruments that have maximum transferability and convertibility and minimum maturity and period of notice, i.e. notes, coins and overnight deposits. The intermediate aggregate M2 includes, additionally, deposits with slightly longer maturity and period of notice: specifically, deposits with maturity of up to two years and deposits redeemable at notice up to three months. This aggregate aims to reflect a definition of money that is still very liquid, since these deposits can be converted into narrow money relatively easily, although with some restrictions such as the need for a short advance notice or penalties and fees. Finally, the broad aggregate M3 is composed of M2 and other marketable financial instruments, such as repurchase agreements, money market fund shares/units and money market paper. This broad aggregate is less affected, with respect to the narrower ones, by the substitution between various assets with very similar degrees of liquidity.

At the end of 1999 the narrow aggregate M1 represented approximately 40 per cent of M3, with the predominant share (34 per cent of M3) represented by overnight deposits (see figure 3.1). The intermediate aggregate M2 is closer to M3, since it represents more than 85 per cent of it. Money market fund shares/units and money market paper account for most of the remaining share of M3 (9 per cent of the total).

3.3   Some tentative evidence on the monetary transmission mechanism in the euro area

The transmission of monetary policy impulses to the economy involves complex adjustments of prices and quantities difficult to write down as a chronological succession of channels of reactions. In addition, it remains unclear whether any of the potential channels of transmission hypothesised in theory can be considered as predominant from a quantitative viewpoint.

In this section, we provide, without any pretence to be exhaustive, a short taxonomy of the channels that are likely to play some role in the transmission mechanism. The exposition is based on ECB (2000a), where the reader can find a more detailed discussion. Subsequently, we summarise the available evidence for the euro area. We focus, in particular, on the macroeconomic effects of a monetary policy shock identified through a structural VAR of the euro area economy. These results are also compared to those of a simulation based on the ECB area-wide model.

Finally, we briefly discuss some tentative evidence on the effects of changes in the exchange rate and in commodity prices. Concerning the exchange rate, we report on the results of simulations performed with the area-wide macroeconometric model. As to commodity prices, we use the experience of the first year of the single monetary policy as an 'event study' showing the combined effect of exchange rate and oil price changes on import prices and the HICP.

It goes without saying that all results should be considered with particular caution, since they are subject to three main caveats. First, the aforementioned necessity to base any area-wide estimation on 'synthetic' data sheds doubts on the reliability of any econometric results. It remains unclear whether economic relationships uncovered on the available data set will continue to hold true for 'proper' euro area data in the future. In addition, available data sets tend to be short for econometric analyses, especially when the behaviour of a large number of variables is investigated. Second, reduced-form econometric relationships estimated at the area-wide level can suffer from an aggregation bias problem, to which we return elsewhere. Finally, the changeover to the single currency can be seen as a textbook example of structural break, thus discouraging any policy evaluation based on estimated reduced form relationships (be it at the national or area-wide level).

3.3.1 The monetary policy transmission mechanism

It is customary to identify two stages of the transmission process: in the first, changes in the monetary policy instrument, typically an interest rate, affect financial market conditions; in the second, the changes in financial market conditions have an impact on nominal expenditure decisions.

Although useful, this simple characterisation is not sufficient to summarise the whole process of monetary transmission. At least one additional direct channel of transmission must be taken into account, notably the effect of policy moves – or lack thereof – on inflation expectations. First, these may have an immediate effect on pricing decisions, for example in the labour markets, where wages are negotiated in a forward-looking fashion. Second, the role of expectations implies that the effects of any policy move will crucially depend, alongside the structural characteristics of the economy, on the credibility of the central bank. If the bank's commitment to price stability is clear to the public, policy moves will be understood as consistent with this goal and will tend to produce the desired effects. Otherwise, the same policy moves are likely to be less effective and, if misinterpreted, they will have perverse effects on private sector decisions.

As explained in more detail in subsequent chapters, the main monetary policy instrument used by the ECB is, together with the 'standing facilities', the interest rate on the main refinancing operations, that have a maturity of two weeks (see chapter 8 for more details on these important policy-related interest rates). In the euro area, a monetary policy impulse can therefore be understood as an unexpected change, or lack thereof, in these interest rates.

The ensuing adjustments in money market conditions quickly affects other financial prices, from yields on long term bonds to the exchange rate and the stock market. The magnitudes and even the directions of these effects are, however, very imperfectly understood. In all cases, the change of arbitrage opportunities caused by the policy move must be weighed against the expected change in future 'fundamentals'. Thus, the reaction of long term interest rates to a policy impulse is strongly affected by the credibility of policy makers. As to the exchange rate, the expected evolution of a large number of economic variables will contribute to shape its response to a policy impulse. Finally, the impact on equity prices will depend on the change in the expected present discounted value of future dividends, which will in turn be affected, possibly in opposing directions, by both the change in the relevant discount rate and the change in the expected future dividend stream.

Following the initial policy impulse, there may be additional non-price adjustments in credit markets, through the repercussions on the whole spectrum of retail interest rates in credit and deposit markets. The structural characteristics of these markets have a determinant role in shaping the direction and timing of these adjustments. We have already stressed the still predominant role played by banking intermediation in the financing of European firms. Historical experience shows that the speed of adjustment of bank rates after monetary policy impulses tends to be different, though always slow, for upwards and downwards changes. The structural features of credit markets, however, are likely to be changing with the profound restructuring process currently experienced by the financial sector of the euro area. Growing competition in financial services and the acceleration in the ongoing process of bank disintermediation are likely to improve the efficiency of pricing in the banking sector, thus inducing banks to transmit faster changes in market conditions to their customers.

The second stage of the transmission mechanism involves changes in nominal spending. Given the gradual adjustment of prices, short term inflation expectations will tend to move slowly after a policy change, which will thus affect the short term real interest rate and real spending through a number of effects. First, cost of capital effects, whereby changes in financial market rates will influence the profitability of business investment and households' spending on consumer durables. Second, income effects, which will depend on the size, the composition, the maturity and cost structure of the balance sheet position of non-financial agents in the economy. The redistribution of income between net creditor and net debtor sectors of the economy will ultimately have an impact on aggregate demand to the extent that the propensity to spend is different across those sectors. The third way in which real spending will tend to change is through wealth effects, arising from potential changes in the market value of real and financial assets after an interest change. Finally, there will be foreign exchange effects, as changes in the exchange rate will affect international trade.

Although no systematic study is available for the euro area, econometric evidence related to a number of countries suggests that cost of capital effects are likely to work through investment, more than through changes in consumption. Income effects are probably very low for households, whose assets and liabilities tend to be at longer-term fixed rates, but somewhat higher for the corporate sector, whose net debt has maturity below one year for one-third. Wealth effects on aggregate consumption are generally estimated to be negligible, unless asset price changes that generate them are sizeable and affect assets held by a large proportion of the population. In the euro area, bonds and real estate meet the latter condition, more than equity. However, wealth effects on bonds tend to be mainly redistributional, while changes in house prices would only become significant if the practice of using the private home as loan collateral became more widespread. As to exchange rate effects, the aforementioned 'large country' character of the euro area implies that these are much smaller than in small and more open economies.

The final impact on prices of these changes in nominal spending will depend on the market frictions that characterise the economy, from the degree of price stickiness to the rigidity of the labour market. Existing econometric evidence on the euro area suggests that the speed of adjustment of real wages to changes in unemployment and productivity is slower than in the United States. This will, in general, lead to more protracted effects on the economy.

3.3.2   A few pieces of quantitative evidence

The structural VAR results discussed here are those obtained by Peersman and Smets (2000). This particular study has been selected for two main reasons: first, it attempts to trace the effect of structural shocks on a relatively wide number of macroeconomic variables; second, it performs a large number of robustness checks. The VAR includes five endogenous variables – namely real GDP, consumer prices, a broad monetary aggregate (M3), a short term interest rate and the real effective exchange rate – and, in order to account for world demand and inflation shocks, three exogenous variables – namely, a world commodity price index, US real GDP and the US short term interest rate.[3] In alternative specifications, other macroeconomic variables are also included in the system.

The results indicate that an unexpected temporary increase by 30 basis points of the average short term interest rate in the euro area tends to be followed, after two quarters, by a real appreciation of the exchange rate and a relatively small and short-lived fall in output. The output effect peaks after five quarters, with a fall of approximately 0.2 per cent with respect to the baseline. The effect on money and prices is much slower: they only start falling significantly below the initial level after two and three years, respectively. These results are comparable to those obtained, within a smaller model and a slightly different sample, by Monticelli and Tristani (1999). The main difference appears to lie in the finding of the latter study of a slow response also for output.

---

[3] The VAR is estimated, in levels, over the period 1980 to 1998 and the basic structural identification is achieved using the Choleski decomposition (with the endogenous variables ordered as described in the text).

Table 3.5. *Impact of selected shocks on euro area inflation and GDP growth (ECB estimates)*

	Prices[1]		Real GDP[1]	
	First year	Second year	First year	Second year
Increase of the short term nominal interest rate[2]	−0.1	−0.2	−0.2	−0.6
Exchange rate depreciation[3]	0.6	1.2	0.4	1.0

Source: Fagan, Henry and Mestre (2001).
Notes: [1] Differences from baseline, in per cent. [2] Increase by 100 basis points sustained for two years. The simulation is conditional on the hypothesis that the exchange rate reacts according to a simple uncovered interest parity condition. [3] Depreciation of 10 per cent in effective terms over two years. The simulation is conditional on the hypothesis of unchanged interest rates.

The various components of GDP tend to follow a similar impulse response pattern. It is noticeable, however, that total investment tends to be much more reactive than total GDP (it falls by a maximum of 0.6 per cent). The response of private consumption is, instead, slower and more muted. Similar patterns characterise the response of investment and consumption goods in manufacturing. Finally, the narrow monetary aggregate M1 displays a strong liquidity effect on impact, while the long term interest rate tends to follow the pattern of the short term rate, although only rising, on impact, by almost 10 basis points.

On the whole, these results are in line with those observed in other industrial countries and mentioned in chapter 1. They also appear broadly consistent with the results of simulations carried out using the area-wide macroeconomic model (see Fagan, Henry and Mestre, 2001). It is important to stress that there are two important differences between the assumptions underlying the VAR impulse responses and those underpinning the macro-model simulations. First, the impulse responses implicitly incorporate the effect of the 'normal' policy response to macroeconomic developments following the initial shock, while the simulations based on the macroeconometric model are conditional on an exogenous path for the policy interest rate. Second, the exchange rate is also free to react to the initial shock in the VAR, while the macro-model simulation is conditional on the assumption that the exchange rate reacts according to a simple uncovered interest parity condition.

In spite of these differences, the results of the simulations based on the macro-model are broadly in line with those of the VAR analysis (see table 3.5). An increase of the short term nominal interest rate by 100 basis points sustained for two years causes a reduction of real GDP by 0.2 per cent after one year and 0.6 after two years (in deviation from baseline). On average, inflation falls by 0.1 per cent per year.

Moving on to consider the effects of an exchange rate shock, we again report some results available from simulations performed by Fagan, Henry and Mestre (2001). Specifically, we consider the simulated effects of a temporary depreciation of the euro by 10 per cent in effective terms for two years. In this case, the simulation is conditional on an unchanged path for the short term interest rate, so that the dynamic reaction of monetary policy to economic developments is not reflected in the results.

Following a drop on impact, GDP increases by approximately 0.4 per cent after one year and by 1 per cent by the end of the second year, with respect to the baseline. As in the VAR results, aggregate investment appears to be the most dynamic component of domestic demand, although the largest effects are obviously observed on imports and exports. The trade balance improves by a maximum of 0.5 per cent after two years. Inflation increases by 0.3 percentage points in the first quarter after the shock, and then by approximately 0.6 per cent in both the first and second years after the shock.

These results point out that, in spite of the relatively closed economy character of the euro area, the exchange rate has a non-negligible role in explaining developments in the HICP (the same property appears to be valid for the United States, according to OECD estimates; see OECD, 1999). In the first year of the single monetary policy this has been confirmed by the impact of the observed dynamics of import and commodity prices. These affect the HICP through two channels. First, they enter directly into private consumption and therefore affect 'mechanically' the HICP. This is the case, for example, for energy prices, whose developments tend to be dominated by changes in the euro price of oil, when the latter are particularly marked. In these circumstances, the pass-through from oil prices to energy prices appears to be very quick, a matter of one or two months (ECB, 2000b). Most of the direct impact of oil price changes is produced on the 'Liquid fuels for households' and 'Fuel and lubricants for personal transport equipment' components of the HICP, with a total effect of approximately 1 per cent on the level of the HICP for the euro area. Hence, the almost immediate mechanical effect of a 10 per cent increase of oil prices is approximately equal to 0.1 percentage points of inflation.

The second effect on the HICP of changes in import and commodity prices derives from the fact that they represent changes of input costs for firms. Their effects on consumer prices will depend on the impact on output pricing decisions at the firm level, which are affected by structural characteristics of product markets, such as their degree of competitiveness or the possibility of firms to price to market. Recent historical experience suggests that a 10 per cent increase in import prices, if sustained, tends to produce approximately 0.5 percentage points of inflation as a cumulative effect over two to three years. This effect is additional to the aforementioned 'mechanical' one.

To summarise, the general features of the monetary policy transmission mechanism in the euro area appear similar to those observed in other industrial countries. As far as more specific characteristics are concerned, however, such as the timing or the size of the dynamic response of macroeconomic variables to a standard monetary policy shock, a lot remains to be learned. The few results available so far have been obtained conditional on a large number of simplifying assumptions and can only be treated as broad reference points for policy analysis.

4   The ECB strategy: defining price stability

With this chapter, we begin describing the actual monetary policy strategy adopted by the ECB. Our starting point is the definition of its primary objective, namely price stability.

At first sight, it may be surprising to find a discussion of price stability within the ECB strategy. Both the objective of price stability and its overriding nature are part of the mandate of the ECB, as defined in the Treaty. As such, price stability is logically distinct from the monetary policy strategy, i.e. the way in which the ECB plans to achieve its mandatory goal. Moreover, the commitment to price stability cannot be subject to revisions at the initiative of the Governing Council. While the latter is in principle free to modify the strategy, the commitment to price stability is 'written in stone'. It has the democratic legitimacy of an international treaty, signed by the governments of the fifteen Member States and ultimately sanctioned either by Parliament approval or by referendum. The role of price stability as an overriding goal of monetary policy, therefore, is taken as given by the ECB (see also Issing, 2000a).

Nevertheless, when devising its monetary policy strategy, the ECB faced the key decision of whether to *announce* a precise, numerical definition of price stability. As we argue in this chapter, the announcement of a quantitative definition for the price stability objective represents an important form of commitment. In this respect, the announcement can be seen as an integral part of the strategy.

4.1   The mandate of the Treaty

The Treaty clearly specifies the mandate of the ECB in Article 105: 'The primary objective of the ESCB is to maintain price stability. Without prejudice to the objective of price stability the ESCB shall support the general economic policies in the Community with a view to contributing to the achievement of the objectives of the Community as laid down in Article 2'. The Treaty's focus on price stability reflects, to a large extent, the economic arguments and the ample empirical evidence in its favour, discussed in previous chapters. It is also the result of the direct awareness of the damage caused by deviations from price stability in the experience of the last century and, most recently, in the seventies and early eighties.

The importance of maintaining price stability has long been clear to economists, in relation to the fundamental role played by money as 'unit of account' for the value of transactions. A popular classic quote on the need for price stability dates back to the seventeenth century:

if there is anything in the world which ought to be stable it is money, the measure of everything which enters the channels of trade. What confusion would there not be in a state where weights and measures are frequently changed? On what basis and with what assurance would one person deal with another, and which nations would come to deal with people who lived in such disorder? (Le Blanc, 1690)[1]

In the classical presentations of the theory of money, it was stressed that the usefulness of a unit of account depends on the stability of its value. For a given (and approximately constant) stock of a certain commodity (e.g., gold), the stability of prices – or, equivalently, of the value of money – in terms of the commodity was a matter that could be dealt with through institutional means. It was analogous to the use of a standard measurement unit for distance or weight. Wicksell (1935) presents a clear formulation of this view. Finally, John Maynard Keynes made the case for the stability of money in a characteristically forceful way:

Lenin is said to have declared that the best way to destroy the capitalist system was to debauch the currency. [...] Lenin was certainly right. There is no subtler, no surer means of overturning the existing basis of society than to debauch the currency. The process engages all the hidden forces of economic law on the side of destruction, and does it in a manner which not a man in a million is able to diagnose. [...] In the latter stages of the war all the belligerent governments practised, from necessity or incompetence, what a Bolshevist might have done from design. (Keynes, 1919, chapter 6)

Focusing on effective ways to ensure price stability, a voluminous academic literature in recent decades has come to the conclusion that it is beneficial for society to appoint an independent central bank with a clear mandate to maintain it (see chapters 2 and 9). Empirically, central bank independence is associated to lower and less variable inflation, whereas there seems to be no evidence of a positive relationship between independence and output volatility.[2]

---

[1] This quote has also been used at least by Einaudi (1953), Konieczny (1994) and an early version of Svensson (1999c).

[2] See, for example, Alesina and Summers (1993), Eijffinger and Schaling (1993) and Pollard (1993).

Many of the recently revised central bank statutes reflect these ideas. They have also been endorsed by an explicit political consensus in Europe, as expressed in the official statements of Community bodies. Specifically, reference to price stability has been included in the European Union's Broad Economic Guidelines since 1995. After substantial progress in disinflation, the 1997 broad guidelines stated that 'Member States should aim at price stability and to target such a level over the medium term'. Moreover, price stability had been an implicit or explicit goal for most NCBs participating in the EMU.

Against the background of the price stability objective – and the rather limited scope for interpretation of the Treaty's letter concerning what exactly price stability should mean – the mandate to 'support the general economic policies in the Community' is of a general nature. The objectives laid down in Article 2 represent a statement of principle, rather than practical monetary policy goals: 'The Community shall have as its task . . . to promote throughout the Community a harmonious and balanced development of economic activities, sustainable and non-inflationary growth respecting the environment, a high degree of convergence of economic performance, a high level of employment and of social protection, the raising of the standard of living and quality of life, and economic and social cohesion and solidarity among Member States.'

The Treaty's mandate is consistent with the core message of the economic literature, as outlined in the first two chapters. The clear and precise statement on price stability as a primary objective corresponds to the widely agreed-upon robustness of the relationship between money and prices in the medium term. The uncertainties on the effectiveness of monetary policy as a means to stabilise output fluctuations are mirrored, instead, by the unwillingness to take a specific stance in this respect.

It would, however, be too simplistic to infer that the ECB is, by mandate, not concerned about output. An economic environment characterised by low and stable inflation is the best contribution that monetary policy can give to reduce the general level of uncertainty and promote an efficient allocation of resources. In this respect, the maintenance of price stability represents the key contribution of monetary policy to 'support the general economic policies in the Community' and it is the best monetary policy can do to foster a high rate of growth of output.

As to output stabilisation – as opposed to output growth – its feasibility as a general goal of monetary policy remains questionable. In his argument for monetary policy rules, Milton Friedman (1959) emphasised that active stabilisation policies easily failed to deliver their promise, because they required a degree of knowledge of the characteristics of the economy that was beyond the reach of economists and central banks.

Orphanides' (2000) results emphasised in chapter 2 point out that this might still largely be the case, since day-to-day policy making is characterised by a high degree of uncertainty that is only resolved after many years.

It remains unclear, moreover, whether more activist anticyclical policies would, in principle, deliver lower output fluctuations than less activist ones. A well-known result of the time inconsistency literature is that the appointment of a *conservative* central banker, i.e. a central banker who cares relatively little about output stabilisation, can be beneficial for society. Clarida, Galí and Gertler (1999) restate this result, drawing attention to the fact that, under certain conditions, in spite of the promise of *less* output stabilisation the conservative central banker can deliver more effective stabilisation, i.e. a more dampened effect of exogenous shocks, *ex post*.

These results clarify why specifying 'output stabilisation' as a clear objective (even though one of secondary importance) for monetary policy proved unappealing for the European legislator. They do not imply, however, that the ECB should completely disregard the consequences of its policy on output. On the contrary, exogenous shocks that create a trade-off between output and inflation developments should be met by a measured, rather than aggressive, response, in order to avoid exacerbating the volatility of interest rates and output. This is consistent with the time frame over which price stability should be maintained according to the Governing Council's announcement of 13 October 1998.

4.2   The ECB's definition of price stability

As seen in the beginning of this chapter, the EU Treaty does prescribe price stability as the ESCB's primary goal. The Treaty, however, does not specify a precise, quantitative definition of price stability or a time frame within which this objective should be attained.

While this is understandable for a legal document, the lack of a quantitative definition of price stability has been interpreted by some authors as leading to an insufficient degree of commitment to the final objective (for example, Romer and Romer, 1996). In the literature on inflation targeting, moreover, it has been pointed out that a precise figure for the rate of inflation to be considered consistent with price stability constitutes an important step towards accountability. Moreover, the definition of price stability increases the transparency of the central bank's objective, thereby increasing the incentive for the central bank to attain its primary goal. Finally, a quantified primary objective helps to co-ordinate inflationary expectations, thus facilitating the achievement of the price stability goal in a world in which agents are forward looking.

A number of similar considerations can be made concerning the announcement of a time frame within which price stability should be
achieved. Following an inflationary shock, price stability can be restored
more or less quickly depending on the aggressiveness of the monetary
policy response. Hence, a quantitative definition of price stability should
be accompanied by a specification of the relevant time frame in order to
prove useful as a co-ordinating mechanism for agents' expectations. As
already mentioned, moreover, this issue is related to the willingness of
the central bank to limit excessive output and interest rate volatility.

In spite of these advantages, however, there are also costs in being
explicit about the quantification of the objective of price stability and
its time horizon. On quantification, as already emphasised in chapter 1,
the economic profession has not come to an agreement on the inflation
rate that would ideally maximise economic welfare. Both theoretical and
practical arguments can be made in support of and against an inflation
rate exactly equal to zero (possibly through a price level objective), or a
small, but positive, rate of inflation.[3] Given this situation, it could appear
wise to refrain from the specification of an exact figure, let alone choose
between zero and small positive inflation.

Similarly, there are also good arguments that discourage the specification of an exact time frame. The reason is that, from the point of view
of society, a different policy response can be optimal depending on the
initial conditions and the source and dimension of the exogenous shocks
that cause deviations from the objective. Although the time frame could
be made conditional on the exact type of shock hitting the economy (and
this solution has indeed been explored in some countries), an exhaustive
classification of shocks is practically unfeasible. As a result, the central
bank must be granted some room for manoeuvre, for example in the interpretation of the nature of the shocks hitting the economy at a given
point in time.

It is interesting to observe that, far from reflecting an extreme position,
the latter conclusion appears to have been implicitly drawn by the US
Federal Reserve. The famous definition proposed by Alan Greenspan
(1989) ('price levels sufficiently stable so that expectations of change do
not become major factors in key economic decisions') can be seen exactly
as an attempt to convey the anti-inflationary resolve of the Fed without,
at the same time, providing too-precise quantitative indications.

In the difficult process of balancing the benefits and costs of credibility
and flexibility, the European Monetary Institute (henceforth, EMI) had

---

[3] As already mentioned, there are also theoretical arguments for pursuing the Friedman
rule, implying mild deflation.

recognised, at a very early stage, that an operational, precise definition of price stability was a necessary element of the future ECB strategy. This conclusion has been endorsed by the ECB, in view of the benefits that it was expected to deliver in terms of clarity and credibility. In this respect, an important difference between the cases of the Fed and of the ECB – which could have played a fundamental role in shaping the different approaches adopted by the two central banks on this matter – is the availability of a track record, or lack thereof. Put differently, while the Fed could rely on its past performance, the explicit announcement of a precise, quantitative definition of price stability was the only means available to the ECB to earn credibility.

One of the most important manifestations of the practical problems encountered when specifying a price stability objective is the choice between the announcement of a range and of a point value. The latter has the obvious disadvantage of clearly exposing the uncertainty of the central bank (and of the economic discipline) concerning which figure exactly should be chosen. A range, however, also creates difficulties. As emphasised by Bernanke et al. (1999, p. 294) concerning inflation targeting central banks: 'with target ranges in place, politicians, financial markets and the public often focus on whatever inflation is just outside or just inside the edge of the range, rather than on the magnitude of the deviation from the midpoint of the range'.

In defining price stability on 13 October 1998, the Governing Council encountered exactly this kind of problem. It was deemed particularly important to clarify that there is no mechanical rule according to which any possible price development outside the price stability range would automatically entail a given policy response. Specifically, the ECB policy could not be considered akin to a simple mechanical rule, in which, for example, interest rates are a simple function of the sole deviations of the rate of growth of the HICP from price stability. While any such deviation would indeed normally entail a policy response, there are cases in which this might not happen. For example, a surprise deviation from price stability in a given month, well known to all economic agents as being of a temporary nature, might not trigger an immediate policy response.

Price stability in the euro area has been defined by the Governing Council as annual price increases of less than 2 per cent, according to the Harmonised Index of Consumer Prices for the euro area as a whole. It has also been clarified that the final objective of price stability is to be pursued over the medium term.

This definition allows a prompt *ex post* verification by an independent third party of whether current price developments are compatible with

it. At each point in time, therefore, it is possible to assess unequivo-
cally whether the economy is, or is not, at price stability. As a result, the
definition of price stability represents an important contribution to accountability, which is crucial in any contract of delegation (see chapter 9
for a more detailed discussion of accountability).

The specific characteristics of the price stability announcement are in
accordance with the past practice of many participating central banks
and of the European Union's Broad Economic Guidelines. Specifically,
the choice of 2 per cent as the ceiling for price increases compatible
with price stability can be justified mainly on grounds of continuity. The
Council of the European Union has, since July 1995, selected a value
of 2 per cent to define the maximum rate of inflation compatible with
price stability: 'Further progress towards price stability must be made
... Those Member States that are currently expected to experience rates
of inflation between 2 and 3 per cent should maintain a policy aimed
at preventing any resurgence of inflationary pressures and at progressing
towards or going below 2 per cent. Other countries need to increase their
efforts, in some cases substantially, if they are to meet the guidelines'
(Council Recommendation of 10 July 1995 on the broad guidelines of
the economic policies of the Member States and of the Community). It is
also a value that has been used in the past by the European central banks
with the best track records in terms of maintenance of price stability,
including the Bundesbank.

The definition of price stability given by the ECB was initially criticised
for being 'asymmetric' owing to the lack of an explicit 'floor' for the
range of rates of inflation compatible with price stability. After a careful
reading of the ECB announcement, however, these criticisms appear to be
misplaced. The definition refers to 'price increases of less than 2 per cent',
and thus excludes the possibility of a fall in prices (that is, the possibility
of deflation). Price stability in the euro area, therefore, excludes both
inflation and deflation and is, in this sense, symmetric.

4.3   Other aspects of the definition of price stability

A related issue, which has recently attracted considerable attention, concerns the choice of whether price stability should be defined in terms
of growth rates or (growing) levels of the price index.[4] According to the
conventional wisdom (see, e.g., Fischer, 1995), defining price stability in

---

[4] Within the theoretical literature on inflation targeting, this issue is referred to as the choice
between inflation and price level targeting.

terms of a path for the price level could increase the volatility of output and inflation. As to an objective defined in terms of growth rate, its most important shortcoming was understood to be that, by treating past deviations from the objective as bygones, it would cause uncertainty about the long run price level.

The inflation vs. price level objective issue is currently an active field of research. Recent contributions, starting from Svensson (1999c), have pointed out that a level objective could be more advantageous than previously thought. Specifically, Woodford (1999a, b, c) demonstrates that, if the forward-looking nature of agents' decisions is acknowledged, the volatility of inflation is lower when the central bank aims to stabilise the price level than when it pursues the stabilisation of the inflation rate. The advantageous effects of a price level objective are maximal when there is no exogenous persistence in inflation (this happens in model economies, such as that described by Clarida, Galí and Gertler, 1999, with Calvo-style pricing), which is therefore completely 'forward-looking'. In these circumstances, the optimal policy rule, under commitment, for a central bank willing to minimise the variability of inflation around the objective, would entail a complete reversal of all shocks to the price level. Vestin (2000) argues, still under the assumption of no inflation persistence, that appointing an independent central bank, acting under discretion, with a price level objective would be beneficial even for a society concerned about inflation, not price level, stabilisation.

Within a more realistic set-up allowing for some exogenous persistence in inflation, Gaspar and Smets (2000) show that the optimal policy under commitment also involves a reversal, though not complete, of shocks to the price level. Under this more general set-up, they also point out that the choice between a price level and an inflation objective for the central bank is not straightforward. It depends on a number of factors, such as the degree of inflation persistence, the credibility of the objective and the horizon over which it is pursued.

It has also been argued that a credible price level objective can be beneficial when deflationary shocks occur (see, e.g., Blinder, 2000). With inflation close to zero, it can alleviate the constraint on policy given by the fact that nominal interest rates cannot fall below zero, because it induces inflation expectations after any unexpected fall in prices.

This debate has clearly not reached the stage of providing clear policy prescriptions (see also Issing, 2000b). The definition of price stability adopted by the ECB, referring to price 'increases' and to the 'medium term', reflects this and provides a pragmatic way of approaching the issue. It is interesting to note, in this respect, that Woodford (1999b) and

Rotemberg and Woodford (1999) show that equivalent results can be obtained if the central bank, though continuing to react to deviations of inflation – not the price level – from the objective, imparts some inertia to its policy by smoothing the interest rate over time. More recently Smets (2000) has argued that responding to deviations from objectives expressed in terms of either level or growth rate of prices leads to similar results in terms of the volatility of inflation and output for suitably different policy horizons. In this framework, the optimal horizon for inflation targeting is about three years whereas for price level targeting it is about six years.

The latter result highlights the important issue of the time reference for the definition of price stability. In the October 1998 announcement, the ECB underlined that 'price stability is to be maintained over the medium term'. The medium term orientation is partly a reflection of the time lag with which monetary policy affects prices – price developments cannot be controlled through monetary policy on a monthly or even quarterly basis. More importantly, a medium term orientation is compatible with the role of monetary policy in the overall framework of stability oriented policies. Svensson (1997b) and Ball (1999) derived, in the context of small theoretical models, a correspondence between the length of time taken in bringing inflation back to target and the central bank's desire to avoid excessive output fluctuations when doing so. The idea is that a longer time horizon allows a more measured response to unforeseen shocks, thereby avoiding 'unnecessary' volatility in output, employment and interest rates.[5] By credibly committing *ex ante* to a medium term orientation in the pursuit of price stability, the central bank is able to respond flexibly to economic conditions while guaranteeing the stability of the value of the currency.

Some countries have followed the alternative route to be more specific about the horizon over which the inflation objective is to be pursued. In order to avoid unnecessarily harsh responses to all inflationary shocks, however, the concept of inflation has been suitably redefined. One possibility is to specify explicit contingencies under which a temporary deviation from the objective can be allowed. Another possibility is to specify the inflation objective in terms of a 'core', rather than headline, measure.

[5] Reference to 'unnecessary' negative consequences of policy is also present in the 'statute' of the most orthodox inflation targeting central bank, the Reserve Bank of New Zealand. The Policy Target Agreement signed in December 1999 explicitly required the Bank to 'seek to avoid unnecessary instability in output, interest rates and the exchange rate' (Article 4c).

These practices have been explored in, for example, New Zealand, where a number of escape clauses have been explicitly included in various 'Policy Targets Agreements' (PTAs), listing the sorts of shocks whose first-round effects on prices could be allowed. The PTA signed in December 1999 included, 'for example, shifts in the aggregate price level as a result of exceptional movements in the prices of commodities traded in world markets, changes in indirect taxes, significant government policy changes that directly affect prices, or a natural disaster affecting a major part of the economy'. Given these factors, the Bank 'will seek to explain the actual inflation outcome in terms of how those temporary factors may have affected the outcome' (background note to the 1997 PTA). Similarly, the Bank of Canada, whose inflation target is expressed in terms of the headline CPI, also uses and reports a core index, which excludes food and energy and the effect of indirect taxes. The inflation target of the Bank of England is expressed in terms of the retail price index excluding mortgage interest payments (RPIX), but an additional series (RPIY), which also excludes the first-round effect of changes in indirect taxes, is also published.

While these practices may appear to define more precisely the central bank's mandate, in the explanation of policy decisions, the explicit provision of escape clauses typically leaves it to the central bank itself to identify whether, at each point in time, the shocks hitting the economy have or have not been of the special nature listed among the escape clauses. As to core inflation, there can be difficulties in convincing the public why the central bank is not concerned with the 'normal' definition of inflation, and it can be confusing to refer to the headline, or the core, index depending on circumstances.

Hence, while these alternative ways to give operational content to the concept of price stability have their positive features, they do not attain the ideal objective of removing all judgmental factors from the assessment of whether the central bank is fulfilling its price stability mandate at each point in time. Specifically, a temporary deviation from price stability of the headline inflation rate and an uninterrupted consistency with price stability, but only in terms of a 'suitably modified' inflation rate, appear to be similar ways to explain economic conditions and motivate the policy response for the benefit of the public.

Two final aspects of the ECB's definition of price stability are worth stressing. First, the definition focuses on the euro area as a whole, as requested by the price stability mandate: no special attention will be paid to country or sector specific shocks, unless they are leading indicators of area-wide developments. This recognises that monetary policy cannot be used as a tool to address idiosyncratic developments.

Second, the definition of price stability refers to annual (year-on-year) price increases. The monthly or quarterly fluctuations in prices are of no direct consequence. The reasons here are that inflation measured in annual terms is prominent in the public debate, and that high frequency price movements are not of primary concern, and in any case cannot be controlled by monetary policy.

5   The role of money

The focus of this chapter is the role played, in the ECB strategy, by monetary analysis, and by the related 'reference value' announced for the monetary aggregate M3. A special role for money, within a full-information framework, is a distinguishing feature of the ECB strategy. We attempt, in this chapter, to clarify the arguments that, in our view, make such a role necessary. This is an area where economic theory, data evidence and policy experience are closely interrelated: money, as we discussed earlier, plays a central role in all well-established theories of inflation; the international evidence confirms these theories, showing a long run link between money and prices; finally, many central banks in recent economic history, particularly when facing inflationary pressures that they were determined to resist, have placed money at the centre of their monetary policy frameworks.

The chapter is organised as follows. First, drawing on the review of the literature presented in earlier chapters, we summarise the main concepts and evidence that suggest that money has a natural role in *any* monetary policy strategy aiming at price stability. At the same time, however, we underscore a number of caveats that suggest caution in interpreting and using monetary data for policy purposes. From this we draw some general implications, moving then to a detailed description of the role that money actually plays in the ECB strategy. Next, we discuss the evidence – still limited – that exists on money demand and the link between money and prices in the euro area.

5.1   What do the literature and policy experiences tell us?

Our starting point in considering the role that money plays in the ECB strategy is to bring together, as in a sort of common denominator, the main theoretical features that characterise money in virtually all models of modern monetary economies. Two such features are, in our view, both of central importance and largely uncontroversial across all main schools of thought.

First, all widely accepted economic models share the property that money is 'neutral' in the long run. This means that changes of the same proportion in the money stock and in all nominal prices in the economy (if we abstract from distortions arising, for example, in the tax system), leave all real variables and all agents' equilibrium positions unchanged.[1] This simply amounts to saying that economic agents are not subject to money illusion: economic decisions don't change according to the units in which money and, conversely, prices are measured.

This statement pertains to the comparison of steady state equilibria. The second feature – related to the first by what Samuelson (1965) called the 'Correspondence Principle' – pertains to dynamics. It can be stated as follows: policy shocks leading to permanent changes in the money stock give rise to sequential changes that eventually lead, after all adjustments have worked through, to a new equilibrium in which money and nominal prices are all changed in an equal proportion. This holds under the assumption that aggregate output has not changed in the process; if aggregate supply of goods and services in the economy is fixed (e.g., at its full employment level), money and prices will have changed proportionally in the new steady state equilibrium. The result says that, after a policy induced change in money, adjustments in the economy will take place after which prices will have changed by an equiproportional amount. The 'dynamic' neutrality property adds to the 'static' one in saying that there is a stable dynamic path bringing the economy from one equilibrium position to another.

These two basic properties have been familiar to, and broadly agreed upon by, economists for a long time.[2] However, they leave ample room for disagreement on the nature and the length of the adjustment path leading to the new steady state equilibrium and on the price/quantity breakdown of the effects of monetary policy shocks. The debate has been (and still is[3]) active on these issues, while it is absent on the two properties mentioned earlier.

Meanwhile, central bank practices concerning the role of monetary aggregates in the design of monetary policy have fallen into three broad categories. A first category of central banks have disregarded monetary

---

[1] We focus, for simplicity, on a closed economy. The extension to open economies does not change the basic thrust of the argument.

[2] The aforementioned discussion relies on the hypothesis that the equilibrium is unique and saddle-path stable. Matters might obviously change if there is a multiplicity of steady states. It should be emphasised, however, that recent models that focus on the role of real indeterminacy entertain the possibility of indeterminacy of the transition path (following an initial shock), not indeterminacy of the steady state. Hence, they do not violate long run neutrality (e.g., De Fiore, 2000).

[3] A 'central banker's' view on this debate is provided by Viñals and Vallés (1999).

aggregates altogether, both in the design and in the implementation of their monetary policy strategies. This is, for example, the case of banks in small, open economies operating under fixed exchange rate regimes or currency boards. It is well known that in such a case the money stock and the price level are determined endogenously. The exchange rate is assumed, in this case, to condense all information relevant for monetary policy.

At the opposite extreme, some central banks operating under floating exchange rates have conducted monetary policies using monetary aggregates as target variables. In this case, the chosen monetary aggregate is treated, within a pre-specified time interval ('control period') as if it was a final target of monetary policy. Frequently quoted examples of monetary targeting in recent history are those enacted by the Fed, during the 'monetarist experiment' between October 1979 and 1982,[4] and by the Bundesbank after 1975.[5]

An intermediate position is occupied by those central banks that use monetary aggregates as information variables. In a pure informational approach, each indicator, including money, is weighted according to the – empirically determined – information content that it proves to possess to predict future values of the final monetary policy goal.

From a theoretical viewpoint, there is a clear-cut distinction between an 'informational' strategy and a 'pure money targeting' one: namely, unlike in the former, in the latter there is a (nonzero) time interval (the 'control period' to which we have referred earlier) in which the intermediate monetary target replaces the final target in driving the central bank's actions. The conditions under which money can be used as an information variable are more general than those in which a pure monetary targeting strategy can efficiently be applied.[6]

From a practical viewpoint, however, the difference between what could be defined as an 'enlightened' targeting strategy, on the one hand, and an informational approach, on the other hand, is less well defined. A clearly identifiable element of difference is that monetary aggregates are naturally given higher prominence in external communication in the case of monetary targeting central banks (the Fed in the 1979–82 period and the Bundesbank illustrate this case) that usually preannounce monetary guidelines, or norms. This does not usually happen for any of the banks that use money as an information variable.

---

[4] See Friedman (1996) for a review of the US experience with monetary targeting. The later Fed experience is described by Kohn (1989).
[5] See Issing (1997).   [6]See, e.g., Friedman (1990).

Nevertheless, it is clear that monetary targeting central banks have continuously monitored a broad set of monetary, financial and real economic indicators in order to check the information contained in money growth. For the Bundesbank, this point is made very clear in von Hagen (1995) who quotes Helmut Schlesinger (1988): '[T]he Bundesbank [has] never, since 1975, conducted a rigid policy geared at the money supply alone; all information about the financial markets and the development of the economy must be analysed regularly zzz Furthermore the Bundesbank had to check the consistency of her original monetary target with the ultimate policy goals.' Some authors have therefore argued that, despite the stated intentions of the German central bank, it never actually pursued a 'true' monetary targeting strategy.[7] Whatever the label adopted to describe this case study, it is certainly true that applied monetary targeting can be judged, in retrospect, to have been relatively flexible and undogmatic.

The experience of the European central banks during Stage Two of EMU is also relevant, considering that continuity with previous practices is one of the factors that have contributed to shape the ECB strategy. In this context, the Bundesbank is the most prominent, but not the only, example of a central bank that attributed a broad monetary aggregate a key role in its strategy. Smaller countries, such as the Netherlands, Austria and Belgium, have implicitly participated in a monetary targeting regime by pegging their currencies to the Deutschmark. Other prospective euro area countries, such as France and Italy, also announced either targets or 'normative' guidelines for the rate of growth of broad monetary aggregates. An increasing number of central banks adopted, after 1992, an explicit direct inflation targeting approach, thereby assigning to money a purely informational role.

5.2   Two implications for the ECB strategy

From the academic debate and the policy experience that we have just described, a number of lessons can be drawn for the design of the ECB monetary policy strategy. We summarise them here, before turning in the next section to the actual description of the role of money in the ECB strategy. To simplify, two main implications can be identified.

First, the central message from the theory, confirmed by the evidence, of a strong and robust long run link between money and prices, cannot be ignored by a central bank that has price stability as its primary goal. This

---

[7] See Bernanke and Mishkin (1992).

relationship is a reminder that it is impossible to have high and sustained inflation without monetary accommodation. Since the relationship holds in the long term, there are obvious difficulties in interpreting the impact of current monetary developments on inflation in the medium term. Concluding, from the acknowledgement of these difficulties, that money should be neglected altogether is, however, a logical *non sequitur*. Ignoring money amounts to disregarding an important piece of information. This information is particularly useful to avoid large mistakes in policy, which could arise when the other available indicators – whose exact relationship with inflation is unknown *both* in the short and in the long run – fail to signal inflationary risks.[8]

It is because of the limitations of economists' and central banks' knowledge of the functioning of the economy that money plays a special role in practical monetary policy making. When future price prospects appear particularly uncertain, the long run relationship between money and prices represents the ultimate, robust policy indicator, which can be trusted on the basis of the simple assumption that agents do not suffer from money illusion. Since monetary developments are consistent with inflationary developments in the long term, they also provide information, admittedly noisier, on developments in the shorter run. The *analysis* of money is therefore important to extract the signal on future price changes from this noisy indicator.

This is the basis for the 'prominence' of money in the ECB strategy – and, consequently, in the analysis leading to policy decisions and in the external communication of such decisions. Attributing a special role to money is ultimately the logical consequence of the notion that the aggregate price level, which is the focus of the statutory objective of the ECB, is nothing else than *the price of money*, expressed in terms of the generality of goods and services that are available in the market. Given certain assumptions concerning the demand, attributing to the dynamics of the supply of money a prominent role in monitoring price dynamics amounts to exploiting an economic relationship that holds whatever the underlying economic structure. In this respect, the usefulness of money is greatest when information about the structure and the functioning of the economy is particularly limited.

The specific nature of the ECB, a central bank with the responsibility for conducting monetary policy for a new monetary area and for a new currency, strengthens this conclusion. This is because basic and robust theoretical and empirical regularities, which have been shown to hold in

---

[8] Brunner and Meltzer (1969) argued in favour of adopting a fixed growth rate of money rule to avoid large mistakes, when the policy maker's knowledge of the economy is particularly poor.

a variety of different circumstances, should be given a dominant weight when specific circumstances (such as the regime shift inherent in the transition to Stage Three of EMU) temporarily increase policy makers' uncertainty about the behaviour of private agents and about the nature of the monetary policy transmission process. Moreover, assigning a central role to money underscores the continuity between the ECB strategy and the strategy of those central banks that have, in the past, successfully used the information coming from monetary aggregates to enact price stability oriented policies.

Second, translating this general premise into practice is a complex exercise, which requires judgment and caution and cannot be approached by relying on overly rigid analytical schemes. The links between money holdings (however defined) and the other main macroeconomic variables can, in the short run, be influenced by a multiplicity of factors, from the nature of the policy regime to the technology of the payment systems, from financial innovation to the tax system. Most of these factors and their impact on money demand are difficult to identify *ex ante*, and therefore they pose a serious challenge to the use of money for policy purposes. The link between monetary developments and monetary policy decisions should in no case be automatic. Decisions should also be supported by an understanding of the broader economic picture, including the factors that may unsettle the demand for money balances in the short run. All available information should be used to ascertain whether, at each point in time, monetary developments entail risks to price stability. This ultimately involves the use of judgmental elements – from the estimation of the existing 'overhang' at each point in time, to the assessment of exogenous 'special factors' – that cannot be summarised in a precise mathematical formula. The empirical evidence of a stable demand for money is important in this context.

Analysing and monitoring a single monetary aggregate is not sufficient. Monetary analysis should take into account, in a comprehensive way, all elements that convey information on the overall degree of liquidity of the economy. This is because it is ultimately such degree of liquidity that may suggest the existence of medium term pressures on prices, or prospective risks to price stability. A single monetary aggregate, such as M3, may not always be sufficient for this purpose. No matter how stable its historical relation with prices may be, its ability to provide an adequate proxy for the economy's liquidity may be weakened by financial innovation, changes in payments technology or fluctuations in portfolio preferences. Eventually, in this case, a redefinition of the monetary aggregate would be needed, though experience shows that it may take a significant amount of time before a new stable aggregate can be identified. Over the shorter time, therefore, the analysis of the developments of the key monetary aggregate needs to be complemented with other information concerning the counterparties of money creation, the supply of credit, and the volume and composition of the asset holdings of households and firms.

5.3   From principles to practice: money in the ECB strategy

The basic concepts regarding the role of money were publicly disclosed by the ECB Governing Council on 13 October 1998, as part of the major statement issued by the Council concerning its monetary policy strategy. After that, many publications by the ECB have further defined and clarified that role.

5.3.1   A 'prominent role' for money

The Council has taken the view that in the ECB strategy money should be accorded a 'prominent role', distancing itself from both theoretical monetary targeting and the pure informational approach.

The developments in the money stock are evaluated against a preannounced 'reference value'. This implies that the interpretation and the implications of monetary developments are logically split in two parts. *Ex ante*, a reference path for the money stock is estimated, conditional on (that is, deemed to be consistent with) certain assumptions concerning the broader macroeconomic picture and the maintenance of price stability. *Ex post*, actual developments in the money stock are compared with the reference path, and the deviations are taken into account in the monetary policy decision process. Under normal conditions, such deviations signal potential threats to price stability.

The prominent role assigned to money and the preannouncement of a reference path for this variable are the two elements of continuity of the ECB strategy with monetary targeting. But here is where similarities with monetary targeting end, and the differences begin. In the ECB strategy, the difficulties involved in the analysis of money over the short run are explicitly acknowledged through the provision of an important role for *other* information (discussed in the next chapter). This openly rules out mechanistic and automatic policy responses to deviations of the money stock from the reference value.

The medium term frame in which the price stability objective is cast makes the use of money as a communication tool particularly appealing. Short term, potentially erratic fluctuations in money are not attributed particular relevance, as they are normally not deemed to have implications for price developments. This is highlighted by the conceptual framework used for communication with the public, which is the 'quantity equation'. This equation can be seen as an identity, defining velocity as a function of other well identified variables. It acquires operational content only if a theory is formulated for the behaviour of velocity. Then, a normative value for money growth (the 'reference value') can be derived, given a desired value of the rate of change in prices ('price stability') and a projected path for the rate of growth of output.

The criteria for calculating velocity and output growth deserve attention in this context. Following the practice established over the years by the Bundesbank, output growth is referred to as *trend* output and it excludes short term cyclical fluctuations. This mechanism is useful because it restates the notion of a medium term orientation for monetary policy, not aiming at fine tuning output or the price level.

The projected value of the rate of growth of monetary velocity is obtained using both structural and time series models. Again, however, short term fluctuations in monetary velocity are excluded from the projected path underlying the calculation of the reference value, for the reasons already discussed above. Sizeable and permanent changes in projected developments of velocity, if they occur, should be incorporated in the calculation of the reference value when they are deemed to be well understood and there is sufficient supporting evidence.

5.3.2   Some technical issues

Some further specific and technical issues need to be addressed. The first of them concerns the identification of the appropriate monetary aggregate to be used to calculate the reference value. The proper definition of monetary aggregates has been the object of considerable controversy, particularly after monetary aggregates became, around the mid-seventies, central to monetary policy frameworks in many countries. Conceptual elements and a wide array of empirical results have been brought into the debate.[9] The longest-contended issue is that relating to the choice of large vs. narrow aggregates. Narrow aggregates, which include only the most liquid components of money (typically, cash and current accounts), have the advantage of being closer to the theoretical definition of 'transaction money' in that they are directly used as means of payment. Moreover, since they are normally characterised by very low or zero own-returns, they are more easily controllable by the central bank, since policy induced changes in money market rates have a direct impact on their opportunity cost. However, the very fact that they do not yield a market determined

---

[9] An earlier review of the relevant concepts was provided by Osborne (1984).

return makes them more vulnerable to instability, when innovations in the financial system or in payment technology allow households and firms to economise on the relatively costly assets of which narrow aggregates are composed. Broad aggregates, which include also certain near-money instruments (such as longer term bank deposits, certificates of deposits, and the like) are not subject to this type of instability. However, from the viewpoint of measuring the existing stock of 'direct purchasing power' they have the drawback of including assets held more for portfolio than for transaction motives. In addition, they are normally more difficult to control using standard monetary policy instruments: changes in short term rates tend to impact more on their maturity composition than on their overall volume.

In the context of the ECB monetary policy strategy, the choice fell on broad aggregates, for several reasons. Unlike in the case of theoretical monetary targeting, controllability is not a key requirement. However, the chosen aggregate must have a stable, predictable long run relationship with prices, as well as good leading indicator properties in the medium term. From this viewpoint, the evidence available for the euro area, to which we will turn shortly, speaks clearly in favour of broader aggregates. This is not surprising, since money markets in several European countries have undergone, in recent years, precisely the type of phenomena that should lead to instability in narrow aggregates: changes in bank structures and behaviour; developments of new money market segments and deregulation of the existing ones; liberalisation of short term capital flows; reforms of the tax systems and of reserve requirements. Conceptual criteria and, in particular, empirical analyses have lead to the identification of a specific broad aggregate, M3, which possesses particularly desirable long run stability properties.[10]

A further set of technical issues relates to the modalities in which the reference value is announced. Specifically: should this be expressed as a single growth rate, thereby defining a single path of M3 compatible with the reference value itself, or should it be a range, implying a band in which actual M3 developments can oscillate? These issues are more presentational than substantive. On the one hand, a range has the benefit of more clearly expressing the uncertainties that exist in projecting future money developments: in fact, the range can be used to express the degree of this uncertainty. On the other hand, it may convey the impression that there exist well-defined limits beyond which deviations would not

---

[10] The maturity threshold and the composition of M3 are also dictated, to some extent, by statistical considerations, linked to the features of the existing bank reporting system. In particular, the econometric evidence does not provide clear-cut indications for or against the inclusion of money market funds.

be tolerated, and that the central bank would become a pure monetary targeter when those limits are reached. Such risk of ambiguity does not arise when a single number is announced.

A subtler alternative is whether the reference value should be expressed in terms of levels of M3, or in terms of rates of changes. This issue is related to the other one, already touched upon in chapter 4, of defining the price stability objective in terms of inflation rates or price levels. A reference value expressed only in terms of rate of change over N months implies that one-time, step deviations from the reference value are automatically disregarded after N months, because the N-month percentage change would not include them. On the contrary, a level-based method has, by construction, an infinitely lived memory. There are, clearly, advantages and drawbacks in both approaches. In particular, looking only at percentage changes, especially over a short period such as a calendar year, implies that changes in the money stock become irrelevant much earlier than they should. In technical jargon, a 'base drift' would be incorporated in the money supply monitoring process. On the other side, a pure 'level' approach may give, in the long run, excessive weight to changes relative to given initial conditions. It seems, therefore, appropriate to adopt a flexible, judgmental approach, according to which percentage changes receive central attention but deviations in the level of the money stock relative to its reference value are also monitored for their potential implications for price stability.

Finally, we turn to the ECB's experience so far with the announcement of the reference value. The interpretation of actual monetary developments, in light of the reference value, during the first year of Stage Three will be discussed in chapter 10.

The ECB's Governing Council has issued so far two major announcements concerning the reference value for M3, the first in December 1998 and the second one year later.

On 1 December 1998, the Governing Council issued the following announcements on the calculation of the reference value applicable at the start of Stage Three (again, the reader can find details in the original statement by the President):

1. The underlying price assumption is consistent with the price stability definition (that is, a year-on-year increase in the Harmonised Index of Consumer Prices for the euro area of less than 2 per cent);
2. real GDP is assumed to grow at a trend rate between 2 and 2.5 per cent in the medium term;
3. the medium term velocity of circulation of M3 should be between 0.5 and 1 per cent at an annual basis;

4. taking all this into account, the reference value for M3 is set at 4.5 per cent. This value will be reviewed at the end of 1999.

It is important to stress that no explicit time horizon is mentioned, but the intention is expressed to re-examine the reference value after the first year. This is consistent with the medium term orientation of the strategy and also contributes to limit the so-called 'base drift'.

On 2 December 1999, the Council decided to confirm the reference value for monetary growth at a rate of 4.5 per cent for the broad aggregate M3. This decision was based on the fact that the components underlying the derivation of the reference value one year earlier, namely, the definition of price stability and the assumptions for trend real GDP growth and for the trend in the velocity of M3, had remained unchanged. Specifically, the reference value continued to be based on the assumption of a real GDP growth between 2 and 2.5 per cent per year, and an annual decline in the velocity of circulation of M3 in the range between 0.5 and 1 per cent. Again, it was decided that the reference value would be reviewed one year later, in December 2000.

5.4   Money demand models for the euro area

The possibility of identifying a 'pan-European' demand for money function has attracted considerable attention in the economics profession in the last ten years.[11] The starting point of this line of research is a pioneering contribution by McKinnon (1982), according to which international currency substitution among financially integrated economies should tend to give rise to stable multicountry money demand relationships, even when money demands relating to individual countries are unstable.

Providing a survey of the money demand literature is outside our scope here.[12] The empirical evidence focusing on the USA suggests that confidence of the economics profession in the stability of money demand relationship has declined in recent years, from Goldfeld (1973) – who argued strongly in favour of money demand stability in the USA – to Estrella and Mishkin (1997) – who point out the weak information content of money. In the USA, the course of the literature, and the growing

---

[11] Following the pioneering papers by Bekx and Tullio (1989) and Kremers and Lane (1990), many contributions focused on Europe have appeared in the early 1990s: see, for example, Monticelli (1993) and Monticelli and Strauss-Kahn (1992). Browne, Fagan and Henry (1997) and Monticelli and Papi (1996) provide detailed discussions and surveys.

[12] Excellent surveys are: Ericsson (1999); Goldfeld and Sichel (1990).

scepticism towards monetary aggregates, seem to have been heavily influenced by two specific episodes: the *over*-prediction of M2 in the USA in the 1970s (the well known 'case of the missing money'[13]) and the equally strong *under*-prediction in the 1980s, stemming from the liberalisation of the bank deposit market. In Europe the picture is different, and somewhat mixed: money market innovation and sizeable short term capital flows, associated at times with exchange rate crises, have contributed to temporarily unsettle money demand relations in a number of countries (such as France and Spain), while in others (e.g., Germany and Italy) money demand has remained relatively more stable.

After the EMU project was conceived, Europe became a natural focus of this research, since the identification of a stable European money demand could potentially become a key building block of the future single monetary policy. Most of the evidence produced in recent years – see, for example, Fagan and Henry (1998) or the survey in Browne, Fagan and Henry (1997) – is broadly supportive of the view that a stable long run relationship between broad monetary aggregates in Europe and the traditional determinants of money demand exists. More recently, the issue has been reconsidered systematically in the comprehensive studies by Coenen and Vega (1999; henceforth CV) and Brand and Cassola (2000; henceforth BC), based on state-of-the-art econometric techniques. Both papers construct a multivariate model for the euro area including real M3 holdings, real GDP, short and long term interest rates, and inflation.

Over the 1980–98 period, CV find that the hypothesis of long run homogeneity of money and prices can be accepted at standard confidence levels. Their results support three conclusions. First, cointegration among real money, real GDP, long and short term interest rates and inflation is not rejected.[14] Second, within the multivariate model, it is possible to identify a long run M3 demand equation which is both simple and plausible on theoretical grounds, in which holdings or real money balances depend on real income, the opportunity cost of holding money relative to competing financial assets and inflation. Thirdly, the model admits also a stable, short term parsimonious formulation, in which M3 holdings depend, through an error correction model, on the same explanatory variables just mentioned.

CV report impulse response functions to study the reaction of M3 following selected macroeconomic shocks. A number of assumptions adopted in their study are worth mentioning. First, aggregate demand

---

[13] Goldfeld (1976).
[14] Unpublished results collected during the preparation of this paper suggest that cointegration may be rejected for narrow monetary aggregates.

shocks are assumed to have only a short-lived effect on *real* money balances and other real variables, while in equilibrium they affect only – and in the same proportion – *nominal* money holdings and the price level. Supply shocks have instead real effects both in the short and in the long run. Second, nominal interest rate shocks do not have effects on real money balances, nor on other real variables, in equilibrium, although they do affect, in the same proportion, nominal money and prices.

The impulse responses show that, in the short run, the 'controllability' of nominal money stock is not ensured: an increase in money market rates does not give rise to a significant decline in the nominal stock of M3. Controllability is, however, satisfied in the longer run, through the joint adjustment to the equilibrium of all the variables in the system.[15]

BC also analyse the properties of money demand in the euro area on the basis of a different econometric specification (including, for example, a different measure of the opportunity cost of holding money and a slightly different sample period, from 1980Q1 to 1999Q3). BC confirm the existence of stable long run relationships between the variables of the system, one of which can be interpreted as a money demand function for M3. It is noticeable that short run deviations from equilibrium of real M3 have an effect on (the change of) the rate of inflation. BC also conduct an impulse response analysis on the basis of a theoretically neutral set of identifying assumptions. Their generalised response profiles show that, whenever M3 happens to grow unexpectedly fast, future inflation ensues. Finally, the short run controllability of M3 is less of a problem within this framework.

Further empirical work on the role of money in the euro area has recently become available. Gerlach and Svensson (2000) propose a direct comparison between money and the output gap in terms of their explanatory power over inflation. To this end, they rely on both the so-called P-star framework and the traditional Phillips curve based view on the transmission mechanism.[16] Since the P-star model can be written in terms of deviations of real money balances from equilibrium (the 'real money gap'), the model provides a direct and testable link between money and inflation. A similar link between the output gap and inflation is obtained through the Phillips curve. Gerlach and Svensson estimate an equation that includes both the real money gap and the output gap as determinants of inflation. Preliminary results show a substantial explanatory power for the real money gap, which is also more significant than that of the output gap.

[15] Cabrero et al. (1998) and Vlaar and Schuberth (1999) obtain similar results.
[16] For the P-star framework, see Hallmann, Porter and Small (1991).

Following this approach and also drawing on CV's results, Trecroci and Vega (2000) estimate an equation for inflation including the real money gap, the output gap and deviations of the real interest rate from equilibrium. Using a variety of measures of the output gap and of the monetary authorities' inflation objective, they confirm a substantive explanatory power of the real money gap over euro area inflation from 1980 to 1998. In addition, the output gap and deviations of the real interest rate from equilibrium also provide useful information on inflationary developments.

In out-of-sample forecasts, the aforementioned three variables also prove useful to predict future inflation up to six quarters ahead. Interestingly, the relevance of the real money gap is robust to changes of measurement of the monetary authority's inflation objective. On the contrary, the importance of the output gap hinges on its correct measurement. Trecroci and Vega also compare their forecast to that obtained in a structural macroeconometric model in which inflation is determined solely by deviations of the economy from potential GDP and the NAIRU (see Fagan, Henry and Mestre, 2001). The latter model clearly outperforms the former at a very short horizon (one or two quarters), but the ranking is reversed for forecasts between three and six quarters. Beyond six quarters, both models provide a very poor indication of future inflationary developments.

Gerlach and Svensson's and Trecroci and Vega's results show a very important role for the real money gap in the euro area. It remains unclear whether these results have uncovered a structural feature of European inflation, given the reduced-form nature of the estimations and the failure of both papers to provide a satisfactory explanation for the strong downward trend of inflation over a large part of the sample period. Nevertheless, the results strongly suggest a key role for money as an indicator of future inflationary pressures in the euro area.[17]

---

[17] Gerlach and Svensson argue that the significant role of the real money gap to predict inflation in the euro area does not necessarily justify the prominent role for money in the ECB strategy. Specifically, they argue that the importance of the *real* money gap does not justify the announcement of a reference value for the rate of growth of *nominal* money. This view, however, appears to be based on a too strict interpretation of the results. Starting from a theoretical equilibrium level, the finding that deviations of real money from this equilibrium tend to anticipate price changes appears consistent with the view that changes in nominal money tend to anticipate changes in prices. Moreover, it should be kept in mind that the prominent role for money in the ECB strategy is 'signalled' by the announcement of a reference value for the rate of growth of M3, but does not coincide with the reference value. An important role for the real money gap is fully consistent with the prominence of money in the ECB strategy.

6   A broadly based assessment

In chapter 5 it was argued that the relation between money and prices in the long run justifies a special role for the analysis of monetary developments in the context of the ECB's strategy. Nevertheless, monetary developments do not exhaust analysis within the strategy: a wide array of models and indicators contribute to define the relevant information.

Given the long run relationship between money and prices, monitoring monetary developments would certainly provide the economy with a nominal anchor. Other factors, however, will influence inflation in the shorter run. The analysis of these developments, including the possibility to respond to them, can improve the efficiency with which price stability is achieved and also ensure that temporary inflationary or deflationary pressures do not become entrenched in the economy.

The range of relevant indicators, and their relative importance, change over time. Consequently, there is no permanently valid way to organise the assessment in a logically consistent manner. For purposes of exposition, we have divided this chapter into two sections. In the first, we describe the analysis of a range of economic variables that have leading indicator properties on inflation in the short to medium term. These, in turn, are organised under four headings: (a) 'gap' measures; (b) measures of cost pressure; (c) international prices and exchange rates; and (d) other asset prices.[1] Finally, we mention the analysis of current price developments, which also has an important role in practical monetary policy making. Section 6.2 describes, instead, the analysis of expectations and forecasts for inflation. Expectations for inflation may be derived from financial markets' information or covered directly through surveys. Forecasts may be produced by the central bank itself (also using econometric models) or by third parties.

---

[1] The role of these indicators is explained in an article published in the ECB's *Monthly Bulletin* in April 1999.

6.1   Leading indicators

As already mentioned the analysis of short term indicators can be usefully grouped into: (a) 'gap' measures; (b) measures of cost pressure; (c) international prices and exchange rates; and (d) other asset prices.

As shown by a wide body of empirical literature,[2] **gap measures** (i.e. measures of the discrepancy between output, or its factors of production, and their equilibrium values) are key elements in predicting inflationary pressures and in guiding central banks' actions. Such measures include output gaps, capacity utilisation and measures of employment and unemployment.[3] Their relevance tends to be higher the lower the degree of external opening of the economy, which determines the extent to which domestic prices are driven by domestic demand and supply conditions. As a consequence, gap measures will be more relevant for the euro area than they were in the past monetary policy experience in each individual participating country. Since the output gap is defined as the difference between potential output and the contemporaneous (demand-determined) output, supply *and* demand conditions are relevant to estimate it. These include national account data, mainly quarterly GDP, industrial production, employment and unemployment, consumer, manufacturing and construction confidence indices and retail sales.

It must be borne in mind, however, that the output gap is a 'latent' variable, which is never measured with precision. Estimation techniques that explicitly recognise this latent variable characteristic are obviously useful, as proven by the recent work by Ehrmann and Smets (2000), Gerlach and Smets (1999) and Smets (1998). Nevertheless, the aggregate output gap remains a theoretically elusive concept, whose practical use in real time monetary policy making should be considered with extreme care (see also the discussion in chapter 2).

Cost measures include wage dynamics, unit labour costs and mark-ups, though the empirical significance of the relationship between inflation developments and changes in mark-ups is relatively less clear. There is empirical evidence available for the euro area showing that unit labour costs are an important determinant for price developments, though mainly at very short horizons (see Fagan, Henry and Mestre, 2001). This evidence confirms that labour costs dynamics tend to be very proximate determinants of inflation and that other indicators can be more

---

[2] See, e.g., Astley and Yates (1999), Stock and Watson (1999) and the recent work on Taylor rules (Bernanke and Mihov, 1997; Clarida, Galí and Gertler, 1998).
[3] We include in this category all the variables that convey information about the current state of the business cycle relative to its trend, or potential trend.

useful in a medium term perspective. Moreover, it should be noticed that the available labour cost data are subject to sometimes-significant revisions, relative to the original release, by Eurostat. Furthermore, they are conditional on available measures of employment indicators, concerning which there are some methodological issues still unresolved for the euro area. Hence, a large degree of uncertainty characterises current estimates of this variable.

Despite the fact that the degree of openness of the euro area is much lower than in any of the participating countries, the **exchange rate** (and, by extension, **international prices**) remains a relevant element of the broadly based assessment. Prolonged exchange rate swings, perhaps inconsistent with fundamentals, can become themselves causes of imbalances and inflationary or deflationary pressures. Nevertheless, the exchange rate has, in the ECB strategy, a very different role with respect to the one it played for the central banks of many EU Member States before EMU. There is no announced target band for either the exchange rate of the euro vis-à-vis a basket of other currencies, such as the ECU during ERM years, or its bilateral exchange rate vis-à-vis other major currencies such as the US dollar or the Japanese yen. Exchange rate developments are monitored not for their own sake, but for the effect they may have on domestic price stability in the euro area. In Fagan, Henry and Mestre (2001) it is shown that import prices, which depend on oil, commodities and other traded goods prices, have a non-negligible effect on internal price developments.

In addition, a key role is assigned to **asset prices** other than exchange rates. The size and the role of bond and stock markets in the monetary policy transmission process suggest that they should be assigned a high weight among relevant indicators. In particular, the yield curve has proved to be an invaluable tool for price stability oriented monetary policy strategies in Europe in the last decade, often providing a yardstick for convergence among potential EMU participants.[4] However, interpreting the yield curve and other asset prices is a particularly complex task, not only in light of the behavioural changes deriving from the transition to Stage Three. Particular caution must be exercised since asset prices are not only a link in the transmission process, but also a measure of market expectations of broad economic developments, including central bank actions. Multiple equilibria and policy-induced instability could occur, if asset prices were used mechanically in monetary policy decision making.[5]

Within the broadly based assessment, attention is also devoted to the analysis of recent price dynamics. Since important variables are only

[4] See Angeloni and Rovelli (1998).
[5] See Bernanke and Woodford (1997); Woodford (1994).

imperfectly observed or only accurately measured after a significant time lag, information on the current state of the economy, price developments in particular, must partly be filtered from other available indicators. In this respect, the empirical stickiness of inflation dynamics is useful to ascertain current trends on the basis of developments in the recent past.

The analysis of recent price developments centres on the information contained in the Harmonised Index of Consumer Prices (although attention is also paid to other price indices, including industrial production prices). From this viewpoint, recent HICP dynamics, together with the advance knowledge of special factors, such as preannounced changes in prices for utilities or in indirect taxation and subsidies, contain, owing to the inherent persistence of price changes, sufficient information to formulate an accurate assessment of inflationary developments in the very near future. Quarterly, sometimes even annual, inflationary patterns are highly autocorrelated, so that developments over these horizons can be captured with a reasonable degree of accuracy through projections of a technical nature.

The main problem faced by a central bank when trying to project ahead recent inflationary developments is to filter out erratic factors, which can determine significant differences between observed developments in headline inflation and the underlying trend. The main source of such discrepancies comes from the impact of changes in relative prices; for example, the behaviour of unprocessed food prices that proves to be, in most cases, the most volatile component of the price index. There are numerous ways of tackling these issues, including the computation of 'core' and 'trend' measures of inflation.

The exact definition of the concept of core inflation, in other words, what exactly a core inflation index should measure, is not immediately clear (see Wynne, 1999, for an insightful discussion). A general approach is to hypothesise that changes in prices of individual goods can be split in the sum of two components: a common one, which is the ultimate rate of inflation of interest to the central bank, and an idiosyncratic one influenced by local market developments. It follows that core inflation can be identified with the common, or trend, component, and different core indices can be distinguished on the basis of the methodology adopted to filter out the idiosyncratic effects.

Bryan and Cecchetti (1993, 1994), Bryan and Pike (1991), Cecchetti (1997) and Quah and Vahey (1995) have popularised alternative measures of core inflation. Some of these try to exploit the information contained in the cross-sectional distribution of prices and, consequently, exclude relatively more volatile components from the price index. The exclusion can be done either according to statistical criteria (using, for instance, trimmed mean or weighted median), or through a more *ad hoc* procedure such as the 'index excluding food and energy' approach. Other methodologies rely on time series information and ultimately amount to smoothing the index over time, through a moving average of the headline index, or other similar filter. Yet another possibility is to exploit both time series and cross-sectional information, and to impose additional assumptions to identify the core component from the rest of the index (for example, the structural VAR approach proposed by Quah and Vahey, 1995).

Ultimately, the key issue is whether the selected concept of core inflation is a leading indicator of future headline inflation (as argued by Blinder, 1997b). The leading indicator properties of alternative measures, however, are particularly difficult to analyse in the euro area because of the relatively short span of available observations on the HICP. In view of the undesirable features of all econometrics-based methodologies, namely that any new data-point added to the estimation can result in a change of past values of the core index, the cross-section based methodologies have mainly been monitored so far. The evolution of different components of the headline index, for example, is systematically discussed in the *Monthly Bulletin* of the ECB.

6.2   Expectations and forecasts

The aforementioned indicators are often used independently, in the sense that they contribute to shape, sometimes (e.g. for financial market prices) in real time, the informal judgment of the Council. They also play a role, however, in forming expectations and forecasts.

There are similarities between the roles of inflation expectations and inflation forecasts within the broadly based assessment. The similarities are self-evident concerning forecasts produced by third parties: like expectations, these represent the best assessment of other agents – from international institutions to 'the market' – of future inflationary prospects. One would expect matters to be different for internal forecasts, whose assumptions may be expected to embody the judgment and the information of the policy maker. Nevertheless, because of the inability of econometric models to provide an accurate description of the functioning of the economy, the relationship between assumptions and outcomes of the forecasting process is not unambiguous. On the contrary, it is severely affected by, for example, changes in the specification of the model or in the choices made to account for past forecasting errors. Consequently, the distinction between internal and external forecasts is, in practice, blurred. The uncertainty of the reliability of any indicator of future price developments is such that, at each point in time, they are all analysed jointly to help ensure internal consistency for the final assessment, which is ultimately informal.

There are two main sources of inflation expectations: survey measures and estimates relying on financial market data. The latter include the so-called 'break even inflation rate' which is obtained as the difference between the yield on a nominal bond and the yield on a real (index-linked) bond. Developments in inflation expectations are also seen as a proxy for the credibility of the central bank.

The ECB looks at the information contained in forecasts produced by third parties, including those formulated by international organisations (the European Commission, the IMF and the OECD, for example), by research institutes (such as the NIESR) and synthetic measures (e.g., Consensus, an average of forecasts made by financial institutions).

The ECB also produces regular economic forecasts for the euro area, conditional on the technical assumption of unchanged interest rates and exchange rates. Forecasts are produced in the context of a procedure named 'broad forecasting exercise' that twice a year involves both ECB staff and staff from the National Central Banks. Projections are produced for all the main macroeconomic variables, including prices, economic activity, employment, etc. The involvement of National Central Banks signals the attempt to take into account, in the forecast, all information available both from the aforementioned indicators and from national expertise.

A careful combination of models and judgments is necessary, for the ECB even more than for other central banks, for at least three reasons. First, structural breaks might have occurred with the move to the single currency. Second, the data series for the euro area are the result of estimation and are subject to a considerable margin of error. Third, models estimated for the euro area as a whole are particularly prone to aggregation biases.

The possibility of structural breaks poses problems that can hardly be avoided, since existing macroeconomic models are never derived entirely from first principles, and therefore are not invariant to changes in economic and policy regimes. Nevertheless, the ECB has made a special effort to deal, at least in part, with the other aforementioned difficulties. Specifically, concerning the availability of time series, an entirely new database has been built, with the aim of maximising consistency of variables across countries (in terms of both definition and length). In an attempt to deal with the aggregation bias, the ECB has chosen to develop at the same time two quarterly macroeconometric models: the 'area-wide model' (AWM), in which behavioural relationships are estimated at the area-wide level, and (in conjunction with the National Central Banks) the multicountry model (MCM), in which behavioural relationships are estimated at the national level.

The distinguishing feature of the area-wide model is, as already mentioned, the fact that it is estimated on the basis of area-wide data (a detailed description of the AWM is provided by Fagan, Henry and Mestre, 2001). The key advantage of the area-wide model is that it is relatively small and easy to manage, so that it represents a flexible tool for policy analysis. For an economic region such as the euro area, however, it also creates special problems in the construction of the data set. For the years preceding 1999, area-wide macroeconomic variables must be constructed aggregating national data. Criteria, arbitrary to some extent, to convert national currency units into a common standard must be applied.

The MCM does not pose this kind of data problem and, in addition, is less prone to aggregation bias. It can, however, suffer of the kind of misspecification bias stressed by Pesaran, Pierse and Kumar (1989). Given the high economic integration between European countries, euro area variables can play an important role in national economic relationships and should therefore, in principle, be included in individual countries' models. The MCM is a key tool used in the broad forecasting exercises. It provides a framework in which different assumptions about exogenous variables and judgments about the current state and dynamics of the economy can be taken into account and assessed. Moreover, it is especially helpful as the natural framework to bring together the specific knowledge and expertise of staff from NCBs concerning developments in their respective economies.

The general architecture of the AWM and the MCM is based on the standard aggregate supply–aggregate demand structure. On the supply side, a vertical 'Phillips-curve' characterises the steady state. Money is therefore both neutral and superneutral in the long run. In the short run, however, there is sluggish adjustment of wages and prices, based on a flexible dynamic structure that does not impose any specific theoretical adjustment mechanism. Given that wages and prices are sticky, output is demand determined in the short run. The adjustment mechanisms involve, *inter alia*, the feedback of disequilibrium terms in labour and product markets into wage and price dynamics.

The current versions of the models are essentially backward looking, since expectations are mainly adaptive. Forward looking elements only enter the equations determining financial variables, namely the exchange rate and the term structure of interest rates. While this feature is not particularly problematic for the purpose of generating short term forecasts conditional on unchanged, or exogenous, paths of the interest rate and the exchange rate, it obviously prevents the execution of fully satisfactory policy simulations, in which private agents' expectations and behaviour depend on the policy followed by the central bank. Extensions of the models aimed at including more explicitly forward looking expectations are included in the ECB's research agenda.

Despite the aforementioned shortcomings, the ECB experience of the first year (likewise, the experience of most central banks in recent decades) suggests that in-house structural econometric models are valuable tools for ensuring consistency in the internal debate.

7   The ECB strategy: an overall view

In previous chapters, we have examined in some detail the main building blocks of the ECB monetary policy strategy. We will take that as our starting point in the attempt to offer, in this chapter, a comprehensive overview of the strategy as a whole. We will focus, specifically, on the interaction among those building blocks in the process leading to monetary policy decisions.[1]

To summarise the discussion of the last two chapters, the ECB's stability oriented monetary policy strategy includes three main elements: (1) a precise definition of price stability; (2) the analysis of monetary developments; (3) the analysis of a wide range of economic and financial indicators.

Price stability is to be maintained over a medium term horizon. The medium term orientation shows two important general features of the strategy. First, the return to price stability after an inflationary or deflationary shock will be gradual, hence avoiding any unnecessary volatility in output and interest rates. Second, the existence of monetary policy transmission lags is explicitly acknowledged. As a result, policy has to be forward looking and react to current developments mainly to the extent that they convey information on future risks to price stability.

In this respect, the prominent role of money and the broadly based assessment assume the symbolic role of 'pillars' of the strategy itself.[2] The two pillars, considered separately, were extensively discussed in previous chapters, and we shall not return to them here. We shall focus, instead, on their interaction and on the role of the strategy as a framework for both internal information processing and external communication.

---

[1] The essential features of the ECB strategy were outlined in the 13 October 1998 press release (see appendix). Further explanations were provided in ECB (1999a, 2000c). Existing critical reviews of the ECB strategy include: Angeloni, Gaspar and Tristani (1999), Baltensperger (2000) and Svensson (1999b).

[2] As already mentioned in previous chapters, two further elements complement the strategy: the 'operational framework', which includes the instruments and the operating procedures used in financial markets, and the 'communication framework', comprising the set of channels that the central bank uses to communicate to the public its actions and to explain the motivations for such actions.

Before discussing these issues, however, it is important to clarify a point that will be developed more extensively later. Designing the strategy is to some extent an ongoing process, which should reflect progress in theoretical and empirical knowledge, policy experience and understanding of the practical working of the economy. The ECB strategy is *also* a reflection of the still limited extent of our knowledge of the economy to which it is intended to apply. This may change – indeed, it will hopefully change – as time goes on. As already stressed, the only element of the strategy that is 'written in stone', because it is an act of law engraved in an international treaty, and therefore not subject to evaluation over time, is the ECB's commitment to price stability.

7.1   The role of uncertainty in the strategy: general aspects

It is useful to consider, as a benchmark, a hypothetical world in which the 'true' economic model of the world is known, i.e. one without uncertainty about the working of the economy and of the monetary policy transmission mechanism. In such a world all agents share a common information set (*common knowledge*) and they all know the relevant *true* characteristics of the economic environment (*complete information*), possibly including the distribution of a few observable, additive exogenous shocks. Such a world is quite similar to those described in many standard economic models. In these models, the actions of the central bank are immediately understood by the public and no need for explanations would arise. The announcement of, and credible commitment to, the monetary policy's final goal would be sufficient to characterise the entire central bank strategy. No other elements – in the form of intermediate targets, inflation forecasts or otherwise – would be needed. Both the central bank and the public would know exactly, at any time, which adjustments in the monetary policy instruments are needed to attain the final goal within a desired time horizon.

Saying that this world is very far from the one in which market agents and policy makers operate is stating the obvious. A less obvious implication is that the structure of any monetary policy strategy must reflect the extent and the nature of the uncertainties faced by the central bank. Different prevailing sources of uncertainty will normally require different strategies, i.e. differences in the way information is processed in order to attain policy decisions. The ECB strategy, in particular, was tailored having specifically in mind the uncertainties existing in the conduct of the single monetary policy at the start of EMU's Stage Three.

Many of these uncertainties are common to all central banks.[3] The first and perhaps most commonly emphasised is the uncertainty related to the current state of the economy, that is not observable except via a limited number of imprecise and untimely indicators ('state' uncertainty). Policy makers, as well as market agents, are always uncertain about the current condition of the business cycle, the dynamics of aggregate demand and supply and their components, and the actual strength of inflationary and deflationary pressures. Information variables must be used to form an educated guess about the true state of the economy. Moreover, in today's world of information and communication technologies, policy makers are not likely to enjoy a systematic informational advantage relative to market participants. Timely and predictable disclosure of statistics, wide availability of sophisticated analytical techniques, real time communication, all quickly erode any available informational advantages that intensely watched policy makers may have.

The second uncertainty concerns the behaviour of economic agents ('parameter' uncertainty). Again, monetary policy makers must formulate 'guesses', typically in the form of parameters of structural econometric models. No matter how sophisticated, these parameters are at best rough estimates, based on historical time series. Aggregation problems are usually ignored. The treatment of parameter variation and structural change is very rudimentary, as the statistical degrees of freedom available to estimate such changes are very limited in most relevant cases.

More fundamentally, uncertainty goes beyond the mere value of parameters and extends to the nature of the 'true' economic model ('model' uncertainty). Alternative and very different theories and models are often offered to the policy maker as rival explanations of the same phenomenon. As argued in earlier chapters, there is no professional consensus around a model that would be appropriate to use for monetary policy purposes. Among the issues debated it is possible to highlight the modelling of money demand or, more generally, the incorporation of money into general equilibrium models, the transmission and propagation of monetary policy, especially through the financial system, the characteristics of price and wage dynamics. The issue is made considerably harder when it is recognised that, in practice, both economic agents and the central bank continuously try to 'learn the model', so that the structure of the economic environment changes in response to behavioural changes.[4]

---

[3] See, in this respect, the proceedings of the conference on Monetary Policy Making under Uncertainty, organised by the European Central Bank and by the Centre for Financial Studies of Frankfurt University, summarised in Angeloni, Smets and Weber (2000).

[4] For completeness, we should mention that market participants and policy makers alike are obviously uncertain about future exogenous events and shocks ('residual' uncertainty).

7.2   Euro area-specific aspects

We have emphasised above some specific types of uncertainty that, though being very important for the ECB from a quantitative viewpoint, characterise the environment in which all central banks operate. There are, however, specific complexities faced at the ECB that can be considered as exceptional, since they are strictly related to the transition to the EMU and to the unique nature of the euro as a single currency shared by many sovereign nations. The institutional setting behind the single monetary policy is, to a significant extent, uncharted territory from a historical perspective. There are significant differences between the ECB and those central banks that, for decades, have exercised their function within their respective national states.[5]

First, the transition to monetary union and the implementation of the single monetary policy constitute a regime shift in the sense of Lucas (1976). This regime shift may, conceivably, have far-reaching consequences on the behaviour of private economic agents. Significant changes may occur, for example, in wage and price behaviour; in the portfolio allocation of savings; in the financing decisions of firms and in the role of financial intermediaries. The plausibility of a significant regime shift potentially affects most economic relations estimated on the basis of historical data. Relevant examples are money demand, aggregate expenditure relations, wages and so on.

Whether a regime shift does take place, and with what implications, cannot be precisely foreseen. It could be argued, for example, that there would be no structural change in private sector behaviour if the monetary policy strategy of the ECB was perceived as the natural extension of those followed by participating central banks just before EMU. Furthermore, the establishment of the single currency is envisaged after a long period of gradual convergence among euro area countries. These arguments suggest that a gradual, rather than a radical, change in the behaviour of economic agents may have occurred. On the other hand, the EMU process took place concurrently with other factors leading to the transformation of the European economy in general, and the financial system in particular.

Second, the creation of the euro area introduces a discontinuity in the available statistical information. We have already mentioned that long time series are not available for the euro area and must be replaced by synthetic aggregates. This raises methodological and conceptual problems. Furthermore, the set of statistics available for the euro

---

[5] See Issing and Angeloni (1999).

area is more restricted than what is normally available to a central bank of an industrialised country, although the Eurosystem, Eurostat and the statistical institutions of the member countries are actively engaged in making the necessary statistical improvements in the shortest possible time.

Third, the ECB faces the difficulty of having to establish its credibility. As an institution without a track record, its strength and prestige do not derive from a reputation acquired in the field, but more from such present day features as independence, the quality of its staff, its ability to communicate and convince outsiders. Another source of credibility for the ECB is the reputation inherited from the constituent National Central Banks. Hence, the effectiveness of the ECB strategy must derive, at least in part, from it being seen to some extent as a coherent development of strategies used previously by the most successful national central banks. The heritage of the Bundesbank plays, in this respect, a special role, for having provided an anchor of stability and making monetary convergence, and ultimately the creation of the single currency, possible.

But at the same time, the ECB is also an entirely new institution, with a new and clear set of statutory assignments. The ECB statute bears strong signs of the experience of recent decades, notably of the period of worldwide currency and price instability that started at the beginning of the 1970s, and of the role played by monetary policies in bringing inflation back under control. The ECB's independence and its mandate to preserve price stability are the fruits of this experience. Moreover, the mandate assigned to the ECB is based not on an exclusive relationship with a state authority (of which currencies are normally an expression and symbol), but on an international treaty. Many policy areas, among them fiscal policy and banking supervision, remain under national responsibility. The operational structure of the Eurosystem is highly decentralised. NCBs carry out all monetary policy operations and national authorities maintain competencies in important fields bordering on monetary policy, such as the organisation of financial markets and the provision of lending-of-last-resort.[6] All these elements add to the complexity of the operational and communication framework of the ECB.

To summarise, whereas central banks operate in a complex and uncertain environment, the special characteristics of the euro area imply that the ECB faces a number of challenges in the fulfilment of its mandate. The result is a particularly high level of uncertainty in the way the single

---

[6] Advantages and drawbacks of decentralisation within regional systems of central banks are examined in Goodfriend (1999) and Angeloni (1999).

monetary policy affects the economy. The characteristics of the monetary policy transmission mechanism for the euro area are less perfectly known than in other long established monetary unions, and likely to be evolving in response to the new monetary regime. These special characteristics called for a monetary policy strategy different from those adopted by other central banks so far.

7.3   A new strategy

In a world characterised by uncertainty and imperfect knowledge, a strategy provides a *framework* to structure the information set relevant for policy. Such a framework is the basis for both the internal policy debate and communication with the outside world. The monetary policy strategy specifies how information is organised and filtered in order to provide the foundation for monetary policy actions aimed at maintaining price stability.

Faced by the sources of uncertainty outlined above, central banks have taken, alternatively, two broad approaches. The first is to adopt guideposts defined in terms of single 'intermediate' variables (typically, monetary aggregates), deemed to have, based on theory and experience, a reliable link with both the instruments and the final objectives of monetary policy. At the opposite extreme, other central banks have taken the view that no individual variable can be attributed a prominent relevance in informing about, or influencing, the developments of the ultimate policy objective. The theoretical framework of reference is, in this case, represented by the recent 'inflation forecast targeting' approach, in which the available models and information are used to obtain inflation forecasts, which are then treated as 'sufficient statistics' of future developments of inflation.

In practical applications, however, both monetary targeting and inflation targeting turn out to be significantly different from the theoretical benchmarks, because they need to take into account the dimensions of uncertainty that characterise the real world.

As we have already argued in chapter 5, the practical experience with monetary targeting has not been dogmatic. Central banks have proven to be fully conscious of the limitations of the theoretical version of this strategy, namely the fact that money is required to be the sole variable, in the transmission process, through which all inflationary pressures are passed to prices. Many studies have pointed out that this is a very restrictive assumption and that, under general circumstances, a mechanistic policy reaction to deviations of money growth from the target value causes unnecessary volatility in inflation and output. In practice, monetary targeting central banks have never implemented this sort of mechanistic monetary policy: judgmental elements have always been part of the decision making process and the evolution of the selected monetary aggregate has had an important role as a communication variable.

Concerning inflation forecast targeting, it is only in some extreme formulations that it can be shown to imply a mechanistic reaction of the policy instrument to deviations of the model-based inflation forecast from the inflation target. As in the case of monetary targeting, however, central banks have never adopted this theoretical version of inflation forecast targeting. The structure of the model is a pedagogic device that gives internal discipline to the central bank, rather than a constraint through which policy decisions have to be funnelled. Once again, judgmental information is systematically used to complement the information of various indicators and econometric models (see chapter 9 and Vickers, 1999).

Inflation forecasts play an important role in external communication for inflation targeting central banks. However, the inflation forecast does not provide operational implications as to the decisions to take. It is not a simple indicator whose knowledge is sufficient to take, or predict, policy decisions. Different policy responses are associated to a given prospective deviation of the forecast from price stability, depending on the source of the exogenous shock(s) and on the horizon over which price stability has to be reached again. If the central bank also wants to avoid unnecessary output fluctuations, the policy instrument will typically be a function not only of deviations of the inflation forecast from the target at a given horizon, but also of other shocks or state variables. It is even conceivable that a reduction of the policy interest rate will be the optimal response to a combination of shocks leading to an increase in expected future inflation.[7] Hence, not unlike the monetary target, the inflation forecast is imperfect as a communication device, and policy decisions might have to be explained in spite of the inflation forecast, rather than because of it.

To summarise, no simple and unique indicator has proven sufficient for central banks to motivate and explain their policy decisions. In spite of the rigidity of theoretical monetary targeting and inflation targeting, judgment has been a crucial component of both monetary policy strategies.

---

[7] This apparent paradox can be seen to arise even in simple frameworks, e.g. Clarida, Galí and Gertler (1999), if an adverse cost-push shock and a negative demand shock occur at the same time in an economy where the output gap is not very sensitive to the real interest rate and cost-push shocks are highly autocorrelated.

Taking stock of these experiences, one of the key characteristics of the ECB's new monetary policy strategy – conceived in order to cope with the particularly high degree of uncertainty and imperfect knowledge prevailing at the beginning of Stage Three of EMU – is to acknowledge explicitly the lack of satisfactory models suitable for policy analysis.

A major shortcoming of all existing models used for policy making seems to be the difficulty to convincingly integrate money, and specifically monetary aggregates, among the factors determining economic activity and inflation in the short run (given the robust long run relationships already emphasised). This characteristic reflects, partly, the fact that, on theoretical grounds, introducing money into micro-founded general equilibrium models has, as is well known, proved difficult. The existence of money is typically assumed rather than derived from basic principles. Yet, a substantial body of other econometric evidence, as well as historical episodes, suggest that monetary aggregates often play a key role in determining price developments.

Important advances in monetary economics have explored the existence of credit, liquidity and balance sheet channels of monetary transmission,[8] which may be a prelude to the better integration of financial factors into standard macro-models. Recent empirical contributions, focused on the role of money as determinant of long run price developments in the euro area and based on the so-called P-star approach, have obtained promising results (see section 5.4).

Until a comprehensive model of the economy – meeting with widespread consensus and backed by convincing empirical evidence – becomes available, the ECB, like any risk-conscious central bank, has chosen to make coherent use of a variety of plausible models, rather that relying on a single one.[9] Accordingly, the stability oriented strategy explicitly acknowledges the connection between money and price developments in the long run as one of the most robust known economic relationships. Policies based on this relationship can be expected to deliver price stability under very general characteristics of the functioning of the economy, though not always in the most efficient manner. Hence, the prominent role for money in the strategy.

The indications provided by the analysis of money are complemented with a broader assessment of potential inflationary or deflationary threats, based on a wide set of economic and financial indicators. Here, a variety of information sources are considered and macroeconometric models

---

[8] See, e.g., Bernanke and Gertler (1995) and Kashyap and Stein (1994).
[9] A similar view is expressed by Engert and Selody (1998).

are used to ensure internal consistency. Scenarios and forecasts typically incorporate a significant amount of judgment, coming from sector specific and country specific information. The broad nature of this assessment is particularly suitable for introducing such specialised information into the policy process.

This structure closely draws on the experience of other central banks. For different reasons, both monetary aggregates and the inflation forecast do not fully reflect all the complex facets of the functioning of the economy. The explicit provision of some aspects of both 'structures' in the ECB strategy is a reminder of the fact that no single indicator provides a satisfactory summary of all the information relevant to assess prospective price developments. Neither the inflation forecasts nor monetary growth, taken alone, represent the whole set of information necessary to the ECB's decision-making bodies. No mechanical link exists between either the outcome of the forecasting process, or the assessment of monetary developments, and monetary policy decisions.

7.4   Two pillars, a single framework

The presence of two pillars within the ECB strategy raises an issue of synthesis: namely, how different signals should be weighted and, when in conflict, reconciled.

The available evidence provides a broad guideline in this respect. The link between money and prices tends to be stronger over the medium term, whereas in the short run several factors may lead to unexpected shifts in the velocity of circulation. Over very short time horizons, a variety of indicators of domestic and international cost and price factors often provide a reasonably accurate account of future price developments. Therefore, it seems natural to attribute a relatively more important (though never exclusive) role to the latter indicators in forming a judgment about short term price developments, while shifting progressively the emphasis on 'money' as the horizon of the assessment lengthens and uncertainty widens. The limited available evidence on the leading indicator properties of money versus other indicators in the euro area tends, as noted above, to support this approach.

In the ECB, the synthesis between the signals coming from different sources begins to take place at the moment in which analyses and options are elaborated and presented to the ECB decision making bodies, the Executive Board and the Governing Council ('analytical level'). At a subsequent stage, the decision making bodies come to the synthesis, adding their own elements of judgment ('decision making level'). The composition of the Governing Council, in which national central bank governors are present, allows entry into the synthesis of a rich spectrum of views relevant for the assessment of euro area developments. These two internal steps are, in turn, closely related to the ECB's external communication, since credibility and transparency require that the public presentation and explanation of monetary policy actions closely mirror the internal analytical and decision making processes ('communication level').

It should be stressed that monetary analysis is not unrelated to the assessment of other indicators. It is not the case, in particular, that the ECB systematically engages in an exercise of partitioning the general information set in order to obtain two separate assessments of future price developments, each based, by construction, on limited information. On the one hand, analyses of the long run link between money and prices cannot completely ignore other variables that have been shown to enter into the long run money demand, such as the trend growth in real GDP or the level and the term structure of interest rates. On the other hand, macroeconomic forecasts computed with the help of structural econometric models typically incorporate information on monetary conditions, in the form of interest rates and, potentially, also in the form of feedback from money and credit aggregates to prices.

The separation between first and second piller should therefore be seen mainly as an organisational framework to structure the available information, both internally and for the benefit of the public.

Concerning external communication, the ECB strategy encompasses, as we have seen, previous successful experiences of central banks in Europe and elsewhere. The experience of the Bundesbank is universally considered prominent in this respect. In this sense, the strategy contains a deliberate element of continuity that does, in the perception of observers and market participants, enhance its credibility. Public presentations of the ECB analyses and policies, primarily in the President's monthly press conference but also in ECB publications, separately highlight the indications of money and of other economic variables. In this respect, the structure of the published documents have a close link with the process of internal assessment and decision making.

In sum, the strategy's logical structure results from an effort to combine many elements. It accounts for the ECB's unique policy environment and for the special elements of uncertainty that derive from the transition to a new monetary regime. It relates to the heritage of credibility existing in the Eurosystem. Not least, it reflects the ECB's understanding of the relevant body of economic theory and empirical evidence. The two pillars symbolise the still insufficient knowledge concerning the functions of the macro-economy and the characteristics of the transmission process. Advances in the understanding of the economy, better theoretical models and statistical data, structural changes in the euro area economy itself may in principle allow, or require, changes in the structure and interpretation of the strategy.

7.5   Recent criticisms and some answers

While the debate concerning the ECB strategy is still active, and it is certainly too early to provide a balanced account of it, it may be useful to briefly mention some of the main critical views that have been raised so far. We will focus on four of the most vocal criticisms that characterised the debate during the first year of EMU's Stage Three.

According to the Centre for Economic Policy Research (see, e.g., Begg et al., 1999), the ECB strategy is unclear because of the existence of two pillars. While there are important links between money growth and inflation in the medium and long run, in practice financial innovation makes these links unpredictable in the short run. Therefore, it is claimed, the ECB will have to frequently ignore the signals coming from the first pillar, just like the Bundesbank has done in the past. It would be advisable, it is concluded, to simply disregard the first pillar and concentrate on the information from the second.

This criticism contains a grain of truth: financial innovation has, indeed, often destabilised money demand relationships in recent decades and any mechanistic reaction to deviations of money growth from the reference value would be unwarranted. As we have already emphasised in chapter 5, however, this line of criticism does not lead, in our opinion, to the conclusion that money should be altogether dismissed from a strategy. It would have been too hasty for a new central bank, mandated to preserve price stability in the euro area, to ignore the special role that money has played in the history of inflation, in Europe and in the world. However, monetary aggregates are not, *cannot be*, the only elements of the decision making process: deviations from the 'reference value' are interpreted as an indication, important but not conclusive, of potential inflationary or deflationary risks. Developments in M3 will never be interpreted rigidly, nor will changes in monetary growth automatically trigger corrections in monetary policy. In addition, money also serves as a useful signal of continuity with those central banks (including, but not only, the Bundesbank) which have, in the past, successfully used monetary aggregates as part of their strategies.

A second line of argument criticises the ECB for excessive flexibility
in interpreting monetary aggregates and pleads for a traditional monetary targeting strategy (Neumann, 1998). Reports prepared by the 'EMU
Monitor' group organised by the Zentrum für Europäische Integrazions-
forschung of the University of Bonn,[10] argue that the reference value for
money 'should be taken more seriously' as a guide for monetary policy decisions (e.g., EMU Monitor, 1999). Specifically, the ECB should
spend more time explaining why there have been deviations of the rate
of growth of money from the reference value whenever such deviations
occur. From this viewpoint, the broadly based assessment is seen as a step
towards a practice of 'looking at everything', which would allegedly pave
the way towards a fully discretionary and short run oriented monetary
policy. This view, opposite to the one previously discussed, is subject to
the same counter-argument. The stability of money demand cannot be
trusted completely: hence the reference value for money must be considered neither as a completely irrelevant policy indicator (the CEPR
view), nor as a sufficient one (the EMU Monitor view). It is precisely for
this reason that the ECB has decided to attribute to money a prominent
role, but to avoid announcing a target value for the rate of growth of a
particular aggregate.

A third line of criticism is presented by, for example, Lars Svensson
(1999b) who, in a recent and widely quoted paper dealing with monetary
policy issues for the Eurosystem, argued against the ECB's choice to as-
sign 'a prominent role to an essentially irrelevant money-growth indicator
in analysis and communication'. Svensson's criticism seems to deny that
money can, in plausible circumstances, play any role in policy. To illustrate his point, Svensson specifies a simple theoretical model in which
money has no role in the monetary policy process, either as a link in the
transmission of monetary policy or as an information variable. The irrelevance of money in the model ultimately rests on the hypothesis that the
'true' model of the monetary policy transmission mechanism mainly operates through an aggregate demand relationship. Accordingly, changes
in the monetary policy instrument affect long term nominal interest rates
and, with sticky inflation and sticky inflationary expectations, long term
real rates, which matter for consumption and investment decisions. The
addition of a money demand equation to this scheme does not change
the substance of the transmission process. Hence the alleged irrelevance
of money as an indicator.

While not denying that coherent models of the monetary policy transmission mechanism can be written in which money is not a useful variable

[10] See the website www.zei.de.

for monetary policy, it remains unclear, in our view, whether these models represent a reasonable approximation of the actual functioning of monetary economies. Many alternatives exist, among the range of plausible models, in which money plays a relevant role. First, as amply demonstrated by the literature of the 1970s referred to in earlier chapters, money does not need to be an active link in the transmission chain to provide useful policy guidance. In particular, in the presence of informational and transmission lags and given that there are substantial uncertainties on the statistical quality of many key indicators,[11] a premium should be placed on variables, such as money, that are observed timely and accurately. Second, modern theories of the transmission mechanism based on the credit supply suggest that bank balance sheets size and composition may play a key role in the propagation of shocks, whether originating from monetary policy or from other sources.

Hence, the conclusion that money is an irrelevant indicator is not robust. The ECB strategy simply reflects this result and, in addition, it adopts the view that the theoretical and empirical long run relationship between money growth and inflation, on the one hand, and the uncertainties surrounding the short run functioning of the transmission mechanism, on the other hand, place the burden of proof on those who *deny* a useful role for money, not on those who *advocate* it. As also emphasised by Baltensperger (2000), showing that money plays no role within a model in which it is excluded *a priori* can hardly be seen as a convincing proof.

Finally, the ECB monitoring group organised by the Centre for European Policy Studies has taken a milder critical position. On the central issue of money, it has claimed that money should indeed play an important role in the ECB strategy, but mainly in view of the apparent link between asset price inflation and excess supply of liquidity.[12] While noting that asset price bubbles can develop and burst without effects on consumer price inflation (as in the Japanese experience), Gros et al. (2000) express the view that it is useful to monitor money growth carefully when it deviates persistently and over extended periods of time from the reference value. This position is not inconsistent with our own. The logical relationship between money and prices is complex and, at least in some circumstances, it could indeed unfold through asset price dynamics that anticipate future developments of aggregate demand incompatible with the maintenance of price stability. Asset price movements could, in other words, represent one of the channels through which the

---

[11] A prominent example in this respect is the output gap, which is as central in modern theories of monetary transmission as it is difficult to measure (see Orphanides, 2000).
[12] See the website www.ceps.be.

link between monetary developments and future threats to price stability manifests itself.

To summarise, the lack of consensus amongst different observers of the ECB often strikes as more profound than the disagreement of each critic with the ECB itself. Within diametrically opposite views, the position of the ECB emerges as a reasonable midpoint, which reflects recent advances in economic research without jumping on the train of the currently most fashionable theory and without forgetting long-established results.

Nevertheless, the ECB continuously makes an effort to be involved in the debate with its critics, through an intense economic seminars programme and through active participation in academic conferences, most notably the ECB Watchers Conferences in Frankfurt. This reflects the view that 'never has the situation been more urgent to exploit the potential gains [from trade in ideas between central bankers and academics] than in the current context as we embark on the hazardous process of monetary union in Europe' (Issing, 1999c).

8 The operational framework

Like every modern central bank, the Eurosystem operates in the financial market to implement monetary policy. The 'operational framework', described in this chapter, comprises the overall set of instruments, procedures and practices that are used by the Eurosystem to intervene in the financial market, in order to achieve its objectives as defined by the monetary policy strategy. It is the 'tool kit' (interpreted in a broad sense, as we shall see) through which monetary policy is implemented.

The operational framework is clearly linked to, and must be consistent with, the monetary policy strategy. However, the link is not simple or rigid. Different sets of operational instruments and procedures could, in principle, be compatible with the price stability goal. It thus follows that the relative merits of alternative frameworks must be judged not only on the basis of whether they fulfil the goals and requirements of the strategy, but also on market related grounds.

In the case of the Eurosystem, a link between the operational framework and the strategy follows from the principle (established at an early stage by EMI, 1997a, b, c) that the implementation of monetary policy in the euro area would be based on the control of a (suitably defined) short term interest rate (or set of rates). Therefore, a key requirement of the Eurosystem's operational framework must be its ability to ensure good control and signalling properties with respect to short term interest rates. Implementing this principle was one of the priorities in the design of the Eurosystem's operational framework, carried out by the EMI and all participating NCBs during EMU's Stage Two, between 1994 and 1998. The preparatory work took stock of the experience in conducting monetary policy operations by the main central banks of the world during the course of recent decades, and carefully pondered the pros and cons of alternative operational settings.

Recent international experience of central banking practices[1] has shown that a successful operational framework must satisfy at least three

---

[1] See, for example, Aspetsberger (1996), Escrivá and Fagan (1996).

broad requirements. *First,* it must be consistent with the strategy, i.e. specifically with the goals of monetary policy. In accordance with the EU Treaty, the framework must therefore be efficient in attaining the price stability objective. This is ensured, in the context of the stability oriented monetary policy strategy, by adequately and timely responding to information coming from the analysis of monetary developments and the assessment of a wide range of economic and financial indicators. *Second,* it must ensure an effective communication between the central bank and the market. This means that through the operational framework the central bank must be able to convey an effective signal of the current monetary policy stance and to influence expectations in a way consistent with the attainment of the final goal; this implies, *inter alia,* that the framework should be simple and transparent. *Third,* the framework must be in line with the principles of a market economy, favouring the efficient allocation of financial resources. These three criteria – *goal efficiency, signalling capability, market compatibility* – have in fact guided the evolution of the operational framework of all main European central banks in recent years.

The design of an appropriate framework for the Eurosystem benefited from the convergence, which had already taken place in the monetary control frameworks used by the main central banks in Europe during the 1990s, towards a set of common patterns that we can refer to as the 'European model' of monetary control. Qualitatively, there are three main elements in this 'model'. First, a 'corridor', defined by two central bank administered rates, constrains (by market arbitrage) money market rates to fluctuate according to demand and supply of interbank short term funds within a predetermined band. Second, the 'model' envisages a predominant use of short term liquidity-providing operations – either repurchase agreements or collateralised loans – against high-quality collateral, to provide refinancing and to regulate the supply of central bank money. Thirdly and finally, reserve requirements with averaging positions are used to smooth daily fluctuations of very short term rates (specifically, the overnight interbank rate) and to create, if necessary, structural shortage of liquidity in the balance sheets of the banking system. On the whole, the 'European model' is characterised by its reliance on self-regulating market mechanisms and by a limited presence of the central bank in the open market.

The Eurosystem's operational framework was constructed around features which emerged in a largely spontaneous fashion among the main European central banks during the 1990s. A further, additional factor shaping the Eurosystem's framework was the Treaty's provisions according to which: 'To the extent deemed possible and appropriate ..., the

ECB shall have recourse to the national central banks to carry out operations which form part of the tasks of the ESCB' (Act 12.1 of the ECB Statute).

The bulk of the Eurosystem's operations are executed by NCBs and affect their (not the ECB's) balance sheets; decentralisation of operations is a distinguishing feature of the Eurosystem's framework. In turn, NCBs are required to 'act in accordance with the guidelines and instructions of the ECB' (Act 14.3 of the ECB Statute), which ensures unity of intent in the single monetary policy. Moreover, the mechanism of the euro area's real-time-settled money market (supported by the TARGET infrastructure) contributes further to ensure that the decentralisation of the sources of central bank liquidity does not interfere with the 'singleness' of the euro area's monetary stance.

8.1   Outline of the Eurosystem's operational framework

A detailed description of the framework adopted by the Eurosystem can be found in the preparatory works published by the EMI before the end of Stage Two. More recently, a comprehensive 'general documentation' has been made available by the ECB.[2] What follows in this section is a brief outline of these documents, focusing only on the key monetary policy instruments, in light of the operational decisions adopted by the Governing Council in late December 1998. Money market developments in the course of 1999 will be commented upon in section 8.4 and the reader will find there further elements that will help in understanding the principles and practice governing the working of the operational framework.

Along the lines of what we referred to as the 'European model', the operational framework of the Eurosystem includes three main instruments: open market operations, standing facilities and reserve requirements. Table 8.1 (based on ECB, 1998) provides an overview of the Eurosystem's open market operations and standing facilities.

8.1.1   Open market operations

The most important open market operations are the *main refinancing operations*, which play a central role in pursuing the goals of (a) signalling the monetary policy stance and steering market interest rates; (b) providing the bulk of refinancing to the financial sector in order to manage liquidity in the money market. The main refinancing operations are executed every week and have a maturity of two weeks. Additionally, open

---

[2] EMI (1997a, 1997b, 1997c) and ECB (2000d).

market operations are executed every month under the form of *longer term refinancing operations*. These have a maturity of three months and, as a rule, do not have a signalling role.

The main refinancing operations and the longer term refinancing operations take the form of reverse transactions (either repurchase agreements or collateralised loans, according to the legal instrument used by the various central banks), i.e. operations in which the system – operating through the NCBs – provides or withdraws liquidity in exchange for preselected collateral assets.[3] Allocation of funds through this channel always takes place through auctions, in order to ensure an efficient distribution of base money among 'eligible' counterparties. Different types of auctions – fixed or flexible rate, with multiple or uniform price, etc. – can in principle be used, according to the needs identified by the ECB governing bodies in each specific case. The choice for reverse operations, as opposed to outright transactions, as the main monetary policy instrument is dictated by the wish to transmit impulses to the interest rate structure *indirectly,* through the market at the short end of the term structure.

Finally, the ECB can decide to implement *fine-tuning operations*. These aim in particular to smooth the effects on interest rates caused by unexpected liquidity fluctuations in the money market. Given their exceptional nature, fine-tuning operations can be executed using different procedures and operational features, depending on circumstances. Specifically, they can be either liquidity-providing or liquidity-absorbing, they can take the form of reverse transactions or collection of fixed-term deposits in the most usual circumstances, and their frequency and maturity are not standardised.[4]

All open market operations are decided by the ECB and executed in a decentralised manner through the National Central Banks.[5] Normally, a tender procedure is implemented, although fine-tuning operations can be executed through bilateral procedures. Tender procedures comprise six operational steps (see figures 8.1–8.2). In step 1, the ECB announces the tender, including a number of issues of detail going from the date to the type of the auction (fixed or variable rate tender), through public wire services. In step 2, counterparties prepare and submit their bids to NCBs, under the understanding that they have sufficient eligible collateral to settle the amount of liquidity that they will be allotted. The bids are pooled

[3] According to the Treaty (Article 18.1 of ECB/ESCB Statute), all credit operations by the Eurosystem must be backed by adequate collateral.

[4] For a description of the remaining sorts of open market operations, including *structural operations* and foreign exchange swaps, see ECB (2000d).

[5] However, in exceptional circumstances, fine-tuning bilateral transactions may be executed by the ECB itself.

Table 8.1. *The Eurosystem's monetary policy operations*

Monetary policy operations	Types of transactions		Maturity	Frequency	Procedure
	Provision of liquidity	Absorption of liquidity			
OPEN MARKET OPERATIONS					
Main refinancing operations	Reverse transactions		Two weeks	Weekly	Standard tenders
Longer-term refinancing operations	Reverse transactions		Three months	Monthly	Standard tenders
Fine-tuning operations	Reverse transactions	Foreign exchange swaps	Non-standardised	Irregular	Quick tenders
	Foreign exchange swaps	Collection of fixed-term deposits			Bilateral procedures
		Reverse transactions			
	Outright purchases	Outright sales		Irregular	Bilateral procedures
Structural operations	Reverse transactions	Issuance of debt certificates	Standardised/non-standardised	Regular and irregular	Standard tenders
	Outright purchases	Outright sales		Irregular	Bilateral procedures

STANDING FACILITIES				
The marginal lending facility	Reverse transactions		Overnight	Access at the discretion of counterparties
The deposit facility		Deposits	Overnight	Access at the discretion of counterparties

Source: ECB (2000d).

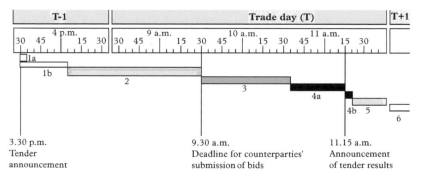

Figure 8.1 Normal time frame for the operational steps for standard tenders
Source: ECB.

and compiled in step 3. In step 4a, the ECB takes the allotment decisions, following different procedures depending on the type of auction, and then announces tender results (step 4b). Finally, in steps 5 and 6, individual allotment results are certified and transactions are settled, respectively.

The main refinancing operations and the longer term refinancing operations are executed through *standard* tender procedures, while the fine-tuning operations, when needed, are normally executed through *quick* tender procedures. The difference lies in the duration of the operational steps of the tender described above, as well as in the set of counterparties authorised to participate (which is narrower in the case of quick tenders). Standard procedures span over three working days, while quick procedures are completed in a matter of three hours.

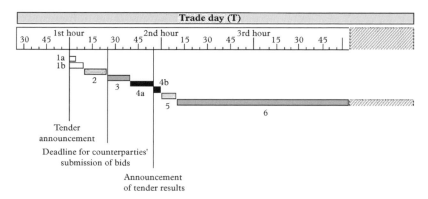

Figure 8.2 Normal time frame for the operational steps for quick tenders
Source: ECB.

8.1.2   Standing facilities

The operational framework also includes two standing facilities. Standing facilities are not activated by the ECB and are not addressed to the market as a whole, but are directed to, and activated by initiative of, individual counterparties.

There are two standing facilities. The *marginal lending facility* is used to provide overnight credit at penalty cost. Credit is conditional only on the presentation of sufficient collateral. The *deposit facility* allows counterparties to place overnight funds with the Eurosystem, earning a rate of return below the market level.

The interest rate on both standing facilities is specified in advance by the ECB, which retains the power to change it at any time. Since the two facilities are constantly available ('standing'), the official interest rates applied to them define a range, or corridor, within which the oscillation of overnight market rates is bounded as a result of money market arbitrage.

8.1.3   Minimum reserve requirement

The third main instrument is the minimum reserve requirement. The ECB imposes minimum reserves on all credit institutions in the proportion of 2 per cent of the reserve base. The latter includes all liabilities by credit institutions vis-à-vis the (non-bank) counterparties with maturity up to two years.

The reserve requirement is mainly intended to contribute to stabilise money market interest rates. It operates, through the 'averaging mechanism', by giving institutions an incentive to smooth the effect of temporary liquidity shortages or surpluses. All institutions subject to the reserve obligation are allowed to deposit or withdraw funds freely, on a daily basis, provided the requirement is fulfilled on average over the monthly maintenance period (from the 24th of each month to the 23rd of the following one). Reserve deposits are remunerated at the money market rate determined in the main refinancing operations.

8.2   How does the framework fulfil its main goals?

Open market operations, standing facilities and reserve requirements are designed to operate together as a consistent set, jointly fulfilling the requirements of goal efficiency, signalling capability and market compatibility referred to earlier in this chapter.

We can look at the instruments described above in the light of the three guiding criteria indicated at the beginning of this chapter. In accordance with the principle of *goal efficiency,* the instruments used by the Eurosystem are designed to ensure effective control of money market rates, and, indirectly, to influence the whole term structure, through the management of liquidity conditions in the money market. The reserve requirement system is used to give flexibility to the money market and, since it is fully remunerated, it contains no penalty element. Therefore, no artificial wedge is introduced between bank deposit and lending rates. Reserve requirements are not intended as an instrument for short run control of the money stock.

The function of *signalling* is performed mainly by the interaction of the repurchase operations and the corridor between the two rates applied on standing facilities. The width of the corridor gives the market an indication of the potential range of variation of money market rates in the very short run. The alternative auction mechanisms for the main refinancing operation also contribute to the signalling function: in particular, the fixed rate auction conveys to the market a clear signal of the level of short term rates deemed appropriate by the central bank; for variable rate auctions, the signalling role is played by the minimum bid rate. The position of market rates inside the corridor defined by the standing facilities may signal market perceptions about the likely future course of the repo rate.

Finally, all the main aspects of the operational framework are designed in a way compatible with the *efficient working of the market mechanism.* The reserve requirement system and its averaging mechanism provide an incentive to credit institutions to optimise their liquidity flows during the monthly computation period, based on their expectations of future market conditions and their attitude towards risk. Not least, the whole structure of the payment system supporting the operation of the single monetary policy, as well as the regulations governing the use of collateral – two important related aspects that are not discussed here – are designed to permit an efficient flow of central bank money and securities throughout the entire euro area.

8.3   Counterparties and eligible collateral

We conclude this brief overview of the operational framework of the Eurosystem with a clarification of the concepts of counterparties and eligible collateral.

The operational framework is designed with a view to ensuring participation of a large number of counterparties. Hence, all institutions subject to the reserve requirement can participate in open market operations based on standard tenders and access the standing facilities.

The ECB can, however, select a limited number of counterparties when implementing a fine-tuning operation.

Finally, all liquidity-providing operations have to be based on adequate collateral. A wide range of assets can be pledged, grouped into two broad categories: 'tier one' and 'tier two'. The main difference rests on the selection of the eligibility criteria. Tier one assets must fulfil uniform area-wide criteria specified by the ECB, while the eligibility criteria for tier two assets are selected by the NCBs, subject to ECB approval. Eligible assets may be used on a cross-border basis, in the sense that counterparties may borrow from the NCB of the State in which they are established by making use of assets located in securities depositories of another Member State.

8.4   The performance of the operational framework in 1999

From several angles, the first year of the euro is an ideal trial period to assess the functioning of the Eurosystem's operational framework. First, the early months after the introduction of the euro provide evidence on how easily and quickly market agents, particularly banks, have adopted the new operating environment; they thus convey information on whether the framework is sufficiently simple and 'market-friendly'. Several indications, commented on below, suggest that the adaptation has been quite easy, particularly considering that the start of Stage Three has coincided with sizeable portfolio adjustments and cross-border payments, both within the euro area and with the rest of the world. Moreover, in the first year, the ECB Council has enacted two changes in official interest rates in opposite directions; the 1999 data thus allow us to judge how the framework has operated around a turning point of the monetary policy cycle, with the ensuing change in market expectations.

An element worth stressing is how quickly and easily the framework has reached steady and normal working conditions. The 'emergency precaution' adopted at the outset – namely, the introduction of an exceptionally narrow corridor, of 50 basis points, between the rates on the two standing facilities – was removed, as announced, after three weeks (22 January 1999). When this happened, and the corridor between the rates in the two standing facilities was adjusted to a 'normal' size (2.5 per cent at the beginning of 1999), the EONIA[6] remained sufficiently stable and close

---

[6] EONIA: 'euro overnight index average' refers to the weighted average of the rates on all overnight (unsecured) lending transactions reported by a panel of large banks. The panel includes the fifty-seven banks with the highest volume of business in the euro area money market. The EONIA is reported on an act/360 day count convention and is displayed to two decimal places (see also www.euribor.org).

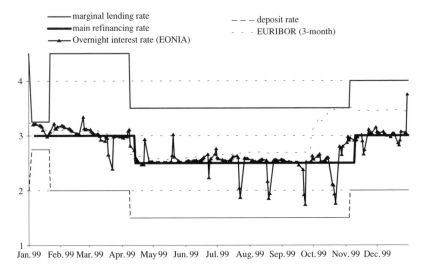

Figure 8.3 ECB interest rates and money market rates
Source: ECB.

to the rate on the main refinancing operations. Since then, the framework has operated according to a steady and preannounced calendar of main and longer term refinancing operations, conducted with a fixed rate and discretionary quantity tender mechanism (with *pro-rata* allotment) and with a variable rate tender mechanism, respectively.[7] No fine-tuning operations were needed to maintain the EONIA sufficiently stable and close to the appropriate values, during the whole course of 1999.[8]

Some summary charts, presented in figures 8.3–8.8, capture the main features in the working of the operational framework during this period. Figure 8.3 depicts the movements of the EONIA, the rate on the main refinancing operations (henceforth MRO), the three-month EURIBOR and the rates on the standing facilities. The figure shows that the EONIA remained close to the main 'guiding rate'.[9] This suggests that the interest rate on the main refinancing operations has performed its key signalling

[7] As discussed below, the auction system for the main refinancing operations has been partially modified on two occasions.
[8] On 5 January 2000, it was decided to conduct the first liquidity-absorbing fine-tuning operation with a maturity of one week, through a quick tender procedure and a variable rate. The operation was intended to adjust the liquidity situation, which was generous both for the ECB's commitment to prevent liquidity constraints from occurring during the transition to the year 2000 and because of autonomous expansionary factors at the beginning of the year.
[9] In principle, no simple relationship exists between a daily market rate, such as EONIA, and a two-week maturity rate defined in relation to the central bank policy, such as the MRO rate. The spread among them depends on various factors, such as interest rate expectations, the cost of collateral, the structure of the interbank market.

function in a satisfactory way. The spread between the EURIBOR and the MRO rate, assuming that the latter clears the market at a two-week maturity, is a proxy of market expectations of future changes in the MRO rate. The chart suggests that this spread seems to have correctly anticipated the future changes in the MRO rate.

At the same time, EONIA presents obvious signs of higher volatility (in both directions) towards the end of the minimum reserve's maintenance period; this is a feature commonly observed, before Stage Three, in national markets (in Germany, for example) characterised by minimum reserve regulations similar to those adopted by the ECB.[10] Though some recent analyses[11] seem to suggest that the volatility of EONIA has so far been lower than the volatility of national day-to-day rates before the introduction of the euro, more evidence is needed before this can be confidently attributed to the working of the Eurosystem's operational framework.

Figure 8.4 is indicative of the ease with which the framework was 'phased in'. The chart indicates the amounts of the recourse to the two standing facilities, within each maintenance period as a whole and, separately, for sub-periods within each maintenance period. The contemporaneous recourse to both facilities within the same period – which is an indicator of malfunctioning in the interbank market, since it should be eliminated by arbitrage – dropped dramatically after the first maintenance period. The growing recourse to the deposit facility at the end of the maintenance periods during the summer months is a result of the generous liquidity policy followed by the ECB during that period.

Figures 8.5–8.6 show the overall volume of bids presented by all banks in the euro area at the weekly MRO tender. During the whole course of 1999, the Governing Council decided that the main refinancing operations were to be executed using fixed rate tenders, while longer-term refinancing operations were carried out through variable rate tenders.[12] The charts show that the tender mechanism has produced a tendency for the amount of bids to grow well in excess of the tender amount. Moreover, the volume of bidding has grown significantly during the course of the year. Although the amount of 'overbidding' seems to be loosely related to the level of the EONIA rate (relative to the MRO rate), the bidding volume remained exceedingly high in almost all weekly tenders of the

[10] For a theoretical model of bank reserve management embodying this feature, see Angeloni and Prati (1996), appendix 1.
[11] See Pérez-Quirós and Rodríguez-Mendizábal (2000).
[12] In March 1999, the American-type (discriminatory) auction replaced the Dutch-type (or single rate) auction for longer-term refinancing operations. The most visible consequence of this change was a slight reduction in the number of participants, as it is natural to expect, given the greater complexity of the American-style auction mechanism.

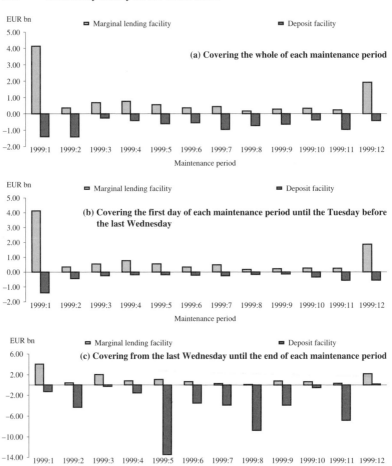

Figure 8.4 Recourse to the marginal lending and deposit facility (averages of the periods as described in each chart's label)
Source: ECB.

year, with the exception only of those immediately preceding the interest cut in April. The phenomenon of overbidding at the weekly tenders was eventually eliminated by the change to the allocation system enacted in June 2000.[13]

---

[13] In June 2000, the Governing Council decided that a new, variable rate auction system would be used for the main refinancing operations. The new system was intended as a technical response to the severe overbidding which had developed in the context of fixed rate tender procedures. For the purpose of signalling the monetary policy stance, the minimum bid rate was designed to play the role performed by the single rate in fixed rate tenders.

EUR bn

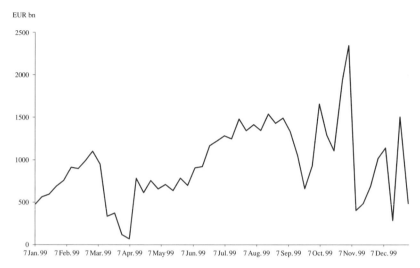

Figure 8.5 Bidding in the main refinancing operations during 1999
Source: ECB.

Finally, figures 8.7–8.8 show the contribution of main and long term refinancing operations in the provision of central bank liquidity in the euro area. The outstanding volume of MRO has oscillated during the year between 100 and 150 billion euros, being managed on a weekly basis to match the oscillation of the so-called 'autonomous factors' of

number of basis points

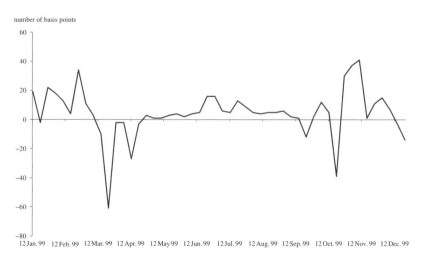

Figure 8.6 Spread EONIA–repo rate (on the day before the submission of the bids for the main refinancing operations)
Source: ECB.

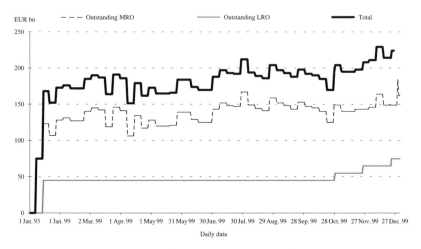

Figure 8.7 Volume of main and long term refinancing operations
Source: ECB.

central bank money, while the overall volume of longer-term refinancing operations was kept constant by the Governing Council over a period of several months. Such compensating action has been successful
in avoiding, on a weekly basis, shifts in the 'autonomous' sources of liquidity (notably, public sector operations in the books of NCBs) that produced undesired fluctuations in money market rates. On a daily basis, this

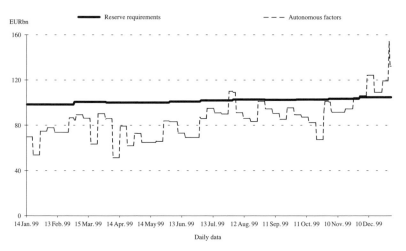

Figure 8.8 Required reserves and autonomous factors
Source: ECB.

stabilisation function was performed by the averaging mechanism of reserve requirements.

Summing up, the Eurosystem's operational framework has worked remarkably well after the start of Stage Three. Operating in a largely self-regulating way, the framework was smoothly accepted by market participants and has proved to be efficient in the pursuit of its goals, capable of correctly transmitting monetary policy signals, and market friendly.

9   Accountability and transparency

Accountability and transparency have become increasingly important issues in the debate on central banking in recent years, alongside the growing degree of institutional independence enjoyed by central banks. In democratic societies, independence goes hand in hand with accountability, i.e. responsibility for the exercise of decision making powers granted through an act of delegation. Thus, while being granted independence, central banks are also made accountable for their outcomes through a number of statutory requirements. On a more general note, the need for transparency is also linked to the large degree of uncertainty that characterises monetary policy. In an uncertain environment, the central banks' assessment of current and future economic conditions is not self evident from the simple observation of their policy decisions. In order to be effective, monetary policy decisions must be understood as part of a more general monetary policy strategy. This implies a constant effort by the central bank to clarify, in a way understandable to the public at large, how its actions contribute to the attainment of its policy goals.

We take up the issue of accountability in section 9.1, beginning with a general discussion of its relationship to independence. The beneficial effects of the latter, both in theory and in the empirical evidence, are also summarised here. We then discuss how the general concept of accountability, which naturally pertains to the political sphere rather than to the economic one, has been 'translated' and interpreted in the academic literature on central banking.

Transparency is addressed in section 9.2. The economic literature is silent on how exactly to achieve transparency in an environment where both the central bank and private agents have very imperfect information on the functioning of the economy. There is no role, in formal models, for verbal explanations and informal discussions, which represent the core of communication with the public in the real world. In order to be effective, transparency needs to satisfy a number of characteristics to an extent that is difficult to accomplish in practice. For the sake of simplicity, the economic literature has sometimes taken a short cut, postulating an equivalence between transparency and publication of the internal inflation forecasts. We discuss the advantages and the difficulties involved in the publication of the internal forecast in section 9.2.1 and argue that, while the forecast can be helpful to explain policy decisions, its publication cannot be considered sufficient (or necessary) to achieve transparency.

Section 9.3 concludes the chapter with an explicit analysis of accountability and transparency of the ECB. We discuss the accountability requirements of the Governing Council of the ECB, as specified by the Treaty, and how they have been abided by in practice. Finally, we mention and discuss a number of critical views that have been put forth on the ECB's transparency practices.

9.1   Accountability and independence

The issue of how best to achieve accountability arises only for independent bodies. It is therefore important to assess, first, why independence of central banks is a desirable institutional attribute.

Institutional independence arises as a general feature of the solutions to the inflationary bias problem, starting with the Rogoff (1985) 'proposal' to appoint an independent weight-conservative central banker (i.e. one with a stronger distaste for inflation than the general public). Independence can ultimately be seen as a way to shield the central bank from the kind of political pressures in favour of aiming at unachievable outcomes (such as output growth systematically above potential).[1]

In theoretical models, the institutional set-up of the central bank is defined once and for all at a given point in time. The inflation goal – which maximises society's welfare – is identified, then this goal is announced and there is no room for changes unless society's preferences change. In practice, however, society will be represented by the elected government, so that the practical issue of how to cope with possible modifications of the goal after changes in the political majority arises. If the change in political majority were to be interpreted as a change in society's preferences, then it could be optimal for the new government to modify the central bank's goal. As argued by McCallum (1997) and Posen (1993), however,

---

[1] In the literature this result can be rationalised on the basis of: (i) the existence of partisan and opportunistic political cycles leading to inflation, politically induced uncertainty on the economy and increased volatility (Alesina and Gatti, 1995; Alesina, Roubini and Cohen, 1997; Waller, 1989, 1992; and Waller and Walsh, 1995); (ii) the possibility of a second best delegation scheme based on a low inflation goal (Svensson, 1997a); (iii) the interaction between the monetary regime and other characteristics of the overall economic regime, in particular fiscal discipline (Fischer, 1995).

granting the government full power to modify at will the contractual relationship with the central bank only shifts the inflationary bias problem from the central bank to the government itself. If one is willing to accept the hypothesis that the central bank needs to be purged from the temptation to engineer surprise inflation, it is not clear why the government (the 'principal' of the contract) should not be subject to the same temptation. As a matter of fact, to the extent that a possible inflationary bias problem is the result of a myopic attitude, this is certainly more likely to characterise politically elected bodies than central banks.

The closest real world equivalent to the kind of institutional set-up devised in the theoretical literature is therefore to cast the mandate of the central bank at the constitutional level. Like a simple parliamentary mandate, this ensures, first, that the goal of monetary policy is ultimately chosen by the citizens, that it is fixed on a 'permanent' basis and that the central bank retains full authority on, and accountability for, its policy decisions. Second, citizens also retain the power to modify the mandate of the central bank, should their aggregate preferences change. However, a constitutional mandate cannot, and should not, be modifiable by simple legislative procedures. Special procedures are necessary to avoid the risk of political pressures favouring myopic, short term oriented amendments.

Besides the theoretical argument, empirical evidence also appears to support the results on central bank independence. At a purely descriptive level, the performance – in terms both of inflation and of output growth – of the German economy under the Bundesbank can be argued to represent an example of the benefits of central bank independence. Moreover, an ample body of literature, starting with Bade and Parkin (1984), and surveyed by Cukierman (1992) and Eijffinger and de Haan (1996), identifies a statistically significant inverse relationship between institutional measures of central bank independence and the level and variability of inflation. Empirically, it has been found (for example, Alesina and Summers, 1993; Pollard, 1993) that the improved inflationary performance does not occur at the expense of higher output volatility. This evidence points to a potential free lunch: delegating monetary policy to an independent central bank with a clear price stability mandate leads to lower and less variable inflation without increasing the volatility of output.[2]

---

[2] There is a debate on whether (a) the empirical finding is robust (in an extended cross-country sample, Campillo and Miron, 1997, are unable to identify an effect of central bank independence on inflation once other determinants are included in the regression); (b) the causal interpretation is correct. Posen (1993) argues that both the monetary institutions and the inflation outcome are the result of attitudes towards inflation. Those attitudes would operate like an omitted variable.

A useful distinction is that between *goal independence* and *instrument independence* (Debelle and Fisher, 1994). The nature of delegation is such that an independent central bank cannot be free to set its own goal. The definition of the objective of monetary policy has to come from outside the central bank, and can be specified in the statute together with the terms and conditions of the mandate. In this sense, the central bank is not 'goal independent', i.e. free to set its goal at will. Independence must be interpreted as 'instrument independence', i.e. the ability to modify at will the policy instrument in order to achieve the given goal. In this setting there is a clear division of competences and responsibility. On the one hand, the legislator chooses the statute of the central bank establishing its aims and the institutional terms of its mandate, possibly including procedures to change the statute itself. On the other hand, the central bank, taking the statute as given, is *accountable* for conducting monetary policy according to its mandate.

Accountability is therefore an inherently *ex post* concept, as it has to do with explanation for, and responsibility over, observed acts and outcomes. As emphasised in Issing (1999b), 'for the purpose of *accountability*, what matters most will be the ... actual track record of stability performance'. Drawing on the terminology proposed by Briault, Haldane and King (1996), Issing argues that accountability is linked essentially to 'deeds', i.e. observable and verifiable actions (whereas transparency refers primarily to 'words', i.e. attempts to convey explanations and the thinking behind the actions).

Accountability is a requisite that is taken as given by any central bank, which must comply with it in accordance with its statutory requirements. Three aspects of accountability have been discussed to some extent in the economic literature. They regard, specifically: how performance should be defined ('accountable for what?'); which subject should enforce accountability of the central bank ('accountable to whom?'); and over which horizon performance should be measured ('accountable when?'). We discuss them in turn in the rest of this section.

9.1.1   Accountable for what?

The central bank should obviously be accountable for the achievement of its statutory objectives. In this respect, a debate has arisen on the desirability of individual vs. collective responsibility.

The case for individual accountability is sometimes presented as a step in the direction of increasing accountability (e.g., Buiter, 1999), since it brings into the open individual motives and responsibilities. There are, however, no simple short cuts to ensure accountability of a monetary policy council, and concerns over individual incentives must be balanced with the need for effective collective decision making. Decisions are the outcome of a process of collective reasoning which is more than a mere exchange of views. This collective process can shape the final outcome (the decision) more than each single vote. Once this feature of councils and committees is recognised, the case for individual accountability becomes debatable.

To begin with, it is not clear what public advantages would derive from the knowledge that, after a certain decision was taken, a particular member of the committee or council was against it, but also unable to convince the other members of his or her opinions. Accountability ultimately means bearing the consequences of *decisions*, not *intentions*. Since choices are made collectively when a committee or council is the decision making body, collective accountability appears to be the natural choice.

Moreover, individual accountability has the cost of increasing the risk that council members be subject to pressure from third parties representing specific political or economic interests. This risk is particularly high for supranational institutions, such as the ECB. National interest groups would find ways to characterise monetary policy as contrary to, or in favour of, the welfare of their own country, thus exercising pressure on council members.

In addition, full transparency on individual contributions to the meetings through the publication of attributed minutes could constrain the efficiency of the decision making process (Bini Smaghi and Gros, 2000). As members of the council would become aware of their personal image and performance over and above that of the council as a whole, it is conceivable that spontaneous interactions and debate would decline. Two different and equally serious risks exist. First, individual council members could become concerned with the implications of their positions not only for the collectively adopted policy decision, but for their own personal image. Second, the disclosure of individual positions (and arguments) could contribute to shift the 'real' debate outside the council room. The risk would be, in other words, that of uninteresting official meetings punctuated by prepared statements little related to each other, and a transfer of the 'true' policy debate to separate informal gatherings.

9.1.2   Accountable to whom?

As a general principle, an independent central bank should be accountable to the public at large and its elected representatives. In practice, however, institutional arrangements in different countries implement this requirement in different ways. In fact, there is 'no single model of accountability that can be applied to all central banks in all cases and circumstances' (Bini Smaghi and Gros, 2000, p. 144).

In this respect, supranational institutions, such as the ECB, present special features, also in connection with the aforementioned issue of collective vs. individual accountability. Bini Smaghi and Gros argue that another unappealing feature of the model of individual accountability, for these institutions, is that different members of the Governing Council would have to be accountable to different bodies. This problem would be particularly challenging for an institution whose members of the Governing Council are appointed according to different, national or supranational, procedures.

9.1.3   Accountable when?

A special issue concerning the accountability of central banks is related to the lags that characterise monetary policy. Since years have to pass by before the effects of a given monetary policy action become fully apparent, it has been pointed out that accountability can become void of content. By the time the judgment on the policy outcome can be made, the central bank governor – or Governing Council – might have changed, thus preventing any effective enforcement of potential 'punishment' schemes.

Some authors have therefore argued for alternative, or additional, forms of *ex ante* accountability and that policy intentions, rather than outcomes, should be subject to judgment. This sort of accountability is sometimes claimed to be superior to the 'standard' alternative, since it would allow the good will of the monetary policy authority to be judged without the disturbing effects of unforeseen shocks that can change the outcomes *ex post*. The internal inflation *forecast* is therefore proposed as a more timely indicator of the performance of the central bank, which would be appropriately fulfilling its mandate as long as its own inflation forecast is on target (and irrespective of inflation *outcomes*).

Whether a published forecast is a necessary and sufficient means to ensure accountability is a debatable issue – also related to the choice of the strategy – which we analyse in section 9.2.1. *Ex ante* accountability should simply be intended as a synonym for transparency. The only way in which the central bank can show its good will is to explain its approach to monetary policy (its strategy), the motivations for its decisions and its view on current and prospective economic developments. The issue of the publication of the internal forecast must therefore be seen in the context of the general problem of how to achieve a high degree of transparency.

9.2   Transparency

The economics literature on transparency has obviously had to face the substantial problem of how exactly to capture an abstract concept such as transparency within a mathematical model. Theoretical results are typically obtained subject to the assumption that a certain random shock is interpreted as the manifestation of some degree of secrecy, an assumption which is often difficult to justify as robust. By and large, however, there seems to be a large consensus on the benefits of transparency in the economic literature. Taking Goodfriend (1986) as a seminal reference, the case for transparency is quite compelling. Goodfriend reviews a number of informal arguments implicitly or explicitly used to favour 'secrecy', as opposed to 'transparency', for central banks in the light of the academic literature. The result is that, under efficient markets and rational expectations, the release of information leads to better outcomes by reducing forecast errors. In practice, there can be occasions when releasing information can cause excess volatility in interest rates, because markets take time to understand the message of the central bank, or because of many other possible reasons. On average, however, these episodes of turbulence should be infrequent, and they do not seem sufficient to outweigh the benefits of transparency in the medium term. One main theoretical argument for secrecy appears to be related to the possibility that central banks should make imprecise announcements in order to retain room for manoeuvre to exploit 'surprise inflation' (Cukierman and Meltzer, 1986). This motivation for secrecy is, however, shortsighted, since the bank would conceivably be 'punished' by financial markets and through the behaviour of forward looking variables, if it tried to implement this kind of monetary policy.

If one accepts this frame of mind the issue is no longer whether transparency is desirable, but how it can best be achieved. If, as stressed by Goodfriend (1986), there is a risk that transparency may induce extra volatility in financial markets, central banks must be careful about *how* they release any private information and express views on the functioning of the economy. Simply publishing everything related to the decision making process – from data to internal analyses, policy notes, memos, briefings and even transcripts of any internal meeting – can lead to undesirable outcomes if markets and the public are not given a guideline on how to interpret this information.

This viewpoint is also presented in Issing (1999a, b), where it is argued that *complete* transparency on the underlying information set, as well as the thinking and ulterior motives behind central bankers' decisions, is practically impossible to achieve. 'This reflects a deeper (philosophical) recognition of the limits of "knowledge" and the impossibility of providing and communicating anything like a full description of reality' (Issing, 1999b). As also pointed out by Vickers (1998), 'there is surely information relevant for policy-making that is simply incapable of being put in the public domain. In that case, and with the best will in the world, optimal monetary policy cannot be absolutely transparent, nor totally boring.'

Hence, achieving the maximum degree of transparency is certainly not simply a question of making the maximum amount of information available. 'What matters most in order to make sense of reality (which is inherently non-transparent to policy-makers and the public alike) and of policy-makers' behaviour is a coherent frame of reasoning to interpret the subset of *relevant* information through *clear* messages' (Issing, 1999b).

Consequently, there are no straightforward and mechanistic ways – related to the *amount* of information published – to assess whether a given central bank is or is not transparent. Winkler (1999) argues that there are many aspects to be taken into account. Specifically, the aforementioned possibility to make public all the available information, described as a need for 'openness', must be weighed against an equally important need to achieve a parsimonious and effective presentation of the relevant information (that is the need to be 'clear'). Also important is the principle of conveying messages that truthfully represent the policy maker's intentions ('honesty'), possibly through the establishment of a common language ('common understanding') between the central bank and the public.

In practice, the principal way in which modern central banks respond to the general public and its elected representatives is through continuous explanations of their analyses, of their views on future prospects and of their policy decisions. Along this route, different central banks have nevertheless decided to use slightly diverse styles (frequency, coverage, titles) for their publications. While some have remained faithful to traditional and sober 'bulletins', other have adopted more innovative 'inflation reports', often written in an informal style or supported by very simple explanatory notes (e.g., the Reserve Bank of New Zealand 'Fact sheets').

9.2.1   *Publication of the internal inflation forecast*

A number of authors have indicated the inflation forecast as the ideal means to release the relevant information in a coherent and structured manner. The reason is that monetary policy decisions could allegedly be characterised as reactions to deviations of the inflation forecast from the given objective. Once formed, typically not only on the basis of econometric models but with the help of judgmental inputs and characterised in a way that reflects the underlying uncertainties, the inflation forecast could be used to provide a description, allegedly a complete description, of the assessment of price stability prospects and to motivate policy decisions. The natural implication of this argument is that the publication of the inflation forecast represents the necessary and sufficient way to ensure transparency of the decision making process. As a result, a simple equivalence is established between (non)transparency and (lack of) publication of the forecast.

The useful role of forecasts is explicitly acknowledged in the ECB strategy through the reference to the need for an 'assessment of the outlook for future price developments' in the 13 October 1998 press release (see appendix). While explicitly acknowledging the potentially useful role of forecasts, the ECB strategy rejects the equivalence between (non)transparency and (lack of) publication of the forecast and the view that the inflation forecast is an all-encompassing communication device. To perform such a role, the inflation forecast should be able to contain and convey the full set of information and judgment that enters policy decisions. In practice, however, an inflation forecast, however elaborate, only tells part of the story, and other elements of information and judgmental factors must integrate it.

We have already argued, in chapter 2, that the inflation forecast does not allow a perfect and simple explanation of policy decisions. Even in simple models, the central bank cannot fully rely on it to argue that, for example, it must tighten (or loosen) its stance at a certain point in time because, if it did not, inflation would eventually diverge from price stability. In practice, there is no straightforward link from the inflation forecast to the policy decision, which also depends, for example, on the choice of how quickly to return to price stability. Hence, the publication of the inflation forecast (be it in the form of a single number or a whole probability distribution) is not, *per se*, a sufficient way of explaining the policy decision.

Nor does the explanation of policy decisions solely in terms of the inflation forecast help to forecast future decisions. The judgmental nature of the sensible forecasts made by all central banks implies that it is never obvious how macroeconomic news feeds into the central bank forecast at each point in time. Hence, the mapping from exogenous information and news to the inflation forecast is also uncertain.

Indeed, while different central banks have taken different decisions regarding the publication of their forecasts, most seem to agree that forecasts have a useful, but limited, role within the decision making process. In particular, no mechanistic reaction to deviations of the forecast from target at a given horizon should be expected from policy. This is the explicit approach of inflation targeting central banks. As Vickers (1998, 1999) argues for the case of the Bank of England, no single model will be adequate for all purposes and each model requires an enormous amount of judgment and a careful specification of assumptions in order to generate the forecast used in the policy process.[3] Forecast numbers will always embody judgmental inputs to a significant extent, so that it is a matter of faith to believe that they indeed convey a complete and truthful representation of the policy maker's evaluation process. As emphasised by Vickers (1999), an outside observer could naturally perceive the risks of 'painting by numbers' or 'numbers by painting'. In the first case, the forecast would simply be the result of feeding data into a computer and 'pressing a button'; in the second, a policy decision would be agreed on first, and a forecast consistent with this decision would be obtained *ex post* by manipulating the relevant assumptions in the model.

With these provisos, information can be usefully organised and structured *also* around an inflation forecast, provided that a number of technical features are adequately conveyed to the public. Specifically, forecasts are *conditional* on a number of assumptions, including the future path of monetary policy variables. The horizon over which the assessment of the outlook for future price developments is made must obviously increase as future, rather than current, decisions are analysed. At the moment, the ability of central banks and independent forecasters to form projections with a minimum degree of accuracy only extends up to approximately two years ahead. Consequently, most central banks have chosen to form their economic forecasts over this horizon, which also prevents any meaningful communication of policy decisions likely to be implemented in the future.

Two conditioning assumptions, both not ideal from the viewpoint of logical consistency, have generally been adopted. One relies on an unchanged policy interest rate path, the other on the interest rate path implicit in the observed term structure of market interest rates.

The case of an unchanged interest rate path does not simply amount to letting the economy evolve without any policy response. Forward looking variables react to expected future policy actions and they would thus react 'today' to an expected future lack of monetary policy response. Hence,

---

[3] Within a Committee, it is not even clear that there would always be agreement on the forecast, once a certain model has been selected. There is, in fact, still room for disagreement on the assumptions on which the forecast must be based. The Minutes of the MPC meeting of the Bank of England held on 4–5 August, for example, report that 'there was considerable uncertainty in the Committee about the inflation outlook, and there was a range of preferred assumptions for the central projection. Various members had different preferred assumptions for the path of the nominal exchange rate, earnings growth, pricing behaviour/profit margins, and the oil price ... Different members preferred different combinations of these assumptions.'

an internally consistent forecast under the hypothesis of no change in the interest rates should filter out any effect on future variables coming from the expected policy response. This creates obvious difficulties owing to the fact that the model must disentangle exogenous economic dynamics from those due to monetary policy responses. It also creates communication problems if the unchanged policy assumption is reflected in a modification of the *current* value of forward looking variables, as these respond now to an unexpected future policy behaviour.

Similarly, a forecast conditional on the interest rate path implicit in the term structure of interest rates relies heavily on the assumption that the expectations hypothesis holds. A large number of studies (see Shiller, 1990, for a survey), however, has found that forward rates are often biased predictors of future rates.[4] For communication purposes, moreover, there are obvious risks of either conveying the impression of following the market, or having to explain why a 'surprise' deviation from the maintained assumption is to be implemented in the absence of shocks.

9.3   Accountability and transparency of the ECB

9.3.1   Accountability

The ECB's formal democratic legitimacy is derived from the Treaty, which was signed by the governments of the fifteen Member States and ratified by their citizens (through the national Parliaments or directly by referendum). Given its European mandate and independent status, the Council of the ECB can only be held accountable by the European public and its elected representatives.

The institution that directly derives its legitimacy from the citizens of the European Union – and which is entrusted to pursue a common European interest, rather than national ones – is the European Parliament. The key channels for accountability of the ECB are the statutory reporting requirements to the European Parliament, which are expected to take the form of an annual report and quarterly reports. The President of the ECB presents these reports to, and discusses them in, the relevant committee of the European Parliament, which can also question other members of the ECB's Executive Board.

Moreover, the ECB maintains an open dialogue with all the bodies that play a role in the European political process: the Council of Ministers and the European Commission in the first place, but also the Economic and Social Committee. The ECB participates in meetings of the Euro-11

---

[4] However, Fuhrer (1996) argues that the expectations hypothesis can be reconciled with the data accounting for changes in the monetary policy regime.

Group, the ECOFIN Council, while the Council President and a member of the European Commission are invited to attend the meetings of the ECB Governing Council. The ECB also reaches out to other relevant groups in society, such as the social partners, by joining, for example, the discussions of the Macroeconomic Dialogue. These contacts allow the ECB to explain its decisions, to share its analysis and receive feedback, thus being involved, within its own realm of responsibilities, in the overall European policy process.

The basis for the ECB's accountability is provided by the mandate, in particular by the overriding 'primary objective to maintain price stability'. A clear mandate contributes simultaneously to independence and accountability. The clearer and more narrowly defined this mandate, easier it is to monitor the performance of the central bank and to justify the delegation of powers to a non-elected body.

While obviously taking these Treaty requirements as given, the ECB has, to enhance its own accountability, decided to go beyond them in a number of directions. We have already emphasised the decision to provide a numerical definition of price stability. Society can then assess the performance of the ECB in terms of this clearly specified measure, since an independent third party can check, at any moment in time, whether price developments are or are not compatible with the published definition.

Moreover, the ECB has chosen to motivate and explain further its monetary policy decisions. Once a month, immediately after the first meeting of the Governing Council,[5] the President of the ECB delivers an introductory statement, providing a summary of the meeting, at a press conference. After the introductory statement a session of questions and answers with representatives of the international press follows. About one week after this, the ECB publishes the *Monthly Bulletin*, including a thorough analysis of economic developments in the euro area from the viewpoint of monetary policy (see table 9.1).

The President's introductory statement and the press conference are comparable, in breadth and content, to the publication of summary minutes of the meetings of the Governing Council. The introductory statement, the conference and the *Monthly Bulletin* list and discuss the various arguments taken into account in the discussion, thus providing a complete summary of the policy debate in which only the possibility of tracing individual opinions is prevented.

The ECB does not publish, however, voting records or individual views of meetings of its decision making bodies. The choice is to communicate on the basis of the presentation of *arguments* rather than *views*. This type of presentation ensures institutional or collective accountability, as opposed to individual accountability. The general arguments in favour of collective

[5] The Governing Council has been meeting twice each month.

Table 9.1. *The ECB's communication policy*

Frequency	Publication	Press releases	Form of distribution
Yearly	Annual Report		Internet/release to media
Monthly	ECB *Monthly Bulletin*	Introductory statement by the President	Internet[1]/release to media
		Transcript of the questions and answers session	Internet[1]
		BOP monthly key items	Internet[1]
		Monetary developments in the euro area	Wire services/internet[1]
		Securities issues statistics	Internet[1]
Fortnightly		Monetary Policy decisions	Wire services/internet[1]
Weekly		Weekly financial statements	Wire services/internet[1]
Occasional	Speeches by the President and the other members of the Executive Board		Internet[1]
	European Parliament hearings		Internet[1]
	Reports; occasional papers; working papers		Internet[1]

Note: [1] Internet address: www.ecb.int.

accountability were outlined in section 9.1. In the context of the ECB, the publication of voting records would, in all likelihood, be given a national connotation: 'Publishing voting behaviour would provide an observable variable, which may allow national politicians or interest groups to verify whether any pressure applied individually had had the intended result. By contrast, it is practically impossible for any individual to demonstrate conclusively that any particular voting behaviour revealed had *not* been affected by any secret or overt influences' (Issing, 1999b).

9.3.2   Transparency

We conclude this chapter with a general description of the route to transparency followed by the ECB. In this context, the special difficulties posed by the international status of the institution must be emphasised, since they can help to explain the innovative and special features of the model of communication adopted by the ECB. Quoting Padoa-Schioppa (2000), the special difficulties can be summarised as follows: having to deal with a *plurality of languages*, a *plurality of communication conventions* and a *plurality of communicators*. The multilingual nature of the euro area is a distinguishing feature of the single monetary policy which is unprecedented in the industrial world. To the different languages and nations correspond, historically, different communication conventions. As a result, each policy message acquires different connotations and is ultimately perceived differently in different countries. An illustrative example is that of the announcement of the stability oriented strategy, which was perceived, in different countries, as giving either too much or too little emphasis to monetary aggregates. Finally, the ECB must address the markets and the public through a plurality of communicators, going from the President to members of the Governing Councils of national central banks.

For these reasons, it is particularly important for a new and supranational institution such as the ECB to set up a coherent frame of reasoning to interpret the subset of *relevant* information through *clear* messages. Honesty requires that such a framework should be used both in the internal process of information filtering and in the communication to the public of policy decisions.

In the ECB, the decision making process starts with the preparation of briefing notes and analyses for the Executive Board by the staff. These notes analyse current economic developments, evaluating the implications of the dynamics of variables according to both the first and second pillars of the strategy, and also of a number of forecasts, coming both from structural econometric models and from a number of smaller and less structural econometric tools. The ultimate synthesis of the available information is made informally by the Governing Council every two weeks.

The ECB has made a considerable effort to provide a clear description of the stability oriented monetary policy strategy, through a number of articles and speeches.[6] In an effort to maximise transparency and reduce policy uncertainty in the run-up to EMU, the strategy has been explicitly characterised and announced even before the start of the single monetary policy. This communication effort responds to the need to ensure that the new strategy – different from those adopted by other central banks – be accurately perceived.

Given the announced strategy, an explanation of the reasoning behind policy decisions, including a careful weighing of the main arguments, can be given against its background. The upside and downside risks in the interpretation of monetary developments and the general outlook for

---

[6] See, for example, ECB (1999a, 2000c) and Angeloni, Gasper and Tristani (1999).

price stability must be interpreted in this context. A particular feature of the model followed by the ECB is that the explanation of policy decisions happens, through a press statement and a press conference, immediately after the Governing Council meetings. In so doing, the President of the ECB provides quasi real-time information on Council deliberations, so that the media, the markets, and the public are not left to guess the motivation behind any particular decision. As to the communication of future policy moves, these are often implicitly mentioned in the press statement after Governing Council meetings or in the speeches of various governors or members of the Executive Board. A more detailed account of the decision making process is provided, in an analytical fashion, in the articles and notes published in the *Monthly Bulletin*.

The model of communication adopted by the ECB attempts to strike a reasonable balance between the objective of maximising transparency and the special constraints deriving from the international character of the institution. This assessment has been criticised on three grounds, mainly, but not only, from supporters of inflation forecast targeting.

The first criticism is the most fundamental one. Since, it is argued, the actual ECB strategy must be based on the inflation forecast, the role of money cannot be justified in economic terms. In this respect, it is concluded, the announced strategy is not truthful and money must be a smokescreen in the attempt to minimise, rather than achieve, transparency (e.g., Svensson, 1999b).

As argued in earlier chapters, the conclusion that a given strategy is not truthful if it attributes an important and special role to money is, in our opinion, a *non sequitur* (see also the discussion in Baltensperger, 2000). Once the correspondence between the 'true' strategy (i.e. that applied internally by the ECB) and that announced on 13 October 1998 is recognised, the transparency of that announcement must also be acknowledged.

The second, and more specific, criticism to the transparency of the ECB concerns the lack of publication of the internal inflation forecast in the first two years.[7] This circumstance has sometimes been given key relevance in terms of transparency, or lack thereof, of the overall monetary policy strategy.

This criticism is not of fundamental importance since, as we have already argued, a published official forecast is useful, but it cannot be seen as the panacea of external communication. Forecasts related to the euro area are subject to especially high uncertainties, owing to the structural

[7] The ECB started publishing Eurosystem economic projections in December 2000. The ECB area-wide econometric model was published in the following month.

changes associated with the transition to Stage Three of Monetary Union. The decision to publish must weigh the advantages with the potential costs of conveying information which, also internally, is treated with special caution. Sufficient confidence in internal models has to be reached before those models can be used as the basis to formulate quantitative forecasts.

The last strand of criticism to the transparency of the ECB relates to a procedural issue, i.e. the lack of publication of the minutes of the meetings of the Governing Council. From an economic viewpoint, it is not clear that the publication of any internal document used as a background or providing a summary for the decision making body should be a desirable goal for the public. This would only be the case if these documents provided information, over and above that supplied through official publications and statements, on the unobserved components of the central bank's preferences or on its information. In the case of the ECB, the President's introductory statement and the press conferences that follow the meetings of the Governing Council provide this kind of information, through an exhaustive summary of the discussion in the meetings.

10 The single monetary policy in 1999

A careful investigation of the evidence and analyses that form the background of actual policy decisions is of crucial importance to understanding in detail the key features of any monetary policy strategy. This exercise is possibly even more important for the strategy of the ECB, since it can show if there is any difference between the strategy actually followed and the one announced. A few observers maintain that the ECB declares that it has adopted the stability oriented strategy, but it is really doing something different. An analysis of the policy actions adopted in the first year of the single monetary policy should be sufficient to illustrate that the stability oriented strategy has represented an effective framework for policy decisions. This chapter mainly draws on discussions and arguments already presented in various issues of the *Monthly Bulletin* of the ECB.

It goes without saying that the outcome of each and every meeting of the Governing Council of the ECB, whether involving a change of policy rates or not, represents in itself a policy decision. Ideally, the analysis should therefore take into account the economic background and the motivations of the outcomes of all fortnightly meetings of the Council. However, this kind of ambitious undertaking goes beyond the scope of this monograph. We will therefore focus on the decisions to modify the level of interest rates, and we will only touch upon the other decisions when this helps to shed light on the motivation for the ensuing changes.

The single monetary policy formally started in January 1999. However, two important decisions announced by the Governing Council at the end of 1998 can be considered *de facto* as decisions of the ECB.

The first one was the announcement of the stability oriented monetary policy strategy in October 1998. This was intrinsically related to the future single monetary policy and it was the first explicit monetary policy signal provided by the Council of the ECB. Although the importance of this signal goes beyond the 'simple' day-to-day policy making, it is useful to briefly analyse it also as such. The economic circumstances of the announcement of the strategy, that is the economic situation at the time the Council of the ECB was established and the reactions of financial markets to the announcement, are therefore reviewed in section 10.1.

The second decision taken *de facto* by the Governing Council was the reduction of interest rates announced in December 1998. Formally, this decision was taken autonomously by the NCBs, who were still independently in charge of monetary policy in their respective countries. However, in their capacity as members of the Governing Council of the ECB, the governors of the NCBs were aware of the fact that they would be starting to take decisions jointly less than a month later. It is not surprising, in this light, that the decision matured in a meeting of the Governing Council of the ECB and that it was underlined as 'joint' by acting at the same time and by issuing a common press release. The latter emphasised that the move was co-ordinated and consensual, that it was the result of a 'thorough discussion in the ECB's Governing Council' and of a 'common assessment of the economic, monetary and financial situation in the euro area'.

Following the timeline, the December 1998 interest rate change is discussed in section 10.2. Sections 10.3 and 10.4 focus on the April 1999 and November 1999 policy decisions, respectively. In each section, we attempt to structure our discussion along the following lines: first, we illustrate the economic developments at the time; we then explain the interpretation of the data made by the Council and leading to the policy decision; finally, we briefly discuss communication issues and the response of financial markets to the policy moves.

10.1   The announcement of the strategy

The importance of the announcement of the strategy on 13 October 1998 mainly stems from the strategic role that the underlying decision retains. It was also, however, the first time the single monetary policy came to the attention of the general public after years of planning and preparation, both at the EMI and within NCBs. As such, it also has a symbolic relevance and its impact on financial markets – as opposed to that on academics discussed so far – can provide important information for the central bank.

In order to understand the impact of the announcement on financial markets, it is important to quickly review the economic situation at the time of the announcement.

The most striking, common feature of economic developments over the nineties in prospective euro area economies is the return to price stability after, in some cases, more than two decades of inflation. In

January 1990, all countries that would adopt the euro nine years later were experiencing inflation rates above the definition of price stability chosen by the Governing Council on 13 October 1998. This common feature obviously hides large differences in historical performance, whereby in some countries inflation had never really been eradicated since the seventies, while in others only recent and clearly exceptional shocks had led to a deviation from price stability. In January 1990 itself, many differences across countries remained: while the twelve-month inflation rate stood between 2 and 4 per cent in Austria, Belgium, Germany, France and the Netherlands, it was up to 4 percentage points higher in other countries, with Portugal still hovering in the double-digit area (figure 10.1).

Nevertheless, and in spite of the occurrence of shocks such as the ERM crisis of 1992–3, all countries succeeded in bringing inflation under control by the end of 1998. This was partly due to the effect of expectations of participation in the EMU, partly fostered by a determined and explicit commitment to price stability on the part of national monetary policies. The medium and long term gains for the regained monetary stability have yet to materialise, but they will certainly do so if we believe the strong evidence presented in chapter 1.

An immediate reward of the regained monetary stability in the whole continent was the descent of long term nominal interest rates to levels consistent with current and prospective price stability. After reaching two-digit levels, in a few cases as recently as the summer of 1996, in September 1998 bond yields in prospective euro area countries stood between 4 and 4.5 per cent, levels that can be considered as consistent with prolonged prospects of price stability. Official interest rates had declined accordingly and, over 1998, a number of interest rate cuts had already been implemented in most countries.

At the time of the announcement of the strategy, the euro area inflation rate, as measured by the Harmonised Index of Consumer Prices for the area, stood at approximately 1 per cent. The threats to price stability were mostly on the downward side, and typically coming from the rest of the world. Growth had been hampered by the Asian crisis, which had led the IMF to revise downwards its estimates for world growth in 1998 to 2 per cent, from 4.3 per cent forecast one year before; lingering fears of a widespread recession had been reinforced by the Russian crisis during the summer. However, the impact of these international events on European economies was not expected to be too disruptive: the economic recovery was under way and, according to the Commission, the euro area would have grown by 2.8 per cent in the first half of 1998. Hence, it appeared unlikely that strong downward shocks to price stability would ensue. Even if growth was still only moderate in some countries, the decreases in real

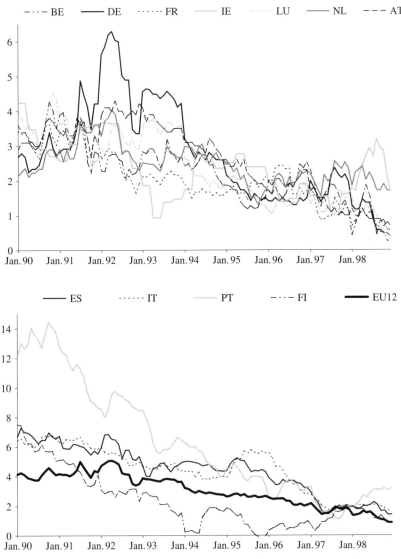

Figure 10.1 Inflation rates in the nineties in euro area countries
Source: ECB.

and nominal interest rates represented an important stimulus for those economies.

Against the background of re-established monetary stability, financial markets interpreted the announcement of the strategy as consistent with the maintenance of this goal. No jumps were observed in financial variables, nor a noticeable change in volatility. Given the pre-existing level of long term interest rates consistent with price stability, the strategy was received simply as a confirmation of that assessment: bond yields continued to fluctuate around 4 per cent in most countries and continued their descent towards this level in the others.

10.2   The first monetary policy actions: 3 December 1998 and 22 December 1998

In the meantime, data signalling a slowdown in production in the third quarter of the year were beginning to be released. Industrial confidence indicators had already been weakening since the summer, registering the reduction of international orders. While these leading economic indicators were not giving encouraging signals, concerns were also deriving from the turmoil in international financial markets. Negative wealth effects were expected to originate in all countries from the marked fall in national stock prices (by up to 25 per cent with respect to the mid-July peaks). These developments raised obvious concerns for a further decrease in the inflation rate, already at a level well below the upper bound for price stability defined in October. Similar concerns had convinced the Federal Reserve to reduce its federal funds target rate by 75 basis points in late 1998, in three successive steps, in spite of the continuing growth in the United States.

Other indicators showed signals broadly consistent with the hypothesis of increasing risks for price stability on the downside. Monetary growth in European countries appeared in line with a subdued outlook for price developments. On the other hand, the recent depreciation of the synthetic euro vis-à-vis the US dollar was not expected to create significant inflation pressures, since it largely reverted the appreciation trend of the first months of 1998.

On 3 December the NCBs, after an agreement reached in the preceding meeting of the Governing Council of the ECB, decided in a co-ordinated fashion to reduce their key central bank rates. This move represented, first, the final step towards convergence of interest rates in the euro area, in preparation for the forthcoming formal start of the single monetary policy. It also meant, however, a further reduction of interest rates towards the lowest levels prevailing in EMU countries: the average three-month interbank rate declined by 70 basis points between August 1998 and the end of 1998 and half of this decline occurred after the decision of 3 December.

Financial markets and general observers reacted favourably to the December decision. They appeared to understand well its motivations

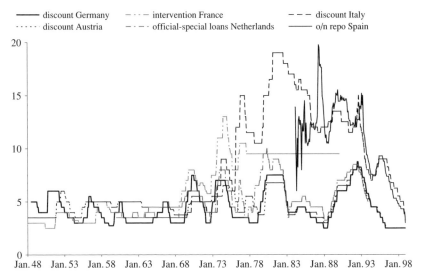

Figure 10.2 Official interest rates in selected euro area countries
Source: ECB.

and to consider it appropriate. In the following days, forward looking financial market variables displayed no signs of receiving the decision as inflationary in the long term. Bond yields continued their gentle descent towards their lowest levels in the post-war period. As already mentioned, the dollar appreciated somewhat against the synthetic euro, but there were already signs that, rather than an indication of loss of credibility of the single monetary policy, this could be read as a direct implication of a potential widening of the growth differential between the euro area and the United States.

By the end of December 1998, official interest rates had reached low levels that were unprecedented in post-war European history (figure 10.2). In most countries, the discount rate was already lower than it had ever been in the Bretton Woods era. These levels had been reached after some-times substantial cuts in the course of 1998: in Italy, the repo rate had come down by over 3 percentage points since the beginning of the year. Even for economies at the early stages of recovery after a stagnant period, at this juncture the level of interest rates appeared low enough comfort-ably to prevent further significant reductions in the inflation rate. In fact, the press release also stressed that this was a '*de facto* decision on the level of interest rates with which the ESCB will start Stage Three of Monetary Union and which it intends to maintain for the foreseeable future'.

The 3 per cent level reached by key policy rates in the move of 3 December was confirmed by the Governing Council on 22 December, when deciding on the levels of the ECB's interest rates for the start of Stage Three of Monetary Union: the rate on the main refinancing operations was set, accordingly, at 3 per cent. Because of the aforementioned consensus that such a level was already low by historical comparison, the corridor around the main refinancing rate was set asymmetrically. While the rate on overnight deposits was set at 2 per cent, that on the marginal lending facility was set at 4.5 per cent. The asymmetry aimed to signal the then prevailing orientation of the Governing Council regarding future movements of the policy interest rates: the already low level of the rate on the main refinancing operations appeared to leave slightly more room for future increases, rather than for a new decrease.

As a temporary measure, aimed to facilitate the smooth transition of money markets to the new environment, the corridor around the main refinancing rate was narrowed to a range of ±25 basis points during the first three working weeks of January 1999.

The monetary policy decisions of December 1998 represented a further easing of the policy stance. In the first months of 1999, the short term real interest rate, as measured by the three-month interbank rate minus the annual rate of HICP inflation, moved below 2 per cent, by far the lowest level reached by short term real rates over the whole decade.

10.3   Second policy move: 8 April 1999

The new information that became available in the months following the first policy move showed that the economic slowdown could be more pronounced than initially believed. Headline HICP inflation declined to 0.8 per cent in December and remained at that level until February, the last month for which the inflation figure was known at the time of the 8 April meeting of the Governing Council. Excluding seasonal food and energy, inflation fell below 1.1 per cent in February 1999, along a downward trend started in June 1998, when it was equal to 1.5 per cent. As a result of the decrease in the inflation rate, the *ex post* short term real interest rate at the end of March had increased to 2.2 per cent.

Not all economic indicators, however, were sending signals of a potential worsening of the outlook for price stability. The assessment of the complex situation was therefore particularly difficult. The reasoning behind the eventual decision to prolong the downward trend in the key ECB's rates can best be analysed in the light of the stability oriented monetary policy strategy.

10.3.1 Monetary developments

M3 growth had been above the reference value since the very beginning of the monetary union, although not by a large amount. This signal of buoyant money growth pointed towards weak risks of upward, rather than downward, pressures on price stability and should have mitigated any worry of new falls in the future inflation rate. However, the assessment of the rate of growth of M3 was complicated by the uncertainty related to the behaviour of this aggregate in the changeover period. In fact, M3 had been growing at annual rates between 4.4 and 4.9 per cent in the four quarters of 1998, all values quite consistent with the reference value for money announced by the Governing Council. Then, at the start of Stage Three, money had sharply accelerated: in January 1999, the twelve-month rate of increase of M3 had been 5.6 per cent. In February, however, it had slowed down, registering a rate of growth of 5.2 per cent (figure 10.3).

In these circumstances, one could not immediately dismiss the hypothesis that the upward jump observed in January was a mechanical effect of the change in regime. There were a few signals that the jump could be due to statistical or institutional factors: substantial reclassification changes for the definition of M3 had been implemented in some countries; the new regime of reserve requirement, moreover, could have led to some portfolio reallocations. However, the quantitative relevance of these factors remained unclear. Concerning the changes of definition,

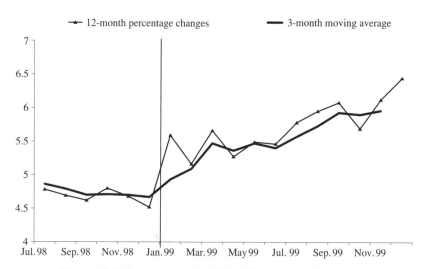

Figure 10.3 Rate of growth of M3, July 1998 to November 1999
Source: ECB.

these had been taken into account in the calculation of the rate of growth of M3 and were thus not likely to play a large role.

Similarly, sizeable portfolio reallocations connected to the switch to the single currency could not be excluded. One could have expected them to be observed already at the end of 1998, since the start of Stage Three of EMU – thus, for example, the ensuing change of regime for reserve requirements – was a largely anticipated event. It was conceivable, however, that some remaining uncertainties about the timing or the successful start of the EMU could have convinced asset holders to wait until January to complete their desired portfolio readjustments. This could support the interpretation of the increase in the rate of growth of M3 in January 1999 as due to exceptional circumstances. In this respect, it must be noted that, after correcting for the January increase, monetary growth would have resulted slightly *below* the reference value in February. However, the slowdown of money growth in February could also be taken as a signal that the increase in January was, at least partly, transitory.

Credit aggregates were sending signals apparently difficult to reconcile with the signs of weaker economic activity and subdued dynamics of M3. In particular, credit to the private sector was growing quickly, at an annual rate of around 10 per cent in both January and February 1999, as a consequence of the low retail bank lending rates. However, credit growth could also have been the result of demand by non-financial firms to finance inventories, which had increased above long term averages according to survey data.

To summarise, the deviation of the rate of growth of M3 from the reference value had to be considered with particular caution. It was not inconsistent with the hypothesis that the macroeconomic situation in the euro area was broadly in line with the maintenance of future price stability or even with the existence of downward risks to price stability. The risk that monetary growth was actually weaker than apparent from the raw data had to be taken into account.

10.3.2   The broadly based assessment

Clearer indications of downside risks to price stability were in the meantime coming from the second pillar.

The exogenous variable of all available forecasts was the uncertain outlook for the world economy. While in the rest of Asia there were increasing signs of a gradual recovery, the economic prospects in Japan remained gloomy, since preliminary figures for the last quarter of 1998 showed a fall of real GDP by 2.8 per cent (year-on-year). At the same time, the economic recession in Russia was expected to deepen.

In the judgment of the IMF, the OECD and the Commission, these factors would not have too large an impact on the euro area, particularly in view of the resilience of economic growth in the USA, which, sustained by the expansion of domestic demand, appeared untouched by the external developments. However, new data released in the first months of 1999 did not appear consistent with this picture.

10.3.2.1 Real GDP growth. Figures that became available in the first months of 1999 all pointed to a significant slowdown in the euro area in the second half of 1998. Real GDP growth had weakened significantly: according to first estimates by Eurostat, it increased by 0.2 per cent in the fourth quarter of 1998 with respect to the previous quarter. This was mainly the result of a substantial decline in export growth, while private consumption had remained the most dynamic component of GDP. Significant differences between countries continued to characterise the aggregate picture: in the first half of 1998, when growth appeared quite vigorous in smaller countries, such as Finland, Austria and the Netherlands, and buoyant in France and Spain, Germany and especially Italy were still lagging behind.

The slowdown was confirmed by the data on industrial production (excluding construction). In the last quarter of 1998, it had decreased by 0.2 per cent with respect to the previous quarter, with particularly marked falls in Germany and Italy, by 2.4 and 1.4 per cent, respectively. The slowdown was even more pronounced in the manufacturing sector.

Meanwhile, developments in the labour market appeared more favourable: the unemployment rate had fallen by more than a percentage point in Ireland, the Netherlands, Portugal and Spain. Changes in unemployment, however, typically follow the cycle, so they were not necessarily inconsistent with a worsening of the outlook for growth.

10.3.2.2 Evidence from survey data. Very negative signals were coming from industrial confidence, which was continuing its monotonic slide started at the beginning of 1998. On the contrary, the euro area consumer confidence indicator, while staying approximately constant in February, remained at the highest level since the series started in 1985. This was probably suggesting that aggregate consumption would continue to remain buoyant in the following months (figure 10.4).

When trying to interpret these signals, however, the differing nature of the two questionnaires had to be taken into account. While in the case of industrial confidence the questionnaire can be seen as sufficiently forward looking, since it includes, for example, questions on production expectations and the assessment of order books, in the case of consumer

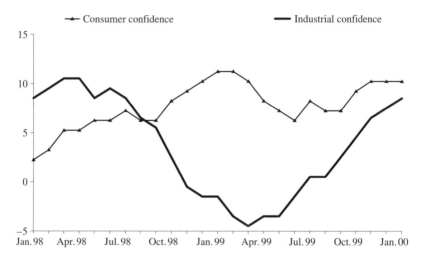

Figure 10.4 Confidence indicators for the euro area, January 1998 to January 2000
Source: ECB.

confidence this is probably less true. Historical analyses have shown that consumer confidence tends to be strongly affected by employment growth, as a determinant of household income. Under this interpretation, the difference between the two confidence indicators could simply be explained in terms of their timing with respect to the cycle, with the industrial indicator leading the consumer indicator. The buoyancy of the latter variable would then represent a misleading signal.

Capacity utilisation in the manufacturing sector had decreased further in the fourth quarter of 1998, although still remaining slightly above its long run average.

In sum, the indicators were signalling that inflationary pressures originating from excess aggregate demand were likely to be substantially weaker than anticipated. Given that all previous inflation projections for 1999 and 2000 were already benign, it would appear that HICP inflation was more likely to remain in the lower range of the definition of price stability.

10.3.2.3 Exchange rate and international prices. On the international scene, a sizeable oil price shock was under way. Oil prices (in US dollars) had been rising steadily since mid-February 1999 and, on 30 March, the increase had reached almost 40 per cent with respect to the February average. This evolution, however, had to be set against the background of the much more pronounced and prolonged fall from January 1997;

since then, oil prices at the end of March 1999 were actually lower by over 40 per cent.

It is interesting to note that the fall in oil prices already appeared to have had an impact on the HICP for the euro area. The headline inflation rate had dropped from 1.5 per cent in December 1997 to 0.8 per cent in February 1999, while inflation in the HICP excluding energy prices had remained broadly constant in the same period. This could be seen as an encouraging sign against the risks of a further fall in the inflation rate, if one was willing to ascribe most of the fall in inflation to oil prices.

A similar effect was produced by the exchange rate of the euro, which had been depreciating in effective terms since the beginning of the monetary union, in particular vis-à-vis the dollar. This indicator, however, had to be treated with particular caution, with regards to its implications for price stability prospects. Preliminary ECB estimates, on the size and the timing of the pass-through of the exchange rate on domestic prices, were not signalling risks of serious inflationary pressures. Even assuming that the depreciation experienced at the beginning of April since the launch of EMU (almost 5 per cent in nominal effective terms) were of a permanent nature, the depreciation could be seen as a compensation for the much more pronounced appreciation of the euro during 1998.

10.3.2.4 Developments in financial markets. The increase of the yield on ten-year bonds, equal to 35 basis points in February, almost stopped in March. The dynamics of long term interest rates mainly appeared to reflect global trends, rather than domestic euro area developments. Yields on euro- and dollar-denominated bonds moved quite synchronously, although the differential had widened somewhat in February.

A more persistent trend could be identified in the dynamics of the yield spread (i.e. the difference between the yield on ten-year nominal bonds and the three-month interest rate), which had narrowed significantly over the previous two years. Judging on the basis of results related to other countries (e.g., Smets and Tsatsaronis, 1997), yield spread dynamics could be interpreted as suggestive of persistently weak economic growth in the future. However, there was no clear evidence on the leading indicator properties of the yield spread in the euro area (figure 10.5).

Internal factors were also likely to have exerted a stabilising role on long term rates. Specifically, the perception of a decrease in the pace of economic activity and the evidence of a new decline in producer price inflation had probably dissipated perceptions of future inflationary pressures. Another signal that financial markets had not significantly altered their outlook for long term inflation was coming from ten-year French index-linked bonds. The implied expected inflation rate, obtained as the

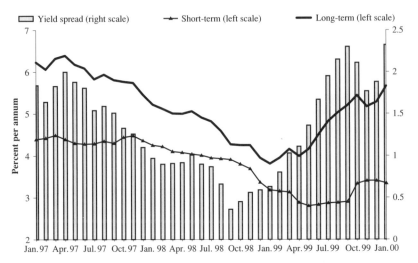

Figure 10.5 Short and long term interest rates and yield spread, January
1997 to January 2000
Source: ECB.

difference between the return on nominal bonds and that on index-linked
bonds had hovered around 1 per cent in the first months of 1999. In
March, the real return on index-linked bonds had remained broadly constant at a level of 3 per cent.

Finally, stock prices only increased slightly in March, by approximately
1 per cent as measured by the EURO STOXX index. The poor performance of euro area equity markets was particularly noticeable when
compared to the relative buoyancy observed in other markets (showing
increases of 4 per cent in the United States and more than 10 per cent
in Japan) and, arguably, another reflection of uncertainties on growth
prospects in the area.

10.3.3   Overall assessment

The particularly high degree of uncertainty faced at this point in time,
and reflected in the difficulties in reconciling the signals coming from
different indicators, can be illustrated through the succession of revisions
of economic forecasts.

The latest forecasts for consumer price inflation in the euro area had
once again been revised downwards to reflect the aforementioned pieces
of evidence. The European Commission was forecasting an increase in
the private consumption deflator by 1.2 per cent in 1999 and 1.5 per cent

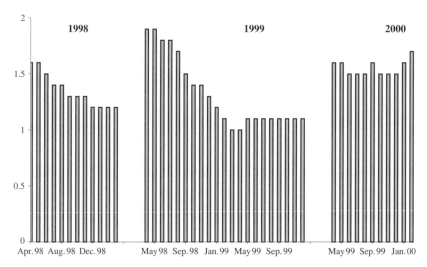

Figure 10.6 Evolution of inflation forecasts for the euro area, 1998–2000
Source: ECB.

in 2000, as opposed to figures of 1.5 and 1.7 per cent, respectively, in the autumn forecast. The latest Consensus forecast had also been revised to 1 per cent in 1999 and 1.5 per cent in 2000, the latest in a sequence of successive downward revisions (figure 10.6).

The outlook for growth was also more pessimistic than previously forecast, at around 2 per cent in 1999 with only a slight improvement in the following year. Again, a sequence of downward revisions had been made in response to the unravelling of events (figure 10.7). The main reason behind the last revision was the conclusion that the impact of the emerging market crisis on the traded goods sector of the euro area economy had been stronger and longer lasting than previously thought. On the other hand, forecasters continued to judge that private consumption and construction investments would remain buoyant.

When meeting on 8 April, the Governing Council was facing a situation in which all inflation forecasts projected the euro area inflation rate to remain around levels well within the definition of price stability in the following two years. These projections, however, were in all cases the result of a sequence of reassessments, always in a downward direction, which were by themselves the manifestation of a trend leading to downward threats to price stability. While there were no *expectations* of the euro area facing deflation, there was the perception of a *risk* that this could happen, and the main risks to price stability remained on the downside. The risk

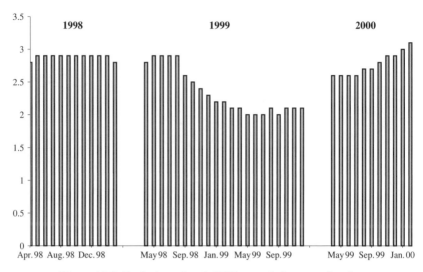

Figure 10.7 Evolution of real GDP growth forecasts for the euro area,
1998–2000
Source: ECB.

could be taken particularly seriously in light of the dangers inherent in a situation in which monetary policy operates at very low levels of inflation (see also Gaspar, 2000).

The Governing Council decided to pre-emptively reduce all policy rates: the main refinancing rate and the deposit rate were both reduced by 50 basis points, to 2.5 and 1.5 per cent respectively; the marginal lending rate was reduced by 100 basis points, to 3.5 per cent. In the press conference, it was clarified that a further fall in the rate of inflation was considered unlikely, so that no further interest rate cuts were foreseen. It was also argued that the size of the cut had brought interest rates to a level deemed consistent with current and expected economic conditions, so that the policy move should not be interpreted as a first step of a renewed declining trend for interest rates. In his answer to a specific question inquiring whether the interest rate had reached a minimum limit, the President explicitly remarked 'we moved from 3 per cent to 2.5 per cent which is maybe a slightly unexpectedly large fall, but I would like to add, and now you be sure: this is it'. This also confirmed that the move had to be read as an insurance against the downside risks, and not as an attempt to tackle an expected fall in the inflation rate.

The timing of the move had been to some extent anticipated by financial markets. Over the course of March, short term interest rates started to reflect the possibility of a general decrease in interest rates. Three-month rates declined by approximately 10 basis points, to touch levels just below the repo rate at the end of March. A further reduction was implicit in the price of three-month interest rate futures for delivery in June, suggesting that markets were expecting a rate cut in the region of 20 basis points in the near future.

The size of the move, however, was to some extent unexpected. Money market rates adjusted to a level consistent with expectations of no further cuts in the forthcoming months. The three-month EURIBOR declined by 24 basis points on 9 April, following the announcement of the Council's decision, bringing about a considerable flattening of the short end of the yield curve.

Once again, markets appeared to understand the pre-emptive nature of the rate cut. Immediately after the announcement, long term interest rates declined slightly and then remained stable in the following weeks. No signals of a change in the assessment of long term inflation expectations were observed.

10.4   The first policy tightening: 4 November 1999

During the summer of 1999, long term rates in the euro area started moving along an upward trend. The driving force was initially the increase of long term interest rates in the United States, but first signs that an economic recovery in the euro area was on its way supported it later on. As a consequence of the rise in bond yields, the yield curve in the euro area steepened considerably. Furthermore, the external environment improved throughout the first part of 1999, as more and more signs of a stabilisation and acceleration of economic activity came from several emerging market economies and even Japan, while in the United States the economy continued to expand at a robust pace. Overall, during the summer of 1999 it became progressively more evident that economic activity in the euro area was set to accelerate significantly in the second part of 1999 and in the year 2000. The downward risks to price stability were gradually fading away and upward risks were beginning to appear.

10.4.1   The evolution of the prospects for price stability

10.4.1.1 Money growth. Monetary growth picked up in the course of the summer to values quite in excess of the reference value. Between February and September 1999, the twelve-month rate of growth of M3 increased from 5.0 to 6.1 per cent (figure 10.3). Even considering the possibility of a structural shift in January 1999, money growth appeared to be in excess of the reference value. Credit growth was also continuing at a steady pace, of approximately 10 per cent, helped by the downward trend in bank lending rates. The low level of interest rates and the low inflation rates also contributed to the growth of the most liquid component of M3: the twelve-month rate of growth of M1 increased from 8.2 per cent in July 1998 to 13.8 per cent in July 1999.

Though M3 growth data continued to be regarded with caution, in light of the possibility of behavioural changes in the previous months, over the summer it became clear that the pace of M3 was no longer consistent with the presence of downward risks to price stability.

10.4.1.2 GDP growth. Even if the expected growth of real GDP in 1999 had not improved dramatically, the balance of risks appeared radically modified. In fact, growth in the last quarter of 1998 and the first of 1999 had first been revised downward to 0.1 and 0.4 per cent, respectively. In the second quarter of 1999, however, GDP growth turned out to be 0.5 per cent, thus pointing to improving prospects. Export volumes also proved more dynamic than expected, reducing to zero, in the second quarter of 1999, the contribution of net exports to GDP growth (with respect to the previous situation of a negative contribution to growth).

Industrial production continued to signal a weak performance of the euro area economy in the first quarter of 1999. Later on, however, evidence showed that it had slightly increased in the second quarter, with noticeable upward revisions in the following months up to August (the latest data available at the time of the meeting of the Governing Council).

In May 1999, the industrial confidence indicator provided by the European Commission increased, for the first time since July 1998. The improvement of the prospects for producers and exporters was confirmed by surveys on the developments of order books. In the meantime, consumer confidence remained high by historical standards. These two pieces of evidence were particularly welcome, since they signalled that the feared fall of the consumer confidence indicator to close the gap with the industrial confidence indicator was unlikely to occur.

10.4.1.3 Commodity prices and the exchange rate. Oil prices had continued to rise steadily, up to levels of $20.8 per barrel in October, and were projected to remain high for the foreseeable future, because of production cuts agreed by OPEC. In euro terms, the price of oil had increased by just over 20 per cent with respect to October 1998.

Until July, the persistently strong growth in the USA kept alive market expectations of future interest rises on dollar-denominated assets. This

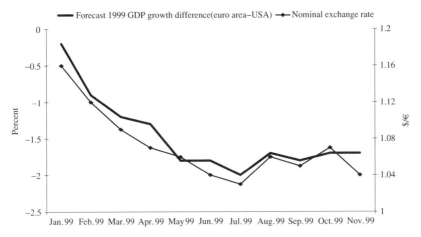

Figure 10.8 Growth differential between the USA and the euro area
and the dollar–euro exchange rate
Source: ECB, Consensus.

compared to the prospect of low interest rates in the euro area for longer
than expected, because of the still ambiguous evidence on growth in the
old continent. In August, however, the euro started to regain ground
against the US dollar; a marked increase of volatility characterised the
exchange rate between the two currencies in the following months. The
contemporaneous improvement of the outlook for growth in the euro area
confirmed the existing perception that the euro–dollar exchange rate was
significantly influenced by relative economic developments in the euro
area and in the United States. The evolution of the exchange rate of the
euro was also affected by official statements of the ECB, as of mid-July,
expressing concern for upward risks to price stability and indicating that
increases in ECB interest rates were more likely in the future than further
reductions.

Corsetti and Pesenti (1999) present graphical evidence that movements
in the dollar–euro exchange rate, at this juncture, were consistent with
relative growth prospects in the USA and the euro area. Using Consensus
data, they show that the progressive widening, in favour of the United
States, in the forecast growth differentials between the two economies
was accompanied by a parallel fall of the euro until July 1999. In the following months, a signal of inversion in the relative growth of the two areas
was mirrored by the slight appreciation of the euro until the November
decision (figure 10.8).

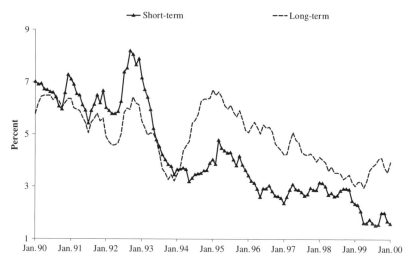

Figure 10.9 Real short term and long term interest rates, 1990–2000
Source: ECB.

10.4.2   Overall assessment

The shift of the balance of risks to price stability towards the upside was signalled consistently by both monetary and credit developments and the indications arising from a broader assessment, including a stronger growth in consumption and investment. International developments were also in line with this picture, given the recent steep rise in oil prices that could potentially feed on to inflation through, for example, wage settlements. It could also be noted that short term real rates had reached particularly low levels. In September, they bottomed at 1.6 per cent, a new historical low over the nineties (figure 10.9)

A corroboration of the hypothesis that these levels were becoming inconsistent with price stability prospects, given the current pace of economic activity, can be illustrated on the basis of simple benchmarks such as the Taylor rule. Based on a variety of assumptions concerning the 'equilibrium' real rate and of estimates of the current output gap, Taylor-type rules suggest that interest rates should have increased significantly.

The signals of financial prices were also consistent with this assessment. Over the summer, long term bond yields increased by more than 1 percentage point, bringing the yield spread to almost 2.5 percentage points in September. At the same time, the inflation rate implicit in French index-linked bonds reached 1.8 per cent in September, with respect to the 1.07 level of April.

In the meantime, the HICP inflation rate had also increased over the summer, reaching the 1.2 per cent level in August and in September.

In the meeting of 4 November, the Governing Council decided to raise the interest rate on the main refinancing operations by 50 basis points, thus bringing it back to the 3 per cent level prevailing before the April decision. The deposit rate and the marginal lending rate were both increased by the same amount, thus leaving the width and the symmetry of the 'corridor' unchanged.

The Council had already announced after previous meetings that its own assessment of the risks to price stability had been revised, and that the downward risks were judged to have disappeared. This assessment was confirmed in the November introductory statement, which also stressed the 'far more favourable' current economic environment that rendered the 'precautionary interest rate reduction made in April no longer justified'. This highlights the fact that the November move can be explained largely by the disappearance of the uncertainty factors that had been behind the decision taken in April.

Moreover, the press conference underlined that the decision to move by 50 basis points (as opposed to, for example, a more gradual 25 basis points) was judged to be 'the best way in which to avoid uncertainties regarding the future course of monetary policy'. This concern was related to the prospects of 'a possible increase in volatility in money markets towards the end of the year'. Three-month interest rates had already increased markedly, at the beginning of October, because of potential Y2K problems. More generally, however, the desire to avoid uncertainties over the future course of policy was also related to the lack of a track record characterising the ECB. In this context, and at a time of exceptionally low interest rates, a too-gradual approach could be misunderstood by the markets as indecision, potentially leading to unjustified jitters at the long end of the yield curve.

The policy tightening had come to be fully expected, regarding both its timing and its size, in financial markets, as witnessed by the increase to approximately 2.8 per cent of the overnight rate in the vicinity of the move.

Appendix: Excerpts from ECB external communications to the press

ECB PRESS RELEASE

A STABILITY ORIENTED MONETARY POLICY STRATEGY FOR THE
ESCB – 13 OCTOBER 1998

1. At its meeting on 13 October 1998 the Governing Council of the ECB agreed on the main elements of the stability oriented monetary policy strategy of the ESCB. These elements concern:
   - the quantitative definition of the primary objective of the single monetary policy, price stability;
   - a prominent role for money with a reference value for the growth of a monetary aggregate; and
   - a broadly based assessment of the outlook for future price developments.

2. As mandated by the Treaty establishing the European Community, the maintenance of price stability will be the primary objective of the ESCB. Therefore, the ESCB's monetary policy strategy will focus strictly on this objective. In this context, the Governing Council of the ECB has adopted the following definition: 'Price stability shall be defined as a year-on-year increase in the Harmonised Index of Consumer Prices (HICP) for the euro area of below 2%.'

   Price stability is to be maintained over the medium term.

   The current rate of HICP inflation in the euro area is in line with this objective.

   Three features of this definition should be highlighted:
   - the HICP is the most appropriate price measure for the ESCB's definition of price stability. It is the only price index that will be sufficiently harmonised across the euro area at the start of Stage Three;
   - by focusing on the HICP 'for the euro area', the Governing Council of the ECB makes it clear that it will base its decisions on monetary, economic and financial developments in the euro area as a whole. The single monetary policy will adopt a euro area-wide

perspective; it will not react to specific regional or national developments;

- an 'increase . . . of below 2%' is very much in line with most current definitions adopted by national central banks in the euro area.

Furthermore, the statement that 'price stability is to be maintained over the medium term' reflects the need for monetary policy to have a forward looking, medium term orientation. It also acknowledges the existence of short term volatility in prices which cannot be controlled by monetary policy.

3. In order to maintain price stability, the Governing Council of the ECB agreed to adopt a monetary policy strategy which will consist of two key elements:

- Money will be assigned a prominent role. This role will be signalled by the announcement of a quantitative reference value for the growth of a broad monetary aggregate. The reference value will be derived in a manner which is consistent with – and will serve to achieve – price stability. Deviations of current monetary growth from the reference value would, under normal circumstances, signal risks to price stability. The concept of a reference value does not imply a commitment to mechanistically correct deviations over the short term.

  The relationship between actual monetary growth and the pre-announced reference value will be regularly and thoroughly analysed by the Governing Council of the ECB; the result of this analysis and its impact on monetary policy decisions will be explained to the public. The precise definition of the reference aggregate and the specific value of the quantitative reference value for monetary growth will be announced by the Governing Council of the ECB in December 1998.

- In parallel with the analysis of monetary growth in relation to the reference value, a broadly based assessment of the outlook for price developments and the risks to price stability in the euro area will play a major role in the ESCB's strategy. This assessment will be made using a wide range of economic and financial variables as indicators for future price developments.

4. This strategy underlines the strong commitment of the Governing Council of the ECB to its primary objective and should facilitate the achievement of this overriding goal. It will also ensure the transparency of the ESCB's decision making and its accountability. Based on its strategy, the Governing Council of the ECB will inform the public regularly and in detail about its assessment of the monetary, economic

and financial situation in the euro area and the reasoning behind its specific policy decisions.

ECB PRESS RELEASE

THE QUANTITATIVE REFERENCE VALUE FOR MONETARY GROWTH –
1 DECEMBER 1998

On 13 October 1998 the Governing Council of the ECB announced the main elements of its stability oriented monetary policy strategy. The Governing Council announced its quantitative definition of the ESCB's primary objective, namely price stability. Price stability was defined as a year-on-year increase in the Harmonised Index of Consumer Prices (HICP) for the euro area of below 2%. Furthermore, the Governing Council outlined the two main elements of the strategy that it will use to achieve the objective of maintaining price stability. First, a prominent role will be assigned to money. This role will be signalled by the announcement of a quantitative reference value for the growth of a broad monetary aggregate. Second, in parallel with the analysis of developments in the monetary data in relation to the reference value, a broadly based assessment of the outlook for price developments and risks to price stability in the euro area will be undertaken. This assessment will encompass a wide range of economic and financial indicator variables.

The announcement on 13 October left two issues unresolved, namely the derivation of the reference value for monetary growth and the definition of the specific broad monetary aggregate for which the reference value will be announced.

At its meeting on 1 December 1998 the Governing Council of the ECB agreed on these remaining issues regarding the ESCB's monetary policy strategy by specifying the details of the quantitative reference value for monetary growth.

1. The reference value will refer to the broad monetary aggregate M3. M3 will consist of currency in circulation plus certain liabilities of Monetary Financial Institutions (MFIs) resident in the euro area and, in the case of deposits, the liabilities of some institutions that are part of central government (such as Post Offices and Treasuries). These liabilities included in M3 are: overnight deposits; deposits with an agreed maturity of up to two years; deposits redeemable at notice up to three months; repos; debt securities with maturity of up to two years; unit/shares of money market funds and money market paper (net).

2. The reference value for monetary growth must be consistent with – and serve the achievement of – price stability. Deviations of current monetary growth from the reference value would, under normal circumstances, signal risks to price stability. To this end, the reference value must be derived in a manner consistent with the ESCB's quantitative definition of price stability, i.e. that the HICP for the euro area increases at a year-on-year rate of below 2%. Price stability according to this definition is to be maintained over the medium term.

3. Furthermore, the reference value for monetary growth must take into account real GDP growth and changes in the velocity of circulation. In view of the medium-term orientation of monetary policy, it appears appropriate to base the derivation of the reference value on assumptions about the medium-term trend in both real GDP growth and velocity growth.

   a. Regarding the trend growth of real GDP in the euro area, a figure is estimated to be in the range of 2% to $2\frac{1}{2}$% per annum. However, non-inflationary growth in the euro area could, in the future, be higher if necessary structural reforms in labour and product markets were realised.

   b. Concerning velocity, medium term trends have to be assessed in the light of the regime shifts and behavioural and institutional changes associated with the convergence towards and transition to Monetary Union. The resulting uncertainties concerning broad money velocity have led to the view that a plausible assumption for the medium term trend in velocity is a decline in the approximate range between 0.5% and 1% per annum. This assumption is consistent with the historical experience of the last twenty years.

4. The derivation of the reference value is based on the contributions to monetary growth resulting from assumptions made for prices ('year-on-year increases of below 2%'), real GDP growth (trend growth of 2% to $2\frac{1}{2}$% per annum) and velocity (a trend decline in the approximate range between $\frac{1}{2}$% and 1% each year).

5. The Governing Council has decided to announce a reference rate for monetary growth, rather than a range. The Council believes that announcing a reference range might be falsely interpreted by the public as implying that interest rates would be changed automatically if monetary growth were to move outside the boundaries of the range.

6. In setting the reference value for monetary growth, the Governing Council emphasised that the ESCB's published definition of price stability limits increases in the HICP for the euro area to 'below 2%'. Furthermore, the actual trend decline in velocity is likely to lie

somewhat below the extreme of the range mentioned above. Taking account of these two factors, the Governing Council decided to set the first reference value at 4½%.

7. The ESCB will monitor monetary developments against this reference value on the basis of three-month moving averages of the monthly twelve-month growth rates for M3. This will ensure that erratic monthly outturns in the data do not unduly distort the information contained in the aggregate, thereby reinforcing the medium-term orientation of the reference value.

8. In December 1999, the Governing Council of the ECB will review the reference value for monetary growth.

ECB PRESS RELEASE

INTEREST RATES IN THE EUROPEAN MONETARY UNION – 3 DECEMBER 1998

All National Central Banks participating in the single monetary policy as from the start of Stage Three lower their key central bank rate today in a co-ordinated decision. These decisions reflect a thorough discussion in the ECB's Governing Council leading to a consensus on the basis of a common assessment of the economic, monetary and financial situation in the euro area.

The joint reduction in interest rates has to be seen as a *de facto* decision on the level of interest rates with which the ESCB will start Stage Three of Monetary Union and which it intends to maintain for the foreseeable future.

ECB PRESS CONFERENCE

THURSDAY, 8 APRIL 1999 – PRESIDENT'S INTRODUCTORY STATEMENT

Ladies and gentlemen, the Vice-President and I are here today to report on the outcome of today's meeting of the Governing Council.

Let me start with the Governing Council's discussion of **recent economic developments and the decisions that the Governing Council has taken today in the field of monetary policy**. After an in-depth review of recent monetary, financial and economic developments, the Governing Council decided that the interest rate for the ECB's main refinancing operations will, from next week on, be set at 2.5%. In addition, the interest rate on the marginal lending facility will be lowered to 3.5% and the interest rate on the deposit facility to 1.5% with effect from tomorrow.

Let me report in some more detail on the reasons for which the Governing Council, in the context of the ECB's monetary policy strategy, deemed it appropriate to lower interest rates.

As regards *monetary developments* in the euro area, the acceleration of monetary aggregates seen in January 1999 was partly reversed in February. The twelve-month growth rate of M3 declined from 5.6% in January to 5.2% in February. This largely reflected a slowdown in the high pace of growth of overnight deposits, presumably reflecting the unwinding of the influence of some special factors related to the start of Stage Three and the introduction of the euro. As the February figures were somewhat higher than those observed in late 1998, the three-month moving average of M3 growth covering the period from December 1998 to February 1999 still increased by 0.2 percentage point to 5.1%. The Governing Council does not regard current monetary trends as constituting a signal of future inflationary pressures, taking into account that the rate of growth of M3 is still close to the reference value of $4\frac{1}{2}\%$ and considering that it may to some extent mirror the specific environment related to the start of Stage Three.

The Governing Council noted that the Harmonised Index of Consumer Prices (HICP) rates of increase for the euro area have now been below 1% for several months, and even though some increases are likely to be seen in coming months owing to the reversal of energy price trends, the more lasting effect on the outlook for future prices comes from the economic environment. Indeed, reflecting the economic environment, many projections for future consumer price increases in the euro area have been revised downwards. In our current assessment of the situation, it appears unlikely that *HICP* increases will be out of line with the Eurosystem's definition of price stability.

With regard to *financial indicators*, both bond and foreign exchange markets were lately under the influence of global factors. After having risen somewhat in February 1999, in tandem with US bond yields, during March euro area government *bond yields* remained broadly unchanged. At the same time the US dollar strengthened further in recent weeks in the light of international developments.

When looking in some more detail at the evolution of the *world economy*, positive signs relate to the continuously strong growth of the US economy, the gradual recovery in some Asian countries and indications of a stabilisation in Latin America. However, there is no noticeable evidence as yet of a turnaround in Japan.

In the *euro area*, overall growth prospects worsened towards the end of last year, as reported when we met in early March. In the meantime, official data confirm that *real GDP growth* in the euro area weakened in the fourth quarter of 1998, when compared with the previous quarter. The weakness is particularly apparent in the *manufacturing sector,* where *confidence* deteriorated further. Partial information covering a substantial part of the euro area appears to confirm this picture. Most recent data on total *employment* in the euro area point to a certain deceleration in net job creation in the last quarter of 1998.

As regards the latest available data on the *HICP,* the annual increase in consumer prices has remained unchanged at 0.8% over several months up to February 1999. Underlying this stable rate of price increases have been offsetting developments at the level of services and goods prices. In February, services price increases moderated further slightly, mainly owing to downward adjustments in prices in the telecommunication area. At the same time, goods prices contributed slightly more to overall *HICP* increases than before, due both to price developments for unprocessed food and a deceleration in the fall in energy prices. It may be worth noting that goods prices may continue to move upwards temporarily, in particular as oil prices increased strongly from mid-February onwards. Such movements reflect the higher volatility of price changes of some categories of goods, in particular imported oil and other commodities.

The interest rate decision has been taken in a forward-looking perspective, focusing on the medium-term trends in inflation and the compatibility of these trends with the Eurosystem's definition of price stability. In the view of the Governing Council, monetary growth is – at the current juncture – not a risk for future price stability.

The decision taken today keeps monetary policy on a longer term stability oriented course and, by doing so, contributes to creating an economic environment in which the considerable growth potential of the euro area could be exploited. Those responsible for other policy areas are urged now even more to take the necessary steps to improve longer term growth prospects for the euro area through strictly and decisively adhering to the aims of the Stability and Growth Pact and through convincing structural reforms in the economy.

I should now like to inform you about some of the **other matters** considered today.

The Governing Council examined the outcome of a test run of the production of euro banknotes. This so-called zero production run involved the printing works of the participating countries. The main purposes of this test were, first, to check the compliance of the 'test banknotes' against the technical specifications and, second, to prove that all printing works are in a position to produce the euro banknotes to the same high quality standards. The result of this test was positive, as only some minor technical specifications need to be modified slightly. The printing works will now start their final preparations for the commencement of the mass production of the euro banknotes.

The Governing Council also decided to establish an Analysis Centre for Counterfeit Euro Banknotes. As is already indicated by its name, the main purpose of this Analysis Centre will be to technically analyse and classify new types of printed counterfeits, and to store the related technical data in a database. The Analysis Centre will be located at the ECB in Frankfurt.

ECB PRESS CONFERENCE
THURSDAY, 4 NOVEMBER 1999 – PRESIDENT'S INTRODUCTORY STATEMENT

Ladies and gentlemen,

The Vice-President and I are here to report on today's meeting of the Governing Council of the ECB.

The **outcome of today's meeting** was that the Governing Council has decided to increase the ECB interest rates. The forthcoming main re-financing operations of the Eurosystem will be conducted as fixed rate tenders at an interest rate of 3.0%, starting with the operation to be settled on 10 November 1999. This increase implies an upward adjustment of 50 basis points from the rate of 2.5% applied to previous such operations. In addition, the interest rate on the marginal lending facility will be increased from 3.5% to 4.0% and that on the deposit facility from 1.5% to 2.0%, both with effect from 5 November 1999.

Overall, on the basis of prospective developments, the Governing Council considers that today's decision will counter the upward trend of the balance of risks to price stability. This decision will therefore contribute to sustaining non-inflationary economic growth in the euro area over the medium term.

The main argument for raising the interest rates was the fact that since around the beginning of the summer the balance of risks to future price stability has gradually been moving towards the upside. In fact, the economic situation in spring 1999 had given rise to concern about downward risks and had led to a precautionary interest rate reduction by 50 basis points on 8 April 1999. However, the current economic environment is far more favourable. Moreover, several indicators, including monetary growth, suggest that there is ample liquidity in the euro area. Inflation rates are expected to increase gradually in the months ahead, mainly as a result of the increase in energy prices earlier this year working its way through to consumer prices. The latest data on industrial producer prices confirm this pattern. Over the medium term, however, it is important to prevent the availability of ample liquidity from translating into upward pressure on prices. In particular, an increase in interest rates now should help to counteract further liquidity growth over the medium term and contribute to maintaining inflation expectations safely below 2%.

With regard to the perception that an increase in interest rates now would endanger the resumption of economic growth, the Governing Council is of the opposite opinion. A timely rise in interest rates will avoid the need for a larger increase in interest rates later and, hence, will contribute to stronger growth over an extended period of time.

Concerning the size of an increase in interest rates, against the background of a fundamentally changed situation, the precautionary interest rate reduction made in April 1999 is no longer justified. Furthermore, today's move by 50 basis points appeared to be the best way in which to avoid uncertainties regarding the future course of monetary policy. In addition, such a move is expected to contribute to reducing any uncertainty premia potentially prevalent in financial markets and also to help to contain a possible increase in volatility in money markets towards the end of the year. Under these circumstances, the alternative of moving by less than 50 basis points now and examining the need for an additional step later on could potentially introduce unwarranted uncertainty for the period ahead.

Let me now provide you with more detailed information on **monetary, financial and other economic developments,** and thereby further explain the decisions taken today.

With regard to *monetary developments* in the euro area, the monetary data up to September 1999 reinforced the view that M3 growth is on a rising trend. The three-month average of the annual growth rates of M3, covering the period from July to September 1999, was 5.9%, which is almost $1\frac{1}{2}$ percentage points above the reference value of $4\frac{1}{2}$%. This deviation from the reference value has steadily increased during 1999. The strong growth of the most liquid components of M3 is particularly noteworthy, suggesting that the very low level of interest rates favoured the strong growth of monetary aggregates. The pick-up in economic activity is likely to have further stimulated M3 growth. Credit to the private sector also continued to expand rapidly in September 1999, at a rate in excess of 10%. The demand for loans remained strong throughout the first three quarters of 1999, supported in particular by the low level of bank lending rates and the ongoing economic recovery. Overall, these developments indicate a generous liquidity situation in the euro area.

Euro area *financial market developments* over the past few months confirm the general change in economic conditions and perspectives for the euro area by also anticipating an acceleration of economic growth. This is reflected in the rise in government bond yields and the associated pronounced steepening of the yield curve since spring 1999. Today's decision should contribute to firming financial market expectations of stronger growth without increasing inflationary pressures.

With regard to *economic activity* itself, current information indeed continues to support the view that there is an ongoing strengthening in the euro area. The outlook for the *world economy* remains positive; this mainly relates to the sustained growth of the US economy, but also to the apparent strengthening of the recoveries in South-East Asia and Japan. Most recent data releases for the *euro area* suggest an acceleration of real GDP growth rates in the second half of this year. This is indicated by confidence and survey data, as well as by production data for the industrial sector extending into the third quarter of the year. Therefore, the prospects for a continued improvement in output growth remain good.

Concerning *consumer prices,* in September 1999 the annual rate of change in the Harmonised Index of Consumer Prices (HICP) was 1.2%, that is to say unchanged from August 1999. On the one hand, upward pressures related to the surge in oil prices in recent months and to the rate of change in prices for seasonal food. On the other hand, in September the increases in both services prices and prices for non-energy industrial goods were more moderate than in August. Countervailing price movements of such a kind may possibly continue in the coming months, while expectations remain that there will be some overall upward movement in the HICP rate in the short term, which will mainly be linked to energy prices.

In **conclusion,** the downside risks to price stability have disappeared. Instead, monetary developments, together with the accumulating evidence of improved economic prospects, confirmed the view expressed earlier by the Governing Council that the balance of risks to future price stability has gradually moved towards the upside. This assessment argued in favour of adjusting the interest rates within the context of a monetary policy stance which is conducive to maintaining price stability over the medium term.

Containing inflationary expectations in a forward looking manner is decisive for ensuring sustainable growth in GDP and employment. This would be greatly facilitated if individual member countries were to make convincing progress in the structural reform of the labour and product markets, which, over the medium term, would enhance the euro area's production potential and thereby curb upward pressure on prices as the recovery proceeds. Together with fiscal consolidation in the context of the Stability and Growth Pact and the necessary moderate wage developments, such reforms could make a crucial contribution towards transforming the current cyclical upswing into a process of longer-term non-inflationary growth.

OTHER BUSINESS

In a press release dated 1 July 1999, the ECB indicated that an announcement would be made in November with regard to the decision on the public relations agency selected to prepare and execute a Europe-wide information campaign for the introduction of the euro banknotes and coins on 1 January 2002. In this regard, I am now pleased to announce that the Governing Council has decided to negotiate the contract with Publicis. Further information on this matter can be found in a separate press release which will be issued this afternoon.

Finally, I should like to draw your attention to the fact that the second meeting of the Governing Council to be held in December has been rescheduled. As announced yesterday, the meeting has been brought forward from Thursday, 16 December 1999, to Wednesday, 15 December 1999, in order to enable several Governing Council members to attend a first gathering of a new forum consisting of ministers of finance and central bank governors (the so-called 'G20'), which is to be held in Berlin on 16 December 1999.

ECB PRESS RELEASE

REVIEW OF THE QUANTITATIVE REFERENCE VALUE FOR MONETARY GROWTH – 2 DECEMBER 1999

At its meeting on 2 December 1999 the Governing Council decided to confirm the reference value for monetary growth, namely an annual growth rate of $4\frac{1}{2}\%$ for the broad aggregate M3. This decision was taken on the grounds that the components underlying the derivation of the first reference value in December 1998, namely the Eurosystem's definition of price stability and the assumptions for trend real GDP growth and the trend decline in M3 income velocity, have remained unchanged.

As before, the Governing Council will assess monetary developments in relation to the reference value on the basis of a three-month moving average of annual growth rates. The Governing Council has decided henceforth to review the reference value on a regular annual basis, with the next review to take place in December 2000.

Against this background, the Governing Council wishes to emphasise that the trend growth potential of the euro area could be considerably enhanced by structural reform in the labour and goods markets. The Eurosystem's monetary policy strategy would take such changes into account, as appropriate.

The derivation of the reference value of $4\frac{1}{2}\%$ is an expression of a medium-term oriented approach. The generous liquidity situation in 1999 will have to be borne in mind.

In the context of the review of the reference value, the Governing Council wishes to recall the following features of the reference value and its role in the monetary policy strategy of the Eurosystem:

1. Given the monetary origins of inflation over the longer term, the Governing Council assigns a prominent role to money. This is the 'first pillar' of the Eurosystem's stability oriented monetary policy strategy.

   To signal the prominent role of money to the public, in October 1998 the Governing Council decided to announce a quantitative reference value for the growth rate of a broad monetary aggregate. In December 1998 the Governing Council announced the first reference value of $4\frac{1}{2}\%$ annual growth for the monetary aggregate M3.

2. The first reference value was derived using the well-known relationship between monetary growth, on the one hand, and developments in prices, real GDP and the income velocity of circulation, on the other.

   The reference value was derived so as to be consistent with – and serve the achievement of – price stability. It was therefore based on the Eurosystem's definition of price stability. The Eurosystem defines price stability as a year-on-year increase in the Harmonised Index of Consumer Prices (HICP) for the euro area of below 2%. Price stability is to be maintained over the medium term.

   To be consistent with the medium-term orientation of the Eurosystem's monetary policy strategy, the reference value was derived using assumptions for the medium-term trend in real GDP and the evolution of M3 income velocity over the medium term. The assumptions were:
   a. real GDP grows at a trend rate of between 2% and $2\frac{1}{2}\%$ per annum over the medium term and
   b. M3 income velocity declines at a trend rate in the range from $\frac{1}{2}\%$ to 1% per annum over the medium term.

   Taking account of the definition of price stability and these two assumptions, the Governing Council decided in December 1998 to set the first reference value at $4\frac{1}{2}\%$.

At its meeting on 2 December 1999 the Governing Council reviewed these assumptions and confirmed that both of them remain valid. The Governing Council therefore saw no reason to change the reference value.

The Governing Council also took the opportunity of this review to re-emphasise that the concept of a reference value is embedded in a monetary policy strategy which is aimed at the maintenance of price stability. The strategy uses two pillars in order to assess the risks to future price stability. The reference value for monetary growth is an important part of the first pillar of the strategy, which assigns a prominent role to the analysis of monetary developments. The information revealed by this analysis has always to be seen in conjunction with the second pillar of the Eurosystem's monetary policy strategy, which includes a broadly based assessment of the outlook for price developments and the risks to price stability, using other available indicators. The reference value therefore does not entail a commitment on the part of the Eurosystem to correct mechanistically deviations of monetary growth from the reference value. Rather, monetary developments are thoroughly analysed in relation to the reference value in order to ascertain their implications for the outlook for price stability over the medium term.

If threats to price stability are identified by this analysis, monetary policy reacts in a manner appropriate to address these threats. Therefore, while substantial or prolonged deviations of monetary growth from the reference value would, under normal circumstances, signal risks to price stability, there is no automatic relationship between short run deviations of M3 growth from the reference value and monetary policy decisions.

The Governing Council will continue regularly and thoroughly to analyse monetary developments in relation to this reference value and will explain the implications of this analysis for monetary policy decisions to the public. Against this background, the confirmation of the reference value implies the continuation of the pursuit of the monetary policy strategy conducted in the past and does not imply any change to the Governing Council's assessment of the current monetary policy stance.

References

Akerlof, G., W. Dickens and G. Perry (1996), 'The macroeconomics of low inflation', *Brookings Papers on Economic Activity*, 1–59

Akerlof, G. A. and J. L. Yellen (1985), 'A near-rational model of the business cycle, with wage and price inertia', *Quarterly Journal of Economics* 100 (supplement), 823–38

Alesina, A. and R. Gatti (1995), 'Independent central banks: low inflation at no cost?', *American Economic Review* 85, 196–200

Alesina, A., N. Roubini and G. D. Cohen (1997), *Political cycles and the macroeconomy*, Cambridge, Mass.: Cambridge University Press

Alesina, A. and L. H. Summers (1993), 'Central bank independence and macroeconomic performance: some comparative evidence', *Journal of Money, Credit, and Banking* 25, 151–62

Andrés, J. and I. Hernando (1999), 'Does inflation harm economic growth? Evidence from the OECD', in Feldstein (1999), 315–41

Angeloni, I. (1999), 'Comments to: The role of a regional bank in a system of central banks', *Carnegie-Rochester Conference Series on Public Policy* 51, 73–77

Angeloni, I., V. Gaspar and O. Tristani (1999), 'The monetary policy strategy of the ECB', in D. Cobham and G. Zis (eds.), *From EMS to EMU*, London: Macmillan, 3–42

Angeloni, I. and A. Prati (1996), 'The identification of liquidity effects in the EMS: Italy 1991–1992', *Open Economies Review* 7, 275–93

Angeloni, I. and R. Rovelli (1998), eds., *Monetary policy and interest rates*, London: Macmillan

Angeloni, I., F. Smets and A. A. Weber (2000), eds., *Monetary policy-making under uncertainty*, Frankfurt: European Central Bank and Center for Financial Studies

Aspetsberger, A. (1996), 'Open market operations in EU Countries', EMI Staff Paper No. 3

Astin, J. (1999), 'The European Union Harmonised Indices of Consumer Prices (HICP)', *Statistical Journal of the United Nations*, ECE 16, 123–35

Astley, M. S. and T. Yates (1999), 'Inflation and real disequilibria', Bank of England Working Paper No. 103, December

Bade, R. and M. Parkin (1984), 'Is sterling M3 the right aggregate?', in B. Griffiths and G. E. Wood (eds.), *Monetarism in the United Kingdom*, New York: St. Martin's Press, 241–86

179

Bagehot, W. (1873), *Lombard street: a description of the money market*, London: P. S. King

Ball, L. (1999), 'Aggregate demand and long-run unemployment', *Brookings Papers on Economic Activity*, 189–236

Ball, L. and D. Romer (1990), 'Real rigidities and the nonneutrality of money', *Review of Economic Studies* 57, 183–203

Baltensperger, E. (2000), 'La Banque centrale européenne et sa politique monétaire', *Swiss National Bank Quarterly Bulletin* 1, 48–73

Barro, R. J. (1993), *Macroeconomics*, 4th edition, New York: Wiley

(1996), 'Inflation and growth', *Federal Reserve Bank of St. Louis Review* 78, 153–69

(1997), *Determinants of economic growth: a cross-country empirical study*, Lionel Robbins Lecture, Cambridge, Mass., and London: MIT Press

Barro, R. J. and D. B. Gordon (1983), 'Rules, discretion and reputation in a model of monetary policy', *Journal of Monetary Economics* 12, 101–21

Barro, R. and X. Sala-i-Martin (1995), *Economic growth*, London and Montreal: McGraw-Hill

Baxter, M. and R. G. King (1999), 'Measuring business cycles: approximate band-pass filters for economic time series', *Review of Economics and Statistics* 81, 575–93

Begg, D., C. Wyplosz, P. De Grauwe, F. Giavazzi and H. Uhlig (1999), *Monitoring the European Central Bank update: May 1999*, London: CEPR

Bekx, P. and G. Tullio (1989), 'A note on the European Monetary System, and the determination of the DM–dollar exchange rate', *Cahiers Economiques de Bruxelles*, 329–43

Benhabib, J., S. Schmitt-Grohé and M. Uribe (1999), 'The perils of Taylor rules', paper presented at the Conference on Expectations, Economic Theory and Economic Policy, Perugia, 23–26 September

Bernanke, B. S. and M. Gertler (1995), 'Inside the black box: the credit channel of monetary policy transmission', *Journal of Economic Perspectives* 9, 27–48

Bernanke, B. S., T. Laubach, F. Mishkin and A. Posen (1999), *Inflation targeting: lessons from the international experience*, Princeton: Princeton University Press

Bernanke, B. S. and I. Mihov (1997), 'What does the Bundesbank target?', *European Economic Review* 41, 1025–53

Bernanke, B. S. and F. Mishkin (1992), 'Central bank behavior and the strategy of monetary policy: observations from six industrialized countries', in O. J. Blanchard and S. Fischer (eds.), *NBER macroeconomics annual*, Cambridge, Mass., and London: MIT Press, 183–228

Bernanke, B. S. and M. Woodford (1997), 'Inflation forecasts and monetary policy', *Journal of Money, Credit and Banking* 29, 653–84

Bini Smaghi, L. and D. Gros (2000), *Open issues in European central banking*, London: Macmillan

BIS (1995), *Financial structure and the monetary policy transmission mechanism*, Basle, March

Blanchard, O. J. and S. Fischer (1989), *Lectures on macroeconomics*, Cambridge, Mass., and London: MIT Press

Blanchard, O. J. and N. Kyotaki (1987), 'Monopolistic competition and the effects of aggregate demand', *American Economic Review* 77, 647–66

Blanchard, O. J. and L. H. Summers (1986), 'Hysteresis and the European unemployment problem', in S. Fischer (ed.), *NBER macroeconomics annual*, Cambridge, Mass., and London: MIT Press, 15–78

Blinder, A. (1997a), 'What central bankers can learn from academia – and vice versa', *Journal of Economic Perspectives* 11, 3–19

(1997b), 'Commentary', *Federal Reserve Bank of St. Louis Review* 79, 157–60

(1998), *Central banking in theory and practice* (Lionel Robbins Lecture), Cambridge, Mass., and London: MIT Press

(1999), 'Central bank credibility: Why do we care? How do we build it?', NBER Working Paper No. 7161, June

(2000), 'Critical issues for modern major central bankers', in Angeloni, Smets and Weber (2000), 64–74

Boskin, M. (1996), *Toward a more accurate measure of the cost of living*, chairman's final report to the US Senate Finance Committee from the Advisory Commission to Study the Consumer Price Index

Brainard, W. (1967), 'Uncertainty and the effectiveness of policy', *American Economic Review* 57, 411–25

Brand, C. and N. Cassola (2000), 'A money demand system for euro area M3', ECB Working Paper No. 39, November

Briault, C. B., A. G. Haldane and M. King (1996), 'Independence and accountability', Bank of England Working Paper No. 49, April

Bronfenbrenner, M. (1961), 'Statistical tests of rival monetary rules', *Journal of Political Economy* 69, 1–14

Browne, F. X., G. Fagan and J. Henry (1997), 'Money demand in EU countries: a survey', Staff Paper No. 7, European Monetary Institute, Frankfurt am Main

Brunner, K. and A. H. Meltzer (1969), 'The nature of the policy problem', in K. Brunner (ed.), *Targets and indicators of monetary policy*, San Francisco: Chandler, 1–26

Bruno, M. (1995), *Inflation, growth and monetary control: non-linear lessons from crisis and recovery* (Banca d'Italia Paolo Baffi Lecture on Money and Finance), Rome: Edizioni dell'Elefante

Bruno, M. and W. Easterly (1998), 'Inflation crises and long-run growth', *Journal of Monetary Economics* 41, 3–26

Bryan, M. F. and S. G. Cecchetti (1993), 'The consumer price index as a measure of inflation', *Federal Reserve Bank of Cleveland Economic Review* 29, 15–24

(1994), 'Measuring core inflation', in N. G. Mankiw (ed.), *Monetary policy*, NBER Studies in Business Cycles 29, Chicago: University of Chicago Press, 195–215

Bryan, M. F. and C. J. Pike (1991), 'Median price changes: an alternative approach to measuring current monetary inflation', *Federal Reserve Bank of Cleveland Economic Commentary*, December

Bryant, R. C. (1991), 'Model representations of Japanese monetary policy', *Monetary and Economic Studies* 9, Bank of Japan, September, 11–61

Bryant, R. C., P. Hooper and C. L. Mann (1993), *Evaluating policy regimes: new research in empirical macroeconomics*, Washington, DC: The Brookings Institution

Buiter, W. H. (1999), 'Alice in Euroland', *Journal of Common Market Studies* 37, 181–209

Cabrero, A., J. L. Escrivá, E. Muñoz and J. Peñalosa (1998), 'The controllability of a monetary aggregate in the EMU', Banco de España, Servicio de Estudios, Working Paper No. 9817

Campillo, M. and J. A. Miron (1997), 'Why does inflation differ across countries?', in C. D. Romer and D. H. Romer (eds.), *Reducing inflation: motivation and strategy*, NBER Studies in Business Cycles 30, Chicago: University of Chicago Press, 335–57

Cecchetti, S. G. (1997), 'Measuring inflation for central bankers', *Federal Reserve Bank of St. Louis Review* 79, 143–55

Christiano, L. J., M. Eichenbaum and C. Evans (1997), 'Sticky price and limited participation models: a comparison', *European Economic Review* 41, 1201–49

(1999), 'Monetary policy shocks: what have we learned and to what end?', in J. Taylor and M. Woodford (eds.), *Handbook of macroeconomics*, vol. IA, Amsterdam: North-Holland, ch. 2

Clarida, R., J. Galí and M. Gertler (1998), 'Monetary policy rules in practice: some international evidence', *European Economic Review* 42, 1033–68

(1999) 'The science of monetary policy: a new Keynesian perspective', *Journal of Economic Literature* 37, 1661–707

(2000), 'Monetary policy rules', *Quarterly Journal of Economics* 115, 147–80

Coenen, G. and J. L. Vega (1999), 'Money demand relationships for the euro area', ECB Working Paper No. 6, September

Coenen, G. and V. Wieland (2000), 'A small estimated euro area model with rational expectations and nominal rigidities', ECB Working Paper No. 30, September

Commission of the European Communities (1998), 'On harmonisation of consumer price indices in the European Union', Report to Council, Brussels

Cooley, T. F. and G. D. Hansen (1995), 'Money and the business cycle', in T. F. Cooley (ed.), *Frontiers of business cycle research*, Princeton: Princeton University Press, 175–216

Corretja, I. and P. Teles (1996), 'Is the Friedman rule optimal when money is an intermediate good?', *Journal of Monetary Economics* 38, 223–44

Corsetti, G. and P. Pesenti (1999), 'Stability, asymmetry and discontinuity: the launch of European Monetary Union', *Brookings Papers on Economic Activity*, 295–358

Craine, R. (1979), 'Optimal monetary policy with uncertainty', *Journal of Economic Dynamics and Control* 1, 59–83

Cukierman, A. (1992), *Central bank strategy, credibility and independence: theory and evidence*, Cambridge, Mass., and London: MIT Press

Cukierman, A. and A. H. Meltzer (1986), 'A theory of ambiguity, credibility, and inflation under discretion and asymmetric information', *Econometrica* 54, 1099–128

Debelle, G. and S. Fisher (1994), 'How independent should a central bank be?', in J. C. Fuhrer (ed.), *Guidelines, and constraints facing monetary policymakers,* Conference Series No. 38, Boston: Federal Reserve Bank of Boston, 195–221

De Fiore, F. (2000), 'Can indeterminacy explain the short-run non-neutrality of money?', ECB Working Paper No. 32, September

De Fiore, F. and P. Teles (1999), 'The optimal mix of taxes on money, consumption and income', Banco de Portugal Working Paper No. 2

Diewert, W. E. (1999), 'The consumer price index and index number purpose', Department of Economics of the University of British Columbia Discussion Paper No. 00–02

Dixit, A. and J. Stiglitz (1977), 'Monopolistic competition and optimum product diversity', *American Economic Review* 67, 297–308

Durlauf, S. N. and D. Quah (1999), 'The new empirics of economic growth', in J. Taylor and M. Woodford (eds.), *Handbook of macroeconomics,* vol. IA, Amsterdam: North-Holland, ch. 4

Dwyer, G. P. and R. W. Hafer (1988), 'Is money irrelevant?', *Federal Reserve Bank of St. Louis Review* 70, 3–17

ECB (1999a), 'The stability-oriented monetary policy strategy of the Eurosystem', *Monthly Bulletin,* January, 39–50

(1999b), 'Euro area monetary aggregates and their role in the Eurosystem's monetary policy strategy', *Monthly Bulletin,* February, 29–46

(2000a), 'Monetary policy transmission in the euro area', *Monthly Bulletin,* July, 43–58

(2000b), 'Price and cost indicators for the euro area: an overview', *Monthly Bulletin,* August, 33–49

(2000c), 'The two pillars of the ECB's monetary policy strategy', *Monthly Bulletin,* November, 37–48

(2000d), 'The single monetary policy in Stage Three: general documentation on Eurosystem monetary policy instruments and procedures', November

Ehrmann, M. and F. Smets (2000), 'Uncertainty about potential output and monetary policy', paper presented at the Conference on Monetary Policy Challenges in the 21st Century – A Transatlantic Perspective, Washington, DC, 27–28 October

Eijffinger, S. C. W. and J. De Haan (1996), *The political economy of central bank independence,* Special Papers in International Economics No. 19, Princeton: Princeton University Press

Eijffinger, S. C. W. and E. Schaling (1993), 'Central bank independence: theory and evidence', CentER Discussion Paper No. 9325, Tilburg University, April

Einaudi, L. (1953), 'The theory of imaginary money from Charlemagne to the French Revolution', in F. C. Lane and J. C. Riemersma (eds.), *Enterprise and secular change,* Homewood, Ill. Irwin, 229–261

EMI (1997a), 'The single monetary policy in Stage Three: specification of the operational framework', available on the Internet: http://www.ecb.int, January

(1997b), 'The single monetary policy in Stage Three: elements of the monetary policy strategy of the ESCB', available on the Internet: http://www.ecb.int, February

(1997c), 'The single monetary policy in Stage Three: general documentation on ESCB monetary policy instruments and procedures', available on the Internet: http://www.ecb.int, September

EMU Monitor (1999), Press Statement No. 4, 24 November, ZEI

Engert, W. and J. Selody (1998), 'Uncertainty and multiple paradigms of the transmission mechanism', Bank of Canada Working Paper No. 98–7, April

Erceg C. J., D. W. Henderson and A. T. Levin (2000), 'Optimal monetary policy with staggered wage and price contracts', *Journal of Monetary Economics* 46, 281–313

Ericsson, N. R. (1999), 'Empirical modelling of money demand', in H. Lütkepohl and J. Wolters (eds.), *Money demand in Europe*, Heidelberg: Physica-Verlag, 29–49

Escrivá, J. L. and G. Fagan (1996), 'Empirical assessment of monetary policy instruments and procedures in EU countries', EMI Staff Paper No. 2

Estrella A. and F. S. Mishkin (1997) 'Is there a role for monetary aggregates in the conduct of monetary policy?', *Journal of Monetary Economics* 40, 279–304

Fagan, G. and J. Henry (1998), 'Long run money demand in the EU: evidence for area-wide aggregates', *Empirical Economics* 23, 483–506

Fagan, G., J. Henry and R. Mestre (2001), 'An area-wide model (AWM) for the euro area', ECB Working Paper No. 42, January

Federal Reserve Bank of Kansans City (1996), 'Achieving price stability', Jackson Hole symposium, Wyoming, 29–31 August

(1999), 'New challenges for monetary policy', Jackson Hole symposium, Wyoming, 26–28, August

Feldstein, M. (1997), 'The costs and benefits of going from low inflation to price stability', in C. Romer and D. Romer (eds.), *Reducing inflation: motivation and strategy*, NBER Studies in Business Cycles 30, Chicago: University of Chicago Press, 123–56

(1999), ed., *The costs and benefits of price stability*, Chicago: University of Chicago Press

Feldstein, M. and J. H. Stock (1994), 'The use of a monetary aggregate to target nominal GDP', in N. G. Mankiw (ed.), *Monetary policy*, NBER Studies in Business Cycles 29, Chicago and London: University of Chicago Press, 7–62

Fischer, S. (1977), 'Long-term contracts, rational expectations, and the optimal money supply rule', *Journal of Political Economy* 85, 191–205

(1981), 'Towards an understanding of the costs of inflation: II', *Carnegie-Rochester Conference Series on Public Policy* 15, 5–41

(1990), 'Rules versus discretion in monetary policy', in B. M. Friedman and F. H. Hahn (eds.), *Handbook of monetary economics*, vol. II, Amsterdam: North-Holland, ch. 21

(1993), 'The role of macroeconomic factors in growth', *Journal of Monetary Economics*, 32, 485–512

(1995), 'Modern central banking', in F. Capie, C. Goodhart, N. Schnadt and

S. Fischer (eds.), *The future of central banking: the tercentenary symposium of the Bank of England*, Cambridge: Cambridge University Press, 262–308 (1996), 'Why are central banks pursuing long-run price stability?', Federal Reserve Bank of Kansas City, Jackson Hole symposium, Wyoming, 29–31 August

Fischer, S. and F. Modigliani (1978), 'Towards an understanding of the real effects and costs of inflation', *Weltwirtschaftliches Archiv* 114, 810–33

Fisher, I. (1920), *Stabilising the dollar*, New York: Macmillan
(1926), *The purchasing power of money*, 2nd edn, New York: Macmillan
(1930), *The theory of interest*, New York: Macmillan

Fisher, M. E. and J. J. Seater (1993), 'Long-run neutrality and superneutrality in an ARIMA framework', *American Economic Review* 83, 402–15

Friedman, B. M. (1975), 'Targets, instruments, and indicators of monetary policy', *Journal of Monetary Economics* 1, 443–73
(1990), 'Targets and instruments of monetary policy', in B. M. Friedman and F. H. Hahn (eds.), *Handbook of monetary economics*, vol. II, Amsterdam: North-Holland, ch. 22
(1996), 'The rise and fall of money growth targets as guidelines for US monetary policy', NBER Working Paper No. 5465

Friedman, M. (1956), 'The quantity theory of money, a restatement', in M. Friedman (ed.), *Studies in the quantity theory of money*, Chicago: University of Chicago Press
(1959), *A program for monetary stability*, New York: Fordham University Press
(1963), *Inflation: causes and consequences*, New York: Asia Publishing House
(1968), 'The role of monetary policy', reprinted in *The optimum quantity of money and other essays*, Chicago: Aldine

Friedman, M. and A. J. Schwartz (1963), *A monetary history of the United States 1867–1960*, Princeton: Princeton University Press

Fuhrer, J. C. (1996), 'Monetary policy shifts and long-term interest rates', *Quarterly Journal of Economics* 111, 1183–209
(1997), 'Towards a compact, empirically-verified rational expectations model for monetary policy analysis', *Carnegie-Rochester Conference Series on Public Policy* 47, 197–230

Fuhrer, J. and B. Madigan (1997), 'Monetary policy when interest rates are bounded at zero', *Review of Economics and Statistics* 79, 573–85

Fuhrer, J. C. and G. R. Moore (1995), 'Inflation persistence', *Quarterly Journal of Economics* 110, 127–59

Galí, J. (1992), 'How well does the IS-LM model fit postwar US data?', *Quarterly Journal of Economics* 107, 709–38

Galí, J. and M. Gertler (1999), 'Inflation dynamics: a structural econometric analysis', *Journal of Monetary Economics* 44, 195–222

Galí, J., M. Gertler and J. D. López-Salido (2000), 'European inflation dynamics', paper presented at the International Seminar in Macroeconomics, Helsinki, 16–17 June

Gaspar, V. (2000), 'The role of monetary policy under low inflation', panel discussion at the Ninth International Conference organised by the Bank of Japan on The Role of Monetary Policy under Low Inflation: Deflationary

Shocks and Policy Responses, http://www.imes.boj.or.jp/english/publication/confsppa.html

Gaspar, V. and F. Smets (2000), 'Price level stability: some issues', *National Institute Economic Review* 174, 68–79

Gerlach, S. and F. Smets (1995), 'The monetary transmission mechanism: evidence from the G-7 countries', CEPR Discussion Paper No. 1219, July

(1999), 'Output gaps and monetary policy in the EMU area', *European Economic Review* 43, 801–12

Gerlach, S. and L. E. O. Svensson (2000), 'Inflation and money in the euro area: a case for monetary indicators?', NBER Working Paper No. 8025

Geweke, J. F. (1986), 'The superneutrality of money in the United States: an interpretation of the evidence', *Econometrica* 54, 1–21

Goldfeld, S. M. (1973), 'The demand for money revisited', *Brookings Papers on Economic Activity*, 577–638

(1976), 'The case of missing money', *Brookings Papers on Economic Activity*, 683–730

Goldfeld, S. M. and D. E. Sichel (1990), 'The demand for money', in B. M. Friedman and F. H. Hahn (eds), *Handbook of monetary economics,* vol. 1, Amsterdam: North-Holland, 299–356

Goodfriend, M. (1986), 'Monetary mystique: secrecy and central banking,' *Journal of Monetary Economics* 17, 63–92

(1999), 'The role of a regional bank in a system of central banks,' *Carnegie-Rochester Conference Series on Public Policy* 51, 51–71

Goodfriend, M. and R. G. King (1997), 'The new neoclassical synthesis and the role of monetary policy', in B. S. Bernanke and J. J. Rotenberg (eds.), *NBER macroeconomics annual,* Cambridge, Mass., and London: MIT Press, 231–83

Goodhart, C. E. A. (1994), 'What should central banks do? What should be their macroeconomic objectives and operations?', *Economic Journal* 104: 1424–36

Greenspan, A. (1989), 'Statement before the Committee on Finance', US Senate, 26 January

Gros, D., O. Davanne, M. Emerson, T. Mayer, G. Tabellini and N. Thygesen (2000), *Quo vadis euro? The cost of muddling through,* second report of the CEPS Macroeconomic Policy Group, Brussels: CEPS

Hall, R. E. and N. G. Mankiw (1994), 'Nominal income targeting', in N. G. Mankiw (ed.), *Monetary policy,* NBER studies in business cycles 29, Chicago and London: University of Chicago Press, 71–93

Hallman, J. J., R. D. Porter and D. H. Small (1991), 'Is the price level tied to the M2 monetary aggregate in the long run?', *American Economic Review* 81, 841–58

Hicks, J. (1937) 'Mr Keynes and the classics, a suggested interpretation', *Econometrica* 5, 147–59

Hoffman, J. (1998), 'Problems of inflation measurement in Germany', Economic Research Group of the Deutsche Bundesbank Discussion Paper 1/98

Hume, D. (1752a), *Of money,* reprinted in *Writings on economics,* edited by E. Rotwein, Madison, University of Wisconsin Press, 1970

(1752b), *Of interest,* reprinted in *Writings on economics,* edited by E. Rotwein, Madison, University of Wisconsin Press, 1970

Issing, O. (1997), 'Monetary targeting in Germany: the stability of monetary policy and of the monetary system', *Journal of Monetary Economics* 39, 67–79

(1999a), 'The euro – four weeks after the start', speech delivered to the European-Atlantic Group, House of Commons, London, 28 January

(1999b), 'The Eurosystem: transparent and accountable or "Willem in Euroland"?', *Journal of Common Market Studies* 37, 503–19

(1999c), 'The ECB and its watchers', speech delivered at the ECB Watchers Conference, Frankfurt am Main, 17 June

(2000a), 'Monetary policy in a new environment', speech delivered at the Bundesbank–BIS Conference on Recent Developments in Financial Systems and Their Challenges for Economic Policy: A European Perspective', Frankfurt am Main, 29 September, available on the Internet: http://www.ecb.int

(2000b), 'Why price stability?', paper presented at the first ECB Central Banking Conference, Frankfurt am Main, 2–3 November

Issing, O. and I. Angeloni (1999), 'The ECB is transparent and accountable', *Wall Street Journal*, 20 October

Kalchbrenner, J. H. and P. A. Tinsley (1976), 'On the use of feedback control in the design of aggregate monetary policy', *American Economic Review* 66, 349–55

Kareken, J. H., T. Muench and N. Wallace (1973), 'Optimal open market strategy: the use of information variables', *American Economic Review* 63, 156–72

Kashyap, A. K. and J. C. Stein (1994), 'Monetary policy and bank lending', in N. G. Mankiw (ed.), *Monetary policy*, NBER Studies in Business Cycles 29, Chicago and London: University of Chicago Press, 221–56

Keynes, J. M. (1919), *The economic consequences of peace*, reproduced in *Essays in persuasion*, London: Macmillan, 1931

Khan, A., R. G. King and A. L. Wolman (2000), 'Optimal monetary policy', paper presented at the Banco de Portugal Conference on Monetary Economics, Oporto, 12–14 June

Kim, S. (1999), 'Do monetary policy shocks matter in the G-7 countries? Using common identifying assumptions about monetary policy across countries', *Journal of International Economics* 48, 387–412

King, M. (1997), 'Changes in UK monetary policy: rules and discretion in practice', *Journal of Monetary Economics* 39, 81–97

King, R. G. and C. I. Plosser (1984), 'Money, credit and prices in a real business cycle economy', *American Economic Review* 74, 363–80

King, R. G. and M. W. Watson (1994), 'The post-war US Phillips curve: a revisionist econometric history', *Carnegie-Rochester Conference Series on Public Policy* 41, 157–219

(1996), 'Money, prices, interest rates and the business cycle', *Review of Economics and Statistics* 78, 35–53

(1997), 'Testing long-run neutrality', *Federal Reserve Bank of Richmond Economic Quarterly* 83, 69–101

Kohn, D. (1989), 'Policy targets and operating procedures in the 1990s', in Federal Reserve Bank of Kansas City, *Monetary policy issues in the 1990s*, proceedings of the Jackson Hole symposium, 129–41

Konieczny, J. D. (1994), 'The optimal rate of inflation: competing theories and their relevance to Canada', in Bank of Canada (ed.), *Economic behaviour and policy choice under price stability*, Ottawa: Author, 1–40

Kormendi, R. C. and P. G. Meguire (1985), 'Macroeconomic determinants of growth: cross-country evidence', *Journal of Monetary Economics* 16, 141–63

Kremers, J. J. M. and T. D. Lane (1990), 'Economic and monetary integration and the aggregate demand for money in the EMS', *IMF Staff Papers* 37, 777–805

Kreps, D. M. and R. Wilson (1982), 'Reputation and imperfect information', *Journal of Economic Theory* 27, 253–79

Kydland, F. E. and E. C. Prescott (1977), 'Rules rather than discretion: the inconsistency of optimal plans', *Journal of Political Economy* 85, 473–91

Le Blanc, F. (1690), *Traité Historique des Monnaies de France*, Paris

Leeper, E., C. A. Sims and T. Zha (1996), 'What does monetary policy do?', *Brookings Papers on Economic Activity*, 1–63

Leiderman, L. and L. E. O. Svensson (1995), *Inflation targets*, London: CEPR

Levin, A., V. Wieland and J. C. Williams (1999), 'The performance of forecast-based monetary policy rules under model uncertainty', paper presented at the joint ECB/CFS Conference on Monetary Policy-Making under Uncertainty, Frankfurt, 3–4 December

Levine, R. and D. Renelt (1992), 'A sensitivity analysis of cross-country growth regressions', *American Economic Review* 82, 942–63

Lockwood, B., M. Miller and L. Zhang (1998), 'Delegating monetary policy when unemployment persists', *Economica* 65, 327–45

Lothian, J. R. (1985), 'Equilibrium relationships between money and other economic variables', *American Economic Review* 75, 828–35

Lucas, R. E. (1972), 'Expectations and the neutrality of money', *Journal of Economic Theory* 4, 103–24

(1973), 'Some international evidence on output–inflation tradeoffs', *American Economic Review* 63, 326–34

(1976), 'Econometric policy evaluation: a critique', *Carnegie-Rochester Conference Series on Public Policy* 1, 19–46

(1980), 'Two illustrations of the quantity theory of money', *American Economic Review* 70, 1005–14

(1987), *Models of business cycles* (Yrjo Jahsson Lectures), Oxford: Basil Blackwell

(1990), 'Liquidity and interest rates', *Journal of Economic Theory* 50, 237–64

(1996), 'Nobel lecture: monetary neutrality', *Journal of Political Economy* 104, 661–82

Mankiw, N. G. (1985), 'Small menu costs and large business cycles: a macroeconomic model of monopoly', *Quarterly Journal of Economics* 100, 529–39

McCallum, B. T. (1984), 'Monetarist rules in the light of recent experience', *American Economic Review Papers and Proceedings* 74, 388–91

(1988), 'Robustness properties of a rule for monetary policy', *Carnegie-Rochester Conference Series on Public Policy* 29, 173–204

(1990), 'Inflation: theory and evidence', in B. M. Friedman and F. H. Hahn (eds.), *Handbook of monetary economics*, vol. II, Amsterdam: North-Holland, 963–1012

(1995), 'Two fallacies concerning central bank independence', *American Economic Review Papers and Proceedings* 85, 207–11

(1996), 'Inflation targeting in Canada, New Zealand, Sweden, the United Kingdom, and in general', NBER Working Paper No. 5579

(1997), 'Crucial issues concerning central bank independence', *Journal of Monetary Economics* 39, 99–112

(1999), 'Issues in the design of monetary policy rules', in J. Taylor and M. Woodford (eds.), *Handbook of macroeconomics*, vol. IC, Amsterdam: North Holland, ch. 23

McCandless, G. T. and W. E. Weber (1995), 'Some monetary facts', *Federal Reserve Bank of Minneapolis Quarterly Review* 19, 2–11

McKinnon, R. I. (1982), 'Currency substitution and instability in the world dollar standard', *American Economic Review* 72, 320–33

Meltzer, A. H. (1984), 'Overview', in Federal Reserve Bank of Kansas City, *Price Stability and Public Policy*, proceedings of the Jackson Hole symposium, 209–22

(1986), 'Limits of short-run stabilisation policy', *Economic Inquiry* 25, 1–14

(1995), 'Monetary, credit and (other) transmission processes: a monetarist perspective', *Journal of Economic Perspectives* 9, 49–72

(1999), 'The transmission process', mimeo, Carnegie Mellon University

Modigliani, F. (1944), 'Liquidity preference and the theory of interest and money', *Econometrica* 12, 45–88

Monticelli, C. (1993), 'All the money in Europe? An investigation of the economic properties of EC-wide extended monetary aggregates', BIS Working Paper No. 19, October

Monticelli, C. and L. Papi (1996), *European integration, monetary co-ordination, and the demand for money*, Oxford: Clarendon Press

Monticelli, C. and M.-O. Strauss-Kahn (1992), 'European integration and the demand for broad money', BIS Working Paper No. 18, April

Monticelli, C. and O. Tristani (1999), 'What does the single monetary policy do? A SVAR benchmark for the European Central Bank', ECB Working Paper No. 2, May

Nelson, E. (2000), 'Direct effects of base money on aggregate demand: theory and evidence', Bank of England Working Paper No. 122, October

Neumann, M. J. M. (1998), 'On the choice of a strategy for the European Central Bank's monetary policy', http://www.zei.de

Obstfeld, M. and K. Rogoff (1995), 'Exchange rate dynamics redux', *Journal of Political Economy* 103, 624–60

OECD (1999), *EMU: facts, challenges and policies*, Paris: OECD

Okun, A. M. (1981), *Prices and quantities: a macroeconomic analysis*, Oxford: Basil Blackwell

Orphanides, A. (2000), 'The quest for prosperity without inflation', ECB Working Paper No. 15, March

Orphanides, A. and R. M. Solow (1990), 'Money, inflation and growth', in B. M. Friedman and F. H. Hahn (eds.), *Handbook of monetary economics*, vol. I, Amsterdam: North-Holland, 223–61

Orphanides, A. and V. Wieland (1998), 'Price stability and monetary policy effectiveness when nominal interest rates are bound at zero', Finance and Economics Discussion Series Papers No. 1998-35, Federal Reserve Board

(1999), 'Inflation zone targeting', ECB Working Paper No. 8, October

Osborne, D. K. (1984), 'Ten approaches to the definition of money', *Federal Reserve Bank of Dallas Economic Review*, March, 1–23

Padoa-Schioppa, T. (1987), *Efficiency, stability and equity*, Oxford: Oxford University Press

(2000), 'An institutional glossary of the Eurosystem', speech delivered at the Conference on The Constitution of the Eurosystem: the Views of the EP and the ECB, 8 March

Patinkin, D. (1965), *Money, interest and prices*, 2nd edn, New York: Harper & Row

Peersman, G. and F. Smets (2000), 'The monetary transmission mechanism in the euro area: more evidence from VAR analysis', mimeo, European Central Bank

Pérez-Quirós, G. and H. Rodríguez-Mendizábal (2000), 'The daily market for funds in Europe: has something changed with the EMU?', paper presented at the conference The Operational Framework of the Eurosystem and Financial Markets, Frankfurt am Main, 5–6 May

Persson, T. and G. Tabellini (1993), 'Designing institutions for monetary stability', *Carnegie-Rochester Conference Series on Public Policy* 39, 53–84

(1999), 'Political economics and macroeconomic policy', in J. Taylor and M. Woodford (eds.), *Handbook of macroeconomics*, vol. IC, Amsterdam: North Holland, ch. 22

Pesaran, M. H., R. G. Pierse and M. S. Kumar (1989), 'Econometric analysis of aggregation in the context of linear prediction models', *Econometrica* 57, 861–88

Phillips, A. W. (1957), 'Stabilisation policy and the time-forms of lagged responses', *Economic Journal* 67, 265–77

Pollard, P. (1993), 'Central bank independence and economic performance', *Federal Reserve Bank of St. Louis Review* 75, 21–36

Posen, A. S. (1993), 'Why central bank independence does not cause low inflation: there is no institutional fix for politics', in R. O'Brien (ed.), *Finance and the international economy*, vol. VII, Oxford and New York: Oxford University Press, 41–54

Quah, D. and S. P. Vahey (1995), 'Measuring core inflation', *Economic Journal* 105, 1130–44

Rich, G. (1997), 'Monetary targets as a policy rule: lessons from the Swiss experience', *Journal of Monetary Economics* 39, 113–41

Roberts, J. M. (1997), 'Is inflation sticky?', *Journal of Monetary Economics* 39, 173–96

Rogoff, K. (1985), 'The optimal degree of commitment to an intermediate monetary target', *Quarterly Journal of Economics* 100, 1169–90

Rolnick, A. J. and W. I. Weber (1997), 'Money, inflation, and output under fiat and commodity standards', *Journal of Political Economy* 105, 1308–21

Romer, C. D. and D. Romer (1989), 'Does monetary policy matter? A new test in the spirit of Friedman and Schwartz', in O. J. Blanchard and S. Fischer (eds.),

NBER macroeconomics annual, Cambridge, Mass., and London: MIT Press, 121–70

(1996), 'Institutions for monetary stability', NBER Working Paper No. 5557

Romer, D. (1996), *Advanced macroeconomics*, New York: McGraw-Hill

Rotemberg, J. J. and M. Woodford (1999), 'Interest rate rules in an estimated sticky-price model', in J. Taylor (ed.), *Monetary policy rules*, Chicago: University of Chicago Press

Rudebusch, G. D. and L. E. O. Svensson (1998), 'Policy rules for inflation targeting', in J. Taylor (ed.), *Monetary policy rules*, Chicago: University of Chicago Press

Samuelson, P. (1965), *Foundations of economic analysis*, New York: Atheneum

Sargent, T. J. and N. Wallace (1975), 'Rational expectations, the optimal monetary instrument and the optimal money supply rule', *Journal of Political Economy* 83, 241–54

Schlesinger, H. (1988), 'Das Konzept der Deutschen Bundesbank', in W. Ehrlicher and D. B. Simmert (eds.), *Wandlungen des geldpolitischen Instrumentariums der Deutschen Bundesbank*, Berlin: Duncker and Humblodt

Schwartz, A. J. (1973), 'Secular price change in historical perspective', *Journal of Money, Credit and Banking* 5, 243–69

Serletis, A. and Z. Koustas (1998), 'International evidence on the neutrality of money', *Journal of Money, Credit and Banking* 30, 1–25

Serletis, A. and D. Krause (1996), 'Empirical evidence on the long-run neutrality hypothesis using low-frequency international data', *Economics Letters* 50, 323–27

Shiller, R. J. (1990), 'The term structure of interest rates', in B. M. Friedman and F. H. Hahn (eds.), *Handbook of monetary economics*, vol. I, Amsterdam: North-Holland, ch. 13

Sidrausky, M. (1967), 'Rational choice and patterns of growth in a monetary economy', *American Economic Review Papers and Proceedings* 57, 534–44

Simons, H. C. (1936), 'Rules versus authority in monetary policy', *Journal of Political Economy* 44, 1–30

Smets, F. (1995), 'Central banks' macroeconometric models and the monetary policy transmission mechanism', in BIS (1995), 225–66

(1998), 'Output gap uncertainty: does it matter for the Taylor rule?', paper presented at the Reserve Bank of New Zealand workshop on Monetary Policy under Uncertainty, 29–30 June

(2000), 'What horizon for price stability?', ECB Working Paper No. 24, July

Smets, F. and K. Tsatsaronis (1997), 'Why does the yield curve predict economic activity? Dissecting the evidence for Germany and the United States', BIS Working Paper No. 49, September

Söderström, U. (2000), 'Monetary policy with uncertain parameters', ECB Working Paper No. 13, February

Stock, J. H. and M. W. Watson (1999), 'Forecasting inflation', *Journal of Monetary Economics* 44, 293–335

Svensson, L. E. O. (1997a), 'Optimal inflation targets, "conservative" central banks, and linear inflation contracts', *American Economic Review* 87, 98–114

(1997b), 'Inflation forecast targeting: implementing and monitoring inflation targets', *European Economic Review* 41, 1111–46

(1999a), 'Inflation targeting as a monetary policy rule', *Journal of Monetary Economics* 43, 607–54

(1999b), 'Monetary policy issues for the Eurosystem', *Carnegie-Rochester Conference Series on Public Policy* 51, 79–136

(1999c), 'Price level targeting vs. inflation targeting: a free lunch?' *Journal of Money, Credit and Banking* 31, 277–95

Svensson, L. E. O. and M. Woodford (2000), 'Indicator variables for optimal policy', ECB Working Paper No. 12, February

Taylor, J. (1979), 'Staggered wage setting in a macro model', *American Economic Review* 69, 108–13

(1993a), *Macroeconomic policy in a world economy: from econometric design to practical operation*, New York: W. W. Norton

(1993b), 'Discretion versus policy rules in practice', *Carnegie-Rochester Conference Series on Public Policy* 29, 173–204

(1996), 'How should monetary policy respond to shocks while maintaining long-run price stability? – Conceptual issues', in Federal Reserve Bank of Kansas City, Jackson Hole symposium, Wyoming, 24-31 August

(1999), 'Staggered price and wage setting in macroeconomics', in J. Taylor and M. Woodford (eds.), *Handbook of macroeconomics*, vol. IB, Amsterdam: North-Holland, ch. 15

Tobin, J. (1970), 'Money and income: *post hoc ergo propter hoc?*', *Quarterly Journal of Economics* 84, 301–17

Trecroci, C. and J.-L. Vega (2000), 'The information content of M3 for future inflation', ECB Working Paper No. 33, October

Vestin, D. (2000), 'Price-level targeting versus inflation targeting in a forward-looking model', Sveriges Riksbank Working Paper No. 106, May

Vickers, J. (1998) 'Inflation targeting in practice: the UK experience', speech delivered at the Conference on Implementation of Price Stability, Frankfurt, 11-12 September, reprinted in *Bank of England Quarterly Bulletin* 38(4), 368–75

(1999), 'Economic models and monetary policy', speech delivered to the Governors of the National Institute of Economic and Social Research, London, 18 March

Vickrey, W. S. (1954), 'Stability through inflation', reprinted in K. Kurihara (ed.), *Post Keynesian Economics*, New Brunswick, Rutgers University Press, 1981, 89–122

Viñals, J. and J. Vallés (1999), 'On the real effects of monetary policy: a central banker's view', CEPR Working Paper No. 2241, September

Vlaar, P. J. G. and H. Schuberth (1999), 'Monetary transmission mechanism and controllability of money in Europe: a structural vector error correction approach', De Nederlandsche Bank, DNB Staff Reports No. 36

Vogel, R. C. (1974), 'The dynamics of inflation in Latin America, 1950–1969', *American Economic Review* 64, 102–14

Von Hagen, J. (1995), 'Inflation and monetary targeting in Germany', in Leiderman and Svensson (1995), 107–21

Waller, C. J. (1989), 'Monetary policy games and central bank politics', *Journal of Money, Credit and Banking* 21, 422–31

(1992), 'A bargaining model of partisan appointments to the central bank', *Journal of Monetary Economics* 29, 411–28

Waller, C. J. and C. E. Walsh (1995), 'Central bank independence, economic behavior, and optimal term lengths', *American Economic Review* 86, 1139–53

Walsh, C. (1995), 'Optimal contracts for independent central bankers', *American Economic Review* 85, 150–67

(1998), *Monetary theory and policy*, Cambridge, Mass., and London: MIT Press

Weber, A. A. (1994), 'Testing long-run neutrality: empirical evidence for G7 countries with special emphasis on Germany', *Carnegie-Rochester Conference Series on Public Policy* 41, 67–117

Wicksell, K. (1907), 'The influence of the rate of interest on prices', *Economic Journal* 17, 213–20

(1935), *Lectures on political economy*, London: Routledge and Kegan Paul

Wieland, V. (1998), 'Monetary policy and uncertainty about the natural unemployment rate', Board of Governors of the Federal Reserve System, April

(2000), 'Learning by doing and the value of optimal experimentation', *Journal of Economics Dynamics and Control* 24, 501–34

Winkler, B. (1999), 'Which kind of transparency? On the need for clarity in monetary policy-making', paper presented at the joint ECB/CFS Conference on Monetary Policy-Making under Uncertainty, Frankfurt, 3 December

Wolman, A. L. (1997), 'Zero inflation and the Friedman rule: a welfare comparison', *Federal Reserve Bank of Richmond Economic Quarterly* 83(4), 1–21

Woodford, M. (1994), 'Non standard indicators of monetary policy: can their usefulness be judged from forecasting regressions?', in G. Mankiw (ed.), *Monetary Policy*, NBER Studies in Business Cycles 29, Chicago: University of Chicago Press

(1999a), 'Inflation stabilisation and welfare', mimeo, Princeton University, June

(1999b), 'Optimal monetary policy inertia', NBER Working Paper No. 7261, August

(1999c), 'Commentary: how should monetary policy be conducted in an era of price stability?', in Federal Reserve Bank of Kansas City, Jackson Hole symposium, Wyoming, 26–28 August

Wynne, M. (1999), 'Core inflation: a review of some conceptual issues', ECB Working Paper No. 5, May

Index